Ian Hamilton was born in 1938 and educated at Darlington Grammar School and Keble College, Oxford. He has published two collections of poetry, two volumes of criticism and, in 1983, a biography of Robert Lowell.

IAN HAMILTON
—— Editor ——

THE NEW REVIEW
ANTHOLOGY

PALADIN
GRAFTON BOOKS
A Division of the Collins Publishing Group

LONDON GLASGOW
TORONTO SYDNEY AUCKLAND

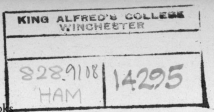
Paladin
Grafton Books
A Division of the Collins Publishing Group
8 Grafton Street, London W1X 3LA

Published in Paladin Books 1987

This collection first published in Great Britain by
William Heinemann Ltd 1985

ISBN 0-586-08569-6

'In Isfahan' by William Trevor reprinted by permission of A. D.
Peters & Co Ltd. 'An Afterwards' and 'The Skunk' reprinted by
permission of Faber & Faber Ltd from *Fieldwork* by Seamus Heaney.
'Sleep If Off Lady' by Jean Rhys reprinted by permission of André
Deutsch Ltd. 'The Soho Hospital for Women' © Fleur Adcock 1979,
reprinted from Fleur Adcock's *Selected Poems* (1983) by permission of
Oxford University Press. 'Lorca' by D. M. Thomas reprinted by
permission of John Johnson Ltd. 'Anniversaries' © Andrew Motion
1978, reprinted from Andrew Motion's *The Pleasure Steamers* by
permission of Carcanet Press Ltd, Manchester.

Printed and bound in Great Britain by
Collins, Glasgow

Set in Bembo

CONTENTS

PREFACE

Since it is our fervent hope that this *New Review* anthology will
enjoy a wider distribution than the magazine did, a few facts
should be stated. *The New Review* made its appearance in April
1974 and ran for fifty issues until 1979. It was monthly,
although now and then money problems forced upon us the so-
called 'double' issue. It was propped up by the Arts Council:
The Review's grant was the largest ever given to a magazine – a
lot of people took personal offence at this – but was never large
enough, alas, to safeguard the enterprise from penury. Although
The New Review was smartly togged-out, and quite plump, it
was all along a 'little magazine'.

And it grew out of an even littler magazine, called *The
Review*, which I had edited from 1962 to 1972. *The Review* was
a poetry magazine, rigorous, combative, the champion of
'intelligent lyricism' in an age of versified prose-poetry and
Pop. Or so we liked to think. After ten years, its polemical
energy began to dim, its young poets were no longer all that
young, and its enemies were beginning to describe it as a
'healthy presence'. Time, surely, to move on.

The New Review was intended to preserve the rigour and
liveliness of *The Review* but to extend its range into 'the arts' –
although literature would be its chief concern. There were few
outlets then (there are maybe even fewer now) for the short
story, for the extended critical essay, or for the sort of 'new
journalism' that was making its mark in the United States. On
the one hand, there were the academic journals; on the other,
the Sunday supplements and culture pages, with their obligation
to be brief. It seemed to us that there was fertile, vacant ground
between the two: it was for this we aimed.

This anthology is meant to give the 'flavour' of the magazine, but at the same time it has to stand up as a book. A magazine's flavour, after all, is often more to do with its ephemera than with its more weighty, lasting contributions. I would like to have preserved something from *The New Review*'s Edward Pygge column – particularly from the period when Julian Barnes so elegantly occupied the sty – but in the end it did seem that even the best throwaway material is justly destined to be thrown away. There were also a number of book reviews – in the later stages very capably commissioned by Craig Raine – which still seem wise and witty; to have reprinted a batch of them, however, would have given this book the kind of 'scrapbook' feel I thought we should avoid.

The New Review printed a number of new plays – by Simon Gray, Harold Pinter, Denis Potter and some others – but considerations of space prohibit their inclusion here. Also, each of them is, I believe, now available at bookshops. This was a difficult decision for me, because I mostly prefer reading plays to watching them, and I have always thought the magazine's record in this area was something to be proud of.

I was not proud of *everything* that went into *The New Review*. Indeed going through the back issues, page by page, has had its few head-hanging moments: a genuine 'little magazine' should probably never let itself be tied to a stiff monthly schedule, a set number of pages, and so on. But finally, I am not ashamed to say, there was enough good stuff to fill half a dozen anthologies. Cutting things out has been the hardest part of this particular editorial assignment.

I am grateful to David Godwin of Heinemann for proposing this celebration of *The New Review*. My list of acknowledgements for the magazine itself would, if properly done, take up at least another page or two, and to name some people and not others would be wrong. The present climate being what it is, though, I would like to offer public thanks to Charles Osborne, Literature Director of the Arts Council throughout the magazine's brief life – without his unflinching personal support that life would have been far briefer, and quite a few of the items in this book might not have seen the light of day.

Ian Hamilton

Annie,
California Plates

———— JIM CRACE ————

The first time I saw Annie was at the Pacific end of the east-bound Interstate 80, about midway between San Francisco and Salt Lake City. Battle Mountain, Nevada, in fact – just to the side of the last diner there. I was eating Kentucky Fried with my thumb out. That was before I got into Health Foods and settled down, more or less, with my old lady in Columbus, Ohio.

I was humming a tune. It was called 'Battle Mountain Here I Come'. I'd got the tune and the title. I was working on the words . . .

> 'Battle Mountain here I come
> Hitching car-rides with my thumb
> That's where my new girl comes from
> Battle Mountain here I come.'

I know songs for near every town in this country – and all the States except Alaska. I used to sit at the side of the road, waiting, humming through the name-songs of the places I'd been through. 'By the Time I get to Phoenix'; 'Twenty-four Hours to Tulsa'; 'San Jose'; 'Alabama Here I Come'; 'Carolina on my Mind'; 'Down by the Banks of the Ohio'. America's full of place-names – and that's about all. You take Phoenix, Arizona. It's a great song but the town itself is a crap-heap. Same with Tulsa and San Jose. It seems that all the bad places have people *leaving* all the time, writing nostalgic songs sure, but never actually *living* there. They're always Goodbye on-the-road songs. You take a good town like Newport, Oregon, or Mackinaw City, Michigan – you never get a song written about them. The people stay there and don't need to write no songs. Songs only get written about bad places in America, places that improve on the leaving. That was why I was writing a song about Battle Mountain, Nevada. It deserved a long song. About 70 verses. I felt the part, too, singing songs about places on the road and wondering all the time whether my old lady was gonna have me when I got home. She said she'd leave me, sure enough. Said so in a letter I got in San Francisco, giving me just seven days to get back to New York City or she'd split. Said she was off to the Adirondacks to live in a commune. She was full of crazy ideas, my old lady. But I knew she wasn't joking, see, because there *were* some cats had a commune up there some place, up by Lyon Mountain I think it was. And if my old lady said she'd leave in a week, she would. That's the way she was.

That gave me seven days to get from San Francisco, California, to New York City, corner of 81st and Amsterdam. Hell, that's no time to cross America, especially when the college kids are out grabbing all the rides. They were shoulder to shoulder on the Berkeley ramp. Kids just getting over the bridge into the City, and the rest with packs and signs for San Diego, Seattle, Chicago, New Orleans, Washington DC – all tight up amongst the parked cars on University Avenue. I got 'EAST' scratched on a bit of card and didn't get a ride till midday. A short one with an ice-truck. The driver wanted to squeeze out as much for me as he could so, instead of dropping me on the highway like I asked, he took me right down-town Sacramento where he said he often saw kids hitching at the lights. If he often saw them there then they weren't getting lifts, I figured, and had to waste the afternoon walking back out to the highway. People are always doing you favours. Who needs it?

Then I got a long ride with two fat girls in a VW. They were going to visit an aunt in Provo, Utah, but it came on to rain midway Nevada. The VW didn't have any wipers so they turned around at Battle Mountain and went back to Sacramento. You meet some crazy people. That left me in Battle Mountain and night coming on. I got a few hours' sleep in my bed-roll till the morning traffic started rolling through, then got back at the side of the road. Nobody'd give me a lift, though I pulled every trick I knew. Roadside Nevada's no place to be with hair and a beard, specially when you're carrying half a K of best Mexican dope like I was. I waited there eight whole hours picturing my old lady packing her bag for the Adirondacks, picking her few books out of mine, leaving me a note saying I could keep her albums. I was getting real nervous. It was then that I treated myself to the Kentucky Fried Chicken and got to work on the Battle Mountain song, and a few moments later, like I said, I first saw Annie.

She came out of Battle Mountain at about sixty, a kind of bean-can gold, California plates, and with her name, Annie, printed in white on the front fender. She was a huge old Chevy station-wagon. She slowed a little when she saw me, accelerated a while, then pulled over on the shoulder about a hundred yards down.

I could see there was this little black cat in the driver's seat, but he didn't turn round and wave me on or back up a bit. He just sat there at the side of Interstate 80 with his blinker going and his foot on the gas. I figured he was one of those tease guys. Get me to shamble up the hot tar with my bag banging up my shin, then put her in drive soon as I got my hand on the door. You get 'em all the time. Best thing to do is to take it real cool — stroll up like you weren't after a ride anyway, as if you just felt like moving out of the shade into that dry old Nevada sunshine. He never pulled off, though. He just sat there looking nervous as hell. Just a little black guy.

'Hey, man,' I said. 'Where you heading?'

'Where *you* heading?'

'East, man,' I said, 'New York City.'

'I'll get you there,' said the little guy, 'New York City, all the way.'

'Far out!' My old lady started to unpack her bag and put her books back in the case.

'I can get you there if you pay for the gas.'

'What, ain't you got no bread?'

'Nope!' He said it like it was the least of his troubles. 'Ain't got no bread. Ain't got no gas.'

'Got none in the tank?'

"Nough for the State line, mebbe.'

'OK. I'll see what I can do.'

I got into the back of Annie and threw my bag into the hatch. Truth is, I only had about six dollars to get me right over to the East coast. I couldn't see any of that filling this cat's tank but I figured I'd ride it out till she dried up on juice.

'Where you headin'?' I tried again.

'Ain't *headin*' no place. I'm leavin'.' He just kept his head down over the wheel and batted old Annie down the nearside lane at a steady 60. I settled down in her back seat and started to figure it out. We were rattling into Emigrant Pass along the side of the Humboldt River. There's an old pioneer song called 'In Emigrant Pass'. I hummed it. Sure was glad to be on the move.

Thing was, it wasn't quite straight with this guy. What was he doing in the middle of Nevada with half a tank of gas and running out of bread, going no place special? He just had a shirt and dungarees, but no bag in the back and nothing under the dash except a mess of wires which should have been a radio. He had a car, though, whatever he was at. Old Annie. Bean-can gold, with enough room in her for a six-piece band, drums and all.

'How much is gas a gallon?' I asked him, working it out in my head.

'Couldn't say.'

'Does she get through much, this old car?'

'Couldn't say.' And he turned around and gave me a 'Button It' look, not to be aggressive but because he didn't like to let on he didn't know the answer to any questions. It was then that I saw the wide scar across the top of his cheek. It looked like a split fig, or how I imagined a split fig because, like I said, that was before I was into Health Foods. We were coming into Elko, Nevada, now and the little negro was keeping his head down like a fox in a hole, acting nervous. When we passed a Highway Patrol wagon parked at a motel he slowed way down and started driving Annie at about an inconspicuous 30 like he was some real careful guy.

Then I had him figured out. Nervous of cops. No bread and no gas. And no travelling bag. Didn't know the price of fuel, and with a six-inch knife scar across the top of his cheek. Going no-place, just getting *away*. Now I don't have to put it to music – this guy was on the run! And this little old Annie, which was riding us across the States, taking him to freedom I guess and me to my old lady getting herself ready for a commune in the Adirondacks, this old bean-can Annie was sure to be a ripped-off Annie. She'd been standing in some up-town parking lot when along had come scarface with the State Police on his ass. And off they'd gone down Interstate 80. Love at first sight. A man and a car. Why he never ripped off a little old Scimitar or one of those big black Plymouths with air-conditioning and cassettes, I don't know. Maybe Annie had her keys in. It wasn't the sort of thing you'd want to ask.

I had it all added up. There I was in a ripped-off car with half the cops in the country hunting down the driver and with half a K of prime Mexican dope in my pack – and running out of gas! I let out this little hiss I do when I'm baffled. It kind of said, 'I know what the score is so far but what happens next?' Scarface loosened up a bit. That was a hiss he recognized.

'They call me Gerald,' he said.

'Well, Gerald,' I said. 'We're in a fix. I've got six dollars to get me to New York City 'n if I throw that into your tank it ain't gonna get us to Salt Lake, even if this little ol' lady'll make it that far.'

'Oh, she'll make it,' he said. 'She's fair set on gettin' east. She's got folks t'see at the motor-mart in Detroit.' He leered at his joke.

'That where you heading?'

'I'm headin' as far as I can get.'

'Give me a minute to think about it,' I said, and I settled back in Annie and started figuring again.

This is how I reckoned it. Chances were that Gerald wasn't that important. He didn't look too mean. In fact he was kind of nice. So maybe, now he was out of California State, things wouldn't be so hot for him or the car. And if they did pick him up for jumping parole or ripping off old beat-up Annie or whatever it was he was supposed to have done, he'd put in a word for me, say I'd only thumbed a ride midway Nevada. Then there was the dope. Any trouble and they might turn me over, find the dope and stick one of those Crossing State Border raps on me. Still I needed the ride bad and if I got out I still had the choice of Wyoming or Colorado to get through. They run you out of those States with a $50 fine just for hitching a ride. Fact is you'd be safer carrying dope in a stolen car than standing on the roadside with a West Coast sun-tan and a back-pack. You can commit murder in some places so long as you do it in a private car. So I'd stick with Annie and see what turned up. But first I had to set my mind to filling her tank. The needle was getting low.

'You figured out the gas yet?' asked Gerald, sinking into his seat as a patrol car hurtled by in the opposite lane.

'Yeah, I got it figured,' I said. 'We pick up every hiker we see, OK? I'll do the talking. We'll see how it goes.'

'Every *hitch*-hiker, is that what you're sayin'?'

'Yeah, every thumb-bum you see.'

We were way down in the red before we saw our first hiker. We'd crossed State border into Wendover, Utah, just before the great white desert of the Bonneville Salt Flats. Last gas station in town and there was a guy fanning himself with a Cheyenne sign.

'This one?' asked Gerald.

'He's our boy,' I said, and rolled down the window like some Texas fat-cat.

'You heading for Cheyenne?'

'Sure am.'

'Waiting long?'

'It's taken me four days since LA!'

'Yeah? Figure it'll take you another four the way things are.'

'Oh, yeah, how's that?' he said, looking like I knew something he didn't.

'Well, I guess you won't have heard. Some hiker on Interstate 80 has been knifing folks.'

'Is that right?'

'Sure as you're stuck here it is. Nobody's giving rides while this guy's on the loose.'

The hiker screwed up his eyes like he was thinking hard. 'Where you folks headed?' he said.

'Well,' I said. 'We was going right past your front porch.

Would have been there first thing tomorrow morning. But now it looks like we're stuck here for a while till I get a bank draft through from New York City.'

'You outta bread?'

'We're outta gas.'

'How long you gonna wait here?'

'Two, maybe three days.'

He was thinking real hard now. 'I could help you out with gas,' he said. 'I got ten dollars to get me home . . .'

'Well,' I said, trying not to sound too keen. 'Climb aboard and we'll see how it goes.'

We backed into the gas station and filled her up with the ten dollars. There was three and a quarter change which I poked in the ash-tray as a kitty.

'My name's Mel,' he said shaking hands all round.

'I'm Bobby,' I said. 'And he's Gerald. And this here,' giving Annie a rap, 'is Annie.'

'Hi,' said Mel. 'You just say if you want me to drive, OK? You guys look pretty bushed.' Gerald moved over and gave him the wheel.

'You want me to drive *now*?'

'Sure, man. We're heading East.'

My old lady used to say that hiking was just a way of getting around, just like any other way of getting around, like taking the bus or riding a bike. The important thing, she reckoned, was getting there, wherever you was headed. That's why she never came on this trip. She would have drove me crazy, hassling for a ride all the time and getting ratty when she never got one. And then when she *did* get a ride she wouldn't say a word, just sit there fingering her watch because the truck wasn't going fast enough. She wasn't very cool when it came to getting a ride, if you wanna know the truth. Now, if you're driving, say, from San Diego to San Francisco, or taking the bus, no matter how many times you do it it'll have the same shape. But hiking'll never be the same twice. It's kind of open-ended, shapeless. You're out on the side of the road with your thumb out and plenty of time to think. If you ain't a thinker you'd best not be a hiker. You'd best get your own motor car and fill your head with gear changes and adjusting the air conditioner. That's what you'd best do.

'Hey, man,' said Mel at the wheel. 'She handles real well. Did you pick her up cheap?' He was talking to me. Gerald was asleep in the front.

'Yeah, real cheap,' I said.

'She don't look much,' he continued, 'but she drives like a star. You got yourself a goodun here.' He jammed his toe hard on the brake.

'Hey! Take it easy, man,' I said.

'There was a hiker back there. You wanna pick him up?'

'Ah, no, man . . .'

'We need the gas.'

'Yeah, but I'm getting to feel bad about offering rides with my hand out for bread.'

'I'll ask.'

So he backed Annie up and flung his door open where the hiker was sitting chewing his lapel.

'Looking for a ride?' asked Mel.

'You bet . . .'

'We're going East . . .'

'That's great. I'm heading for Indianapolis.'

'Wow, that's about twelve hundred miles . . .'

'At least.'

'Can you help out on gas?'

'Well, you can have what I can spare and that ain't much.'

'Every little bit helps when you've got an empty tank, man. Get in.'

Mel threw the door open and the new hiker got in the back next to me.

'Hi, there,' he said. I nodded and Gerald kept on sleeping.

'Hey, man.' He leant over and carried on talking with Mel. 'There's another couple of cats over in that diner trying to get a ride into Des Moines. Two girls, pretty nice chicks. You got room for them?'

'They got money for gas, you think?' asked Mel.

'Well, they've got money for steak and french fries. You got money for french fries, you got money for gas.'

'Go get 'em,' I said. It was the first word I'd spoken and the

— 16 —

new hiker looked at me as if it was none of my business. Gerald just kept on sleeping.

He turned again to Mel in the driving seat. 'You got room, man?'

'Yeah, man, we got all the room in the world.'

The two girls came over with their new smart rucksacks and walking shoes and Mel and the Indianapolis cat started getting hot across the neck bullshitting the chicks with all their hard travellin' and the places they'd seen. I used to be into that when I was a few years younger and before my old lady got me so hung up, threatening to walk out on me all the time and getting me so nervous I didn't have the sweat to look at another chick let alone spin her a yarn, especially the sort that the Indianapolis cat was laying down on *these* chicks. Everyone was getting different ideas of who was who on this journey and, I guess, Gerald was the only one who knew the whole story but he was keeping his head down and his mouth shut and not letting on. If the man from Gallup Poll had come along and asked the question: 'Who owns this car and where's it heading?' I don't think he'd have got the same answer twice.

As the days and States got passed through and my old lady in New York City got closer and closer, I began to feel as if old Annie was moving away from me and Gerald – not, of course, that *I* had any claim. It was Gerald ripped her off, but it was me got her moving halfway across America and moving still with new people getting in and out the whole time and laying their claim on her, taking their turn at the wheel and throwing their bread in the kitty.

Three days later, just east of Indianapolis, with a new bunch of faces inside Annie and her back-seat ash-tray overflowing with quarters and dollar bills, Annie's kettle started to boil and the man who was driving pulled off into a side road so that she could cool off and the rest of us could snatch some sleep. There were too many of us to get comfortable inside, so those who had bed-rolls spilled out on to the grass and concrete. At about five in the morning I was waking with the dew bringing my stiff legs tight up into my chest for the warmth. I had it figured out with my old lady. I was going to arrive in plenty of time.

Maybe I'd have half a day in hand. I'd get myself brushed up and sorted out, then phone her from the call-box opposite the apartment just as her deadline was up. I'd have to unload some of the dope first so that I had some bread to splash around. I had it all figured. Then I heard Annie's door click and I saw Gerald easing it open and getting his hand, over the sleeping bodies, into the gas kitty. He took all the dollar bills and left the quarters. He eased her old door shut again and set off across the gravel to the highway. Gerald was cutting out, heading north for Detroit like he said, I guess, and leaving old Annie behind at the side of the road with her cargo of hikers sleeping at her side and in her cushions. I gave him a little silent wave and he gave me a little smiling nod and put his head down against the dawn.

Hell, you should have heard the language in the morning when they found he'd gone and taken the kitty with him.

'What a bastard trick,' I said. 'I always thought he had a mean look on him.'

'We was lucky,' said a college girl from Boston checking her bag. 'He could have cut all our throats and stolen the car . . .'

'Yeah,' I said. 'You're right there. We should never have given him a ride.'

They dropped me on the Pennsylvania Turnpike when the driver and most of the riders decided to head south on 70S to Washington. She drove off, bean-can gold with her name Annie painted in white on her fender and her California plates dusty from the road. I watched her go. She was a real hitch-hikers' car. Never ending. She'd go go go, back and forth across the States picking up and dropping every highway rider with a thumb to wave and some cents for her tank. People'd get out and people'd get in and nobody'd be too sure whose she was or where she'd come from. Some little black cat called Gerald had ripped her off in uptown San Francisco and set her free to see the land. I was thinking all that, *humming* it to tell you the truth, till my last ride picked me up at the side of the road and ran me into New York City to catch my old lady redecorating the kitchen and not giving a thought to the Adirondacks or communes or the letter she'd sent, bringing me three thousand miles across the land with my heart in my mouth and a half K of prime Mexican in my bag.

For Christmas she bought me *The Whole Earth Catalog* so we got into Health Foods and settled down, more or less, in Columbus, Ohio, not far from where I'd last seen Gerald rifling the kitty and setting off across the motorway dawn.

It's hard for me to believe, but two summers later my old lady and I were down in Louisiana catching a ride on the highway out of Baton Rouge up to Lafayette where a friend of mine was growing cantaloupes. I was singing that song that Janis Joplin used to squeeze out before she drank herself to death, 'Me and Bobby McGee' . . .

> 'Busted flat in Baton Rouge
> Waiting for a train
> Feeling near as faded as my jeans.'

My old lady was humming along in the shade. She didn't know the words. And I was out at the road's edge looking into the glare of windshields with my thumb out. At first I couldn't be sure, but the dirty gold Chevy station-wagon that was drawing out of the gas station looked a lot like Annie. I screwed up my eyes and told my old lady to shut up. She was cussing the highway, the way she does. The car turned towards us and accelerated into the traffic. There were California plates and, fainter but still there, those five white letters on the fender. I just kept my thumb out but she didn't stop to give us a ride. She was full of people.

June 1974

Two Poems

DOUGLAS DUNN

The Tear

Dawn comes remembering the dawn, and you.
At dawn you feel nothing. Blue eye burning
Like gas, flicker-flame, his eye is burning blue
Where the dawn's moisture climbs dripping spirals
To the mist that spreads and is turning
Into a bird-delivered light that falls.
Why is his one good eye wet? Is it dew?
Will he die of it, that acid on the blue
Hole through to him? Blue as the butterfly
Morning, blue as the blue of his dead eye,
That eye through which he dreams the blossom-shade,
That orchard again. The tall kimono-girl,
The girl in the white dressing-gown, parade
His filthy eye one blink would blind or kill.

The Arbitration

Where grasses roll down an unwooded slope,
Arrested by the spell of poppies, cornflowers' heads,
His lady walks in white, a natural trope
That utters images of cool Monet.
She stops to pick, and in the sun, the reds
Bleach to her dress, a hundred spots of blue
Vanish with her in the light she steps into.

Only a shadow gives her back to you,
Darkening her backwards from the day
Where she was lost, or spread out everywhere.
You knew the shadow – it was you – would fall
Just when you asked it; and, for all these fair
And neutral grasses in the summer air,
Your dithering long wait was terrible.

April 1974

Wild Life Studies

—— JAMES FENTON ——

1. The Wild Ones

Here come the capybaras on their bikes.
They swerve into the friendly, leafy square
Knocking the angwantibos off their trikes,
Giving the old-age coypus a bad scare.
They specialize in nasty, lightning strikes.
They leave the banks and grocers' shops quite bare,
Then swagger through the bardoors for a shot
Of anything the barman hasn't got.

They spoil the friendly rodent rodeos
By rustling the grazing flocks of mice.
They wear enormous jackboots on their toes.
Insulted by a comment, in a trice
They whip their switchblades out beneath your nose.
Their favourite food is elephant and rice.
Their personal appearance is revolting.
Their fur is never brushed and always moulting.

And in the evening when the sun goes down
They take the comely women on their backs
And ride for several furlongs out of town
Along the muddy roads and mountain tracks,
Wearing a grim and terrifying frown.
Months later, all the females have attacks
And call the coypu doctors to their bed.
What's born has dreadful capybara heads.

2. Song

The killer snails
Have slung their silver trails
Along the doormat, out across the lawn
Under the bushes
Where the alarming thrushes
Give night its notice, making way for dawn,
And the obliging lizards drop their tails.

On webs of dew
The spiders stir their pots of glue
And drag their quartered victims to the shade.
Soaked in their rugs
Of grass and moss the slugs
Wind up another night of sluggish trade
And young ingredients get into a stew.

The sorrel bends.
The path fades out but never ends
Where brambles clutch and bracken wipes your feet.
It goes in rings.
Its mind's on other things.
Its ways and its intentions never meet.
Meetings of friends?
It gives no undertaking. It depends.

3. Of Bison Men
with apologies to Roy Fuller

A bison in the bath, the image noted
Reminds one that it's time to go to bed.
One's home from dinner, feeling rather bloated.
One's had to drive the babysitter back.
Naturally one's resolve is fairly slack.

Next day, with some surprise, one finds it there
Soaping its fourfold armpits with a will
And whistling some infuriating air.
It's probably used up all one's shampoo,
And look, its soggy hooves have turned to glue.

Quite obviously it came up through the waste,
Emerging through the sponges and the loofahs,
And found the wire bathrack to its taste.
It's quite at home. The children are enthralled.
The dirty uncle has been badly mauled.

One jibs at murder, so one writes a letter
Begging a friend to take it for a week.
'It's bound to get on well with your red setter
And you can exercise it on Blackheath.
I find wire wool is splendid for its teeth.'

We certainly would like thus easily
To palm our troubles off on our acquaintance.
But just as one's prepared its flask of tea
The kids rush in to collar the grownups.
The airing cupboard's full of bison pups!

4. Lullaby for a Summer Recess

'Something comes crawling from St James's Park,
Dragging its dripping flippers through the street
With lengths of pondweed trailing from its feet.
It cracks its knuckles in the gathering dark.

A human shadow is the only mark
On walls where this and the nightwatchmen meet.
Oh no mother, shield my eyeballs from the heat!
It's coming for me. I can hear it bark.'

'Hush child, here come the army in their jeeps,
The nice barbed wire and the barricades.
Your evil godfather takes out his pad.

The 1922 Committee sleeps
And pallid faces, mooning from the shades,
Are smiling on the kingdom of the sad.'

5. This Octopus Exploits Women

Even the barnacle has certain rights
The grim anemones should not ignore,
And the gay bivalves in their fishnet tights
Are linking arms with fins to ask for maw.

The hectic round of rockpools is disrupted
By the addresses of the finny vicars,
With which the limpet choirboys were corrupted.
The knitting-fish produce their eight-leg knickers.

And somewhere in the depths a voice keeps shouting
'By Jove! that was a narrow bathyscaphe.'
What made the Junior Sea-Slugs give up scouting?
The *Daily Seaweed* tells us nowhere's safe.

Beneath the shimmering surface of the ocean,
The thoroughfare of ketches, sloops and luggers,
With their thick boots and hair smothered in lotion,
Are gathering hordes of ruthless ichthic muggers.

The workers on the derricks live in terror.
You can't stroll out across the sea at night.
Professor Walrus writes (see *Drowned in Error*)
'The lemon sole are taught to shoot on sight.'

The lobsters at the water polo club
Sip their prawn cocktails, chatting over chukkas.
The octopus rests idly in its tub.
The Tunny Girls are lounging on its suckers.

May 1974

Out of the War

—— FRANCIS WYNDHAM ——

It was about six o'clock in the evening when I was brought into the orthopaedic ward. The two girls in the ATS who had taken it in turns to drive the ambulance carried me in on a stretcher, which they laid down on the floor, so that the room seemed very big to me, and the ceiling very high. The girls did not know what to do next, and whispered together uneasily. At length one went to fetch my papers, which had been left in the ambulance, and the other disappeared in search of a nurse.

The walls of the ward were white; so were the bedspreads and the patients' faces and their huge bandaged limbs suspended a few inches from the beds. As it was evening, all these things seemed grey, and there appeared to be a light grey mist filling the room. Nobody spoke or moved while I lay on the floor. The ten patients sat still, propped up by many pillows, and some had the black earphones which hung behind each bed clamped to their ears. These had an abstracted air, but the wireless programme, inaudible to me, seemed not to prevent them from reading their magazines, and, turning a page of *Picture Post* or *Everybody's*, one would lift his head for a moment to attend to the broadcast buzzing at his ears; then, no longer seeking meaning in the noise, transfer his mind to the printed page lying on the white counterpane.

Not far from me a man stood upright. His body from the waist to the neck was encased in smooth plaster of Paris, and one of his arms was supported at an angle, shoulder-level. He had the look of an enamel model in a draper's window or a cardboard advertisement propped upright in a cinema foyer. When he blinked, or turned his head, the effect was therefore rather sinister.

A ward maid came into the room. I knew that she was a ward maid because of the dinginess of her dress; her halo-like cap was on askew at the back of her head. She bent over me a kind, intelligent face; then she looked at the man who was standing, and, moving her lips with care, she uttered a strange babbling noise, a string of vowel sounds slightly distorted by a gurgle in her throat as though there were a bubble there, continually bursting and reforming. I learnt for certain later, what I guessed then, that many of the ward maids at the hospital were patients who were deaf and dumb.

The ambulance driver came back with a tall nurse (from where I lay she looked a giantess) who approached the ward maid and shouted into her ear, 'You'll find Sister in her office, Elsie.' Elsie went away and the nurse and the drivers helped me into bed (for the other driver had returned, munching a biscuit bought at a Church Army mobile canteen which stood at the hospital entrance). I was to know that this nurse was called Nurse Bennett. She had a long, freckled face, and crinkly sandy hair. Always smiling and humming to herself, she was brisk, efficient and good-humoured.

One of the drivers, a fat, dark girl, said, 'Cheerio, laddie,' and went away with her friend. I knew that they were bound for a restaurant opposite, where they would drink some tea, as they had arranged this on the way to the hospital, and I wished that I could go with them.

The ward was divided by a partition built across it which had an open space in the middle for the aisle to run through. I was next to the partition, which was as high as the bed; above it there was a curtain which, when drawn, separated one set of six beds from the other – each division consisting of three beds against the two opposite walls. Nurse Bennett had drawn this curtain, cutting me off from one half of the room, with some idea that I might prefer the semi-privacy it afforded while the stretcher was lifted to the level of the bed and while I rolled off it, on to the rubber ring which had been placed beneath the sheet.

'All right, old chap?' she asked.

'Yes, thank you.'

'Good man.' She strode away, leaving the curtain still drawn.

I lay back on the pillows and the feeling of weakness caused by the jolting ambulance drive began to pass away. I was conscious of a muttering noise just above my head; this came from my earphones, which stuttered away distantly and maddeningly, only to assume volume and coherence when actually over my ears.

A red-haired man, evidently a soldier, looked up from his magazine. 'She sang that well,' he said appreciatively, and I gathered that an invisible crooner had that moment finished her song. It was then that the curtain beside me began to twitch. I understood that the man in the bed beyond it was trying to draw it. I saw a hairy hand with a ring on one finger jerking it back nervously, but the hand could only draw the curtain half way and its owner remained invisible to me. I drew the curtain all the way back. In the bed next to mine a dark-haired man of about 50 was smiling at me. Both his legs were supported by a kind of pulley so that they should not touch the bed.

'I don't like to have the curtain drawn like that,' he said. 'I can't see what's going on. But they're always drawing it. It cuts me off from half the room and I like to see what's going on.'

Almost at once he told me his story, the reason for his presence in the hospital. He told me it in an unemotional voice, not at all the sort of voice usually used to describe catastrophes, and while doing so he continued to smile his nervous smile, baring uneven teeth in a haggard face.

He was a postman in the town, a widower with an only son, a boy of 15. They had been walking together one evening, returning home from a public house, when an army lorry which was passing had swerved into the side of the road and run them over. This was some months ago. His legs and arms had been badly injured, but he was now doing surprisingly well, and although it had at first been predicted that he would be crippled for life, it seemed likely that he would make a complete recovery. His son had lain in the bed on the other side of mine. The doctors had operated on the boy, taking off both his legs, without asking his father's consent. Shortly after that the boy had died. The postman repeated, 'It was very wrong of them not to ask my permission. I was very poorly then and perhaps they didn't want to worry me, but they should have told me they were going to take off his legs.'

It seemed that the shock of the discovery of this operation had been so great that it still outweighed in the postman's mind that of his son's subsequent death.

I offered him a packet of cigarettes, of which I had a store, because it appeared that he had no money at all in the world, and depended entirely on his friends who came to see him every visitors' day. He refused them, and seemed rather embarrassed. A few minutes later he in his turn offered me a biscuit, saying, 'My neighbour brought me these yesterday. She's very good to me.' I refused, and he seemed satisfied; I understood that it worried him to borrow from someone whom he would think it necessary somehow to pay back.

He repeated his story to me the next morning, and after that every morning and evening. Whenever my curtain had been drawn to screen me while I was washed, used the bedpan, or was visited by a doctor, I could sense his uneasiness on the other side of it. The nurses never remembered to draw it back. When whatever private activity I had been engaged in was over, there would be a short time of suspense; then the hand would start its ineffectual twitching. The curtain drawn, he would smile apologetically. 'I hate to be cut off like that. I like to see what's going on.'

Shortly after my arrival in the ward, another stretcher was brought in, and the patient deposited on the bed next to mine, which had till then been empty. At first it seemed that the newcomer was a young man, probably a soldier; but when the time for the evening wash came, and he took off his pyjama jacket and sat up in bed, the thinness of his arms and the whiteness of his chest showed that he could not be more than 14. This pleased the postman.

'It's funny,' he said, 'there always seems to be a lad in that bed. That was the bed my boy was in, and after him there was another lad of 15. He was a nice boy, he left before you came. Now there's another laddie.' He leant forward and smiled at the boy, and would have liked to have spoken to him, only my presence between them made this difficult. He did shout a remark, but the boy did not know it was meant for him, although several of the other patients looked up.

I soon found that the only nurse who made any impression on the ward was Nurse Bennett, the tall one with red hair. She was always addressed as Nurse Bennett, while the others were merely known as 'nurse'. She was very friendly with the patients, who loved to tease her. One day the red-haired soldier called her as she passed his bed.

'Nurse Bennett.'

'Yes, Ginger?'

'I want to ask you something.'

'Well, buck up about it, because I'm busy.'

'It says in the Bible that Adam and Eve were the first people on earth, doesn't it?'

'Yes,' said Nurse Bennett guardedly.

'And they had two sons, Cain and Abel, didn't they?'

'Yes.'

'Cain killed Abel, is that right?'

'Yes, Ginger.'

'Then Cain went off somewhere and got married. Who,' Ginger asked triumphantly, 'did he marry?'

Nurse Bennett pulled a face. 'You've got me there, I'm afraid, Ginge. But I think I can explain. You see, we're not supposed to take the Bible too literally. It describes things how they probably did happen, but it can't know for certain, and all it says isn't strictly true. But it is true, though not always absolutely true. Do you see?'

'I see, Nurse Bennett,' said Ginger, grinning and winking at the other patients.

'Now I want to ask you something,' said the nurse. 'Adam and Eve and Pinchme . . .' but she was interrupted by Ginger who pinched her arm. She gave a little shriek then walked off smiling; her voice could be heard shouting orders to a nurse in the passage.

The red-haired soldier would often tell Nurse Bennett coarse jokes, to see how she would react. She never laughed at these, but continued to smile indulgently, only saying, 'I think you're revolting', or 'I'm surprised at you, Ginge. You wouldn't talk like that to your mother, now would you?' Ginger would say of her when she was out of the room, 'She's a caution, that Nurse Bennett. She's got red hair like me, we're a pair. We get along all right.'

There was one subject about which the ward liked to tease Nurse Bennett which offended her and made her cross. She was the captain of a hockey team made up by the nurses at the hospital. She took this very seriously. Before a match, there would be an atmosphere of restrained excitement in the ward. Nurses, while washing patients, would talk about the game to each other over their bodies. 'My dear, I haven't played for *years*. Not since school . . .' After the match, Ginger would say to Nurse Bennett, 'Who won?'

'They did.' The opposite team was that of the Technical College in the town.

'How many goals did you score, then?'

'I didn't score any. I nearly got one just before half time, though.'

'How many goals did your side get?'

'None,' she answered angrily. 'They beat us 6−0 if you really want to know.'

'Don't you ever win a match then?'

'Only when we play South Gate.' (This was a girls' school near the town.) 'That's because they've got about three teams, and they send their C team along to play us. Even then it's a struggle. Still, it's all good fun.'

'And what do they call you in the field? Slasher Bennett?'

Someone suggested, 'Tiger Bennett?'

'Or just the Dumb Blonde?'

Nurse Bennett went red with anger. 'Oh come on, be sports,' she said. 'I can take a joke, but you go on too much about it. Anyway, I can always get my own back, can't I?'

'What would you do, Tiger?'

'Well, next time you want the bottle, I can keep you waiting for it, can't I?'

'Oh, you wicked old cuss!' Nurse Bennett walked out of the ward, taking long strides and muttering to herself.

In the evening, Nurse Bennett read prayers in the ward. The only light still lit was a green-shaded lamp on the table where the night-nurse was to sit all through the night. Nurse Bennett read well, and the atmosphere in the ward was suitably devotional, because the patients liked the prayers, and repeated the 'Amens' clearly and reverently. But before Nurse Bennett, walking steadily on creaking shoes, head bent and hands folded over prayer-book, had left the room, this atmosphere would immediately be dissipated by an exaggerated belch from Ginger's bed, and a giggle from the postman. 'That's the beans we had for supper, eh, Ginge? They repeat something terrible.'

In a bed in one corner of the room there lay an old man, who was in hospital owing to a poisoned leg. The postman, who always referred to him as 'that bloody old man', told me about him on my first night in the ward. 'He's a nuisance, because you see he's ill in the head and thinks he's still at home. He's always taking off his bandages, and he gives the nurses a lot of trouble. He gets out of bed because he thinks he has to get in the coal.' This was embarrassing, because the hospital was short of pyjama trousers, and few of the patients, among them the old man, wore any. He would choose a moment when there were no nurses in the ward to get out of bed and would then make for the door which led to the women's ward, and which he believed to be the coal shed in his own backyard. The old man usually fell down on the floor before reaching the door and then all the patients would shout, 'Nurse! Nurse! Dad's on the move again.' Nurse Bennett would then appear and, smiling cheerfully, and saying, 'Come on, Pop. That's all right, you'll be OK,' would lift him up and carry him in her arms back to his bed.

One day there was a new nurse on duty, a young, small girl who seemed struck dumb and almost paralysed by shyness. Nurse Bennett had explained her duties to her kindly and at great length. The new nurse, biting her lip, breathing heavily and staring at the watch which she pulled up from her bosom, clasped my pulse with an iron grip. She took the thermometer from my mouth and brought it into the middle of the room, frowning at it worriedly. Then, her breast heaving, she marked the results of these investigations on my temperature chart with care, terrified that her fountain pen would make a blot. While this was happening, the old man had been slowly climbing out of bed. I called her attention to it. She stared at him, blushing and frightened of his thin hairy legs and shaking movements, and seemed unable to move. Sister passed the door at that moment, and said to her angrily, 'One of your patients is getting out of bed, nurse. Please will you see to it.' She approached the old man with diffidence, and could be heard muttering something to him. Ginger called out, 'Pack it in, Pop. You've 'ad it!' This seemed to frighten the nurse even more. Fortunately Nurse Bennett came in then, and lifted the old man's legs with her strong arms back into the bed.

From the moment, after prayers had been read and the night staff had arrived, when there was silence and semi-darkness in the ward, until half past five the following morning when the impatient night-nurse began to take the morning temperatures half an hour before she was supposed to, the old man in the corner talked to himself, loudly and without pausing, whether in his sleep or not it was difficult to determine. His words were impossible to make out; this endless, meaningless conversation continued all night, and made sleep possible only for those patients who had grown accustomed to the noise. The others could sleep for a few minutes now and again, and then the old man's voice mingled with their dreams to disturb them.

I had only one night disturbed in this way. On my second evening in the ward, a doctor, tired of the complaints of the other patients, gave the old man a morphia injection, to keep him quiet for the night. The injection did have this effect; but on the following morning, there was still no sign from the old man's bed, and he lay in this condition quite still, for three days and nights. The others in the ward missed the diversion which his continual journeys across the room had afforded; they glanced uneasily at his silent bed, and did not mention him. The nurses whispered together: 'It appears he has heart; doctor didn't know.'

On the third day, when we had grown accustomed to the old man's silence, an orderly hid his bed behind three of the green screens which slid along the floor on castors and were always used when it was necessary to isolate a patient for some reason. This was one of the two visitors' days in the week. At two o'clock I could see pass the window a procession of friends and relations, all carrying parcels containing eatables. Some of these penetrated into the ward and clustered round the different beds for two hours. Conversation was at first lively, but at three o'clock it began to flag, and it was usually with a feeling of relief that the visitors rose from their chairs at four, hearing a nurse march up and down the passage ringing a hand bell to announce that their time was up. The postman had more visitors than anyone else in the ward, but they came singly and in shifts, and did not stay the full two hours. They were mostly men connected with the post office where he had worked; sometimes his neighbour came with a bag of biscuits, sometimes a sister-in-law with a packet of Woodbines; once a solicitor had arrived, with some papers for the postman to sign, as he had been trying since his accident to get some compensation money, but had so far been unsuccessful.

This afternoon the visitors watched the screens being wheeled round the old man's bed, and everybody knew, without saying anything about it, that he had died under the morphia. The day which had been looked forward to by everyone was therefore spoiled; patients and visitors were depressed by the knowledge that the nurses were washing a corpse behind the screens, and many of them were unhappy that the old man whom they had thought such a bore was dead, as they would miss him. Later on, a woman dressed in green arrived, and disappeared behind the screens. These were then stretched end to end, from the corner to the doorway, and we could hear a stretcher being wheeled behind them. Then they were folded up, and leant against the wall, revealing an empty bed, newly made, the sheet turned down ready for the next patient. The woman in green, who might have been the old man's sister, wife or landlady, sat down in a chair by the fire. She was crying. Nurse Bennett brought her a cup of tea. 'Now, dear, you must drink this.' The woman shook her head. 'No, you must, it will give you strength.' Nurse Bennett's voice comforted the woman, and she began to sip the tea. 'I'm going to fetch Sister to speak to you now. You stay there, dear.' But when the nurse had gone, the woman laid the teacup carefully down on the floor, rose and left the room. Sister came in, and finding her gone, sent a nurse to fetch her. She could not be found in the hospital. She must have walked blindly through the confusing passages, by instinct finding the entrance, and then hurried home through the town to her house in one of the suburbs.

These events were the only things that disturbed the monotony of the hospital routine during the week I spent there. The time was passed staring at the white walls, waiting for the next meal to be wheeled in by Elsie. I was to be taken by ambulance to a Convalescent Home five miles away. My life in the hospital had been lived in a void; in fact, I had hardly lived a life of my own at all, and felt as though I consisted only of eyes and ears to record the few things that happened around me. I had been carried as it were blindfold into the ward, and would be carried in the same condition out of it; I did not know my way about the hospital, or even what it looked like from outside; and if I had been put down at the entrance, and walked out into the town which I hardly knew, I should not have known where to go, and would have lost my way. For a week I had just been part of this white room, like a chair or table in it.

On my last morning there, when I felt as though I had already left the place, an orderly was told to give me a blanket bath, so that I should arrive clean enough to make a good impression on the Convalescent Home. Usually, the blanket baths were done by nurses, and then they were very slapdash affairs. Blankets were modestly heaped on one's shivering body, and only one's arms and legs were washed in tepid water by reluctant feminine hands. The orderly, however, did it thoroughly, and washed every part of me vigorously and conscientiously, even taking the water away to be changed half way through. He wore a linen mask over his mouth and nose. He had a bad cold, and sniffed and breathed with difficulty behind the mask. When he had finished, he wheeled away the screen, but left the curtain by my bed still drawn. I had only now to wait for the ambulance, and I longed for it to arrive.

As on my first day there, the postman's hand began to draw the curtain back. I would have liked to have spent my last hours in the ward with the curtain drawn, so that I could almost imagine myself alone, and I felt irritated and did not help him to draw it. When he had done so, I waited for the usual explanation.

'I hate to have that thing drawn. It cuts me off from what's going on.' Then he added, 'They used to draw it when my boy lay in that bed by you, so that I shouldn't see him. My hands were bad then so I couldn't pull it back. I reckon it was silly of them to do that, because even if I couldn't see him, I could still hear him call out, couldn't I?'

June 1974 (written 1944)

Sleep It Off Lady

———— JEAN RHYS ————

One October afternoon Mrs Baker was having tea with a Miss
Verney and talking about the proposed broiler factory in the
middle of the village where they both lived. Miss Verney, who
had not been listening attentively said, 'You know Letty, I've
been thinking a great deal about death lately. I hardly ever do,
strangely enough.'

'No dear,' said Mrs Baker. 'It isn't strange at all. It's quite
natural. We old people are rather like children: we live in the
present as a rule. A merciful dispensation of providence.'

'Perhaps,' said Miss Verney doubtfully.

Mrs Baker said 'we old people' quite kindly, but could not
help knowing that while she herself was only 63 and might,
with any luck, see many a summer (After many a summer dies
the swan, as some man said) Miss Verney, certainly well over
70, could hardly hope for anything of the sort. Mrs Baker
gripped the arms of her chair. 'Many a summer, touch wood
and please God,' she thought. Then she remarked that it was
getting dark so early now and wasn't it extraordinary how time
flew.

Miss Verney listened to the sound of the car driving away,
went back to her sitting room and looked out of the window at
the flat fields, the apple trees, the lilac tree that wouldn't flower
again, not for ten years they told her, because lilacs won't stand
being pruned. In the distance there was a rise in the ground –
you could hardly call it a hill – and three trees so exactly shaped
and spaced that they looked artificial. 'It would be rather lovely
covered in snow,' Miss Verney thought. 'The snow so white,
so smooth and in the end so boring. Even the hateful shed

wouldn't look so bad.' But she'd made up her mind to forget the shed.

Miss Verney had decided that it was an eyesore when she came to live in the cottage. Most of the paint had worn off the once-black galvanized iron. Now it was a greenish colour. Part of the roof was loose and flapped noisily in windy weather and a small gate off its hinges leaned up against the entrance. Inside it was astonishingly large, the far end almost dark. 'What a waste of space,' Miss Verney thought. 'That must come down.' Strange that she hadn't noticed it before.

Nails festooned with rags protruded from the only wooden rafter. There was a tin bucket with a hole, a huge dustbin. Nettles flourished in one corner but it was the opposite corner which disturbed her. Here was piled a rusty lawnmower, an old chair with a carpet draped over it, several sacks, and the remains of what had once been a bundle of hay. She found herself imagining that a fierce and dangerous animal lived there and called aloud: 'Come out, come out, Shredni Vashtar, the beautiful.' Then rather alarmed at herself she walked out as quickly as she could.

But she was not unduly worried. The local builder had done several odd jobs for her when she moved in and she would speak to him when she saw him next.

'Want the shed down?' said the builder.

'Yes,' said Miss Verney. 'It's hideous, and it takes up so much space.'

'It's on the large side,' the builder said.

'Enormous. Whatever did they use it for?'

'I expect it was the garden shed.'

'I don't care what it was,' said Miss Verney. 'I want it out of the way.'

The builder said that he couldn't manage the next week, but the Monday after that he'd look in and see what could be done. Monday came and Miss Verney waited but he didn't arrive. When this had happened twice she realized that he didn't mean to come and wrote to a firm in the nearest town.

A few days later a cheerful young man knocked at the door, explained who he was and asked if she would let him know exactly what she wanted. Miss Verney, who wasn't feeling at all well, pointed. 'I want that pulled down. Can you do it?'

The young man inspected the shed, walked round it, then stood looking at it.

'I want it destroyed,' said Miss Verney passionately, 'utterly destroyed and carted away. I hate the sight of it.'

'Quite a job,' he said candidly.

And Miss Verney saw what he meant. Long after she was dead and her cottage had vanished it would survive. The tin bucket and the rusty lawnmower, the pieces of rag fluttering in the wind. All would last for ever.

Eyeing her rather nervously he became businesslike. 'I see what you want, and of course we can let you have an estimate of the cost. But you realize that if you pull the shed down you take away from the value of your cottage?'

'Why?' said Miss Verney.

'Well,' he said, 'very few people would live here without a car. It could be converted into a garage easily or even used as it is. You can decide of course when you have the estimate whether you think it worth the expense and . . . the trouble. Good day.'

Left alone, Miss Verney felt so old, lonely and helpless that she began to cry. No builder would tackle that shed, not for any price that she could afford. But crying relieved her and she soon felt quite cheerful again. It was ridiculous to brood, she told herself. She quite liked the cottage. One morning she'd wake up and know what to do about the shed, meanwhile she wouldn't look at the thing. She wouldn't think about it.

But it was astonishing how it haunted her dreams. One night she was standing looking at it changing its shape and becoming a very smart, shiny, dark blue coffin picked out in white. It reminded her of a dress she had once worn. A voice behind her said: 'That's the laundry.'

'Then oughtn't I to put it away?' said Miss Verney in her dream.

'Not just yet. Soon,' said the voice so loudly that she woke up.

★ ★ ★

She had dragged the large dustbin to the entrance of the shed and, because it was too heavy for her to lift, had arranged for it to be carried to the gate every week for the dustmen to collect. Every morning she took a small yellow bin from under the sink and emptied it into the large dustbin, quickly, without lingering or looking around. But on one particular morning the usual cold wind had dropped and she stood wondering if a coat of white paint would improve matters. It might look a lot worse, besides who could she get to do it? Then she saw a cat, as she thought, walking slowly across the far end. The sun shone through a chink in the wall. It was a large rat. Horrified, she watched it disappear under the old chair, dropped the yellow bin, walked as fast as she was able up the road and knocked at the door of a shabby thatched cottage.

'Oh Tom, there are rats in my shed. I've just seen a huge one. I'm so desperately afraid of them. What shall I do?'

When she left Tom's cottage she was still shaken, but calmer. Tom had assured her that he had made an infallible rat poison, arrangements had been made, his wife had supplied a strong cup of tea.

He came that same day to put down the poison, and when afterwards he rapped loudly on the door and shouted: 'Everything under control?' she answered quite cheerfully, 'Yes, I'm fine and thanks for coming.'

As one sunny day followed another she almost forgot how much the rat had frightened her. 'It's dead or gone away,' she assured herself.

When she saw it again she stood and stared disbelieving. It crossed the shed in the same unhurried way and she watched, not able to move. A huge rat, there was no doubt about it.

This time Miss Verney didn't rush to Tom's cottage to be reassured. She managed to get to the kitchen, still holding the empty yellow pail, slammed the door and locked it. Then she shut and bolted all the windows. This done, she took off her shoes, lay down, pulled the blankets over her head and listened to her hammering heart.

> 'I'm the monarch of all I survey.
> My right, there is none to dispute.'

That was the way the rat walked.

In the close darkness she must have dozed, for suddenly she was sitting at a desk in the sun copying proverbs into a ruled book: 'Evil Communications corrupt good manners. Look before you leap. Patience is a virtue, good temper a blessing', all the way up to Z. Z would be something to do with zeal or zealous. But how did they manage about X? What about X?

Thinking this, she slept, then woke, put on the light, took two tuinal tablets and slept again, heavily. When she next opened her eyes it was morning, the unwound bedside clock had stopped, but she guessed the time from the light and hurried into the kitchen waiting for Tom's car to pass. The room was stuffy and airless but she didn't dream of opening the window. When she saw the car approaching she ran out into the road and waved it down. It was as if fear had given her wings and once more she moved lightly and quickly.

'Tom. Tom.'

He stopped.

'Oh Tom, the rat's still there. I saw it last evening.'

He got down stiffly. Not a young man, but surely, surely, a kind man? 'I put down enough stuff to kill a dozen rats,' he said. 'Let's 'ave a look.'

He walked across to the shed. She followed, several yards behind, and watched him rattling the old lawnmower, kicking the sacks, trampling the hay and nettles.

'No rat 'ere,' he said at last.

'Well there was one,' she said.

'Not 'ere.'

'It was a huge rat,' she said.

Tom had round brown eyes, honest eyes, she'd thought. But now they were sly, mocking, even hostile.

'Are you sure it wasn't a pink rat?' he said.

She knew that the bottles in her dustbin were counted and discussed in the village. But Tom, whom she liked so much?

'No,' she managed to say steadily. 'An ordinary colour but very large. Don't they say that some rats now don't care about poison? Super rats.'

Tom laughed. 'Nothing of the sort round 'ere.'

— 42 —

She said: 'I asked Mr Slade, who cuts the grass, to clear out the shed and he said he would but I think he's forgotten.'

'Mr Slade is a very busy man,' said Tom. 'He can't clear out the shed just when you tell him. You've got to wait. Do you expect him to leave his work and waste his time looking for what's not there?'

'No,' she said, 'of course not. But I think it ought to be done.' (She stopped herself from saying: 'I can't because I'm afraid.')

'Now you go and make yourself a nice cup of tea,' Tom said, speaking in a more friendly voice. 'There's no rat in your shed,' and went back to his car.

Miss Verney slumped heavily into the kitchen armchair. 'He doesn't believe me. I can't stay alone in this place, not with that monster a few yards away. I can't do it.' But another cold voice persisted: 'Where will you go? With what money? Are you really such a coward as all that?'

After a time Miss Verney got up. She dragged what furniture there was away from the walls so that she would know that nothing lurked in the corners and decided to keep the windows looking on to the shed shut and bolted. The others she opened but only at the top. Then she made a large parcel of all the food that the rat could possibly smell – cheese, bacon, ham, cold meat, practically everything – she'd give it to Mrs Randolph, the cleaning woman, later.

'But no more confidences.' Mrs Randolph would be as sceptical as Tom had been. A nice woman but a gossip, she wouldn't be able to resist telling her cronies about the giant, almost certainly imaginary, rat terrorizing her employer.

Next morning Mrs Randolph said that a stray dog had upset the large dustbin. She'd had to pick everything up from the floor of the shed. 'It wasn't a dog,' thought Miss Verney, but she only suggested that two stones on the lid turned the other way would keep the dog off.

When she saw the size of the stones she nearly said aloud: 'I defy any rat to get that lid off.'

★ ★ ★

Miss Verney had always been a careless, not a fussy, woman. Now all that changed. She spent hours every day sweeping, dusting, arranging the cupboards and putting fresh paper into the drawers. She pounced on every speck of dust with a dustpan. She tried to convince herself, that as long as she kept her house spotlessly clean the rat would keep to the shed, not to wonder what she would do if, after all, she encountered it.

'I'd collapse,' she thought, 'that's what I'd do.'

After this she'd start with fresh energy, again fearfully sweeping under the bed, behind cupboards. Then feeling too tired to eat she would beat up an egg in cold milk, add a good deal of whisky and sip it slowly. 'I don't need a lot of food now.' But her work in the house grew slower and slower, her daily walks shorter and shorter. Finally the walks stopped. 'Why should I bother?' As she never answered letters, letters ceased to arrive, and when Tom knocked at the door one day to ask how she was: 'Oh I'm quite all right,' she said and smiled.

He seemed ill at ease and didn't speak about rats or clearing the shed out. Nor did she.

'Not seen you about lately,' he said.

'Oh I go the other way now.'

When she shut the door after him she thought: 'And I imagined I liked him. How very strange.'

'No pain?' the doctor said.

'It's just an odd feeling,' said Miss Verney.

The doctor said nothing. He waited.

'It's as if all my blood was running backwards. It's rather horrible really. And then for a while sometimes I can't move. I mean if I'm holding a cup I have to drop it because there's no life in my arm.'

'And how long does this last?'

'Not long. Only a few minutes, I suppose. It just seems a long time.'

'Does it happen often?'

'Twice lately.'

The doctor thought he'd better examine her. Eventually he left the room and came back with a bottle half full of pills. 'Take these three times a day – don't forget, it's important.

Long before they're finished I'll come and see you. I'm going to give you some injections that may help but I'll have to send away for those.'

As Miss Verney was gathering her things together before leaving the surgery he asked in a casual voice: 'Are you on the telephone?'

'No,' said Miss Verney, 'but I have an arrangement with some people.'

'You told me. But those people are some way off, aren't they?'

'I'll get a telephone,' said Miss Verney making up her mind. 'I'll see about it at once.'

'Good. You won't be so lonely.'

'I suppose not.'

'Don't go moving the furniture about, will you? Don't lift heavy weights. Don't . . .' ('Oh Lord,' she thought, 'is he going to say "Don't drink!" because that's impossible!') . . . 'Don't worry,' he said.

When Miss Verney left his surgery she felt relieved but tired and she walked very slowly home. It was quite a long walk for she lived in the less prosperous part of the village, near the row of council houses. She had never minded that. She was protected by tall thick hedges and a tree or two. Of course it had taken her some time to get used to the children's loud shrieking and the women who stood outside their doors to gossip. At first they stared at her with curiosity and some disapproval, she couldn't help feeling, but they'd soon find out that she was harmless.

The child Deena, however, was a very different matter.

Most of the village boys were called Jack, Willie, Stan and so on – the girls' first names were more elaborate. Deena's mother had gone one better than anyone else and christened her daughter Undine.

Deena – as everyone called her – was a tall plump girl of about 12 with a pretty, healthy but rather bovine face. She never joined the shrieking games, she never played football with dustbin lids. She apparently spent all her time standing at the gate of her mother's house silently, unsmilingly, staring at everyone who passed.

Miss Verney had long ago given up trying to be friendly. So much did the child's cynical eyes depress her that she would cross over the road to avoid her, and sometimes was guilty of the cowardice of making sure Deena wasn't there before setting out.

Now she looked anxiously along the street and was relieved that it was empty. 'Of course,' she told herself, 'it's getting cold. When winter comes they'll all stay indoors.'

Not that Deena seemed to mind the cold. Only a few days ago, looking out of the window, Miss Verney had seen her standing outside – oblivious of the bitter wind – staring at the front door as if if she looked hard enough she could see through the wood and find out what went on in the silent house – what Miss Verney did with herself all day.

One morning soon after her visit to the doctor Miss Verney woke feeling very well and very happy. Also she was not at all certain where she was. She lay luxuriating in the feeling of renewed youth, renewed health and slowly recognized the various pieces of furniture.

'Of course,' she thought when she drew the curtains. 'What a funny place to end up in.'

The sky was pale blue. There was no wind. Watching the still trees she sang softly to herself: 'The Day of Days'. She had always sung 'The Day of Days' on her birthday. Poised between two years – last year, next year – she never felt any age at all. Birthdays were a pause, a rest.

In the midst of slow dressing she remembered the rat for the first time. But that seemed something that had happened long ago. 'Thank God I didn't tell anybody else how frightened I was. As soon as they give me a telephone I'll ask Letty Baker to tea. She'll know exactly the sensible thing to do.'

Out of habit she ate, swept and dusted but even more slowly than usual and with long pauses, when leaning on the handle of her tall, old-fashioned, carpet sweeper she stared out at the trees. 'Goodbye summer. Goodbye, goodbye,' she hummed. But in spite of sad songs she never lost the certainty of health, of youth.

All at once she noticed, to her surprise, that it was getting dark. 'And I haven't emptied the dustbin.'

She got to the shed carrying the small yellow plastic pail and saw that the big dustbin wasn't there. For once Mrs Randolph must have slipped up and left it outside the gate. Indeed it was so.

She first brought in the lid, easy, then turned the heavy bin on to its side and kicked it along. But this was slow. Growing impatient, she picked it up, carried it into the shed and looked for the stones that had defeated the dog, the rat. They too were missing and she realized that Mrs Randolph, a hefty young woman in a hurry, must have taken out the bin, stones and all. They would be in the road where the dustmen had thrown them. She went to look and there they were.

She picked up the first stone and, astonished at its weight, immediately dropped it. But lifted it again and staggered to the shed, then leaned breathless against the cold wall. After a few minutes she breathed more easily, was less exhausted and the determination to prove to herself that she was quite well again drove her into the road to pick up the second stone.

After a few steps she felt that she had been walking for a long time, for years, weighed down by an impossible weight, and now her strength was gone and she couldn't any more. Still she reached the shed, dropped the stone and said: 'That's all now, that's the lot. Only the yellow plastic pail to tackle.' She'd fix the stones tomorrow. The yellow pail was light, full of paper, eggshells, stale bread. Miss Verney lifted it . . .

She was sitting on the ground with her back against the dustbin and her legs stretched out, surrounded by torn paper and eggshells. Her shirt had ridden up and there was a slice of stale bread on her bare knee. She felt very cold and it was nearly dark.

'What happened,' she thought. 'Did I faint or something? I must go back to the house.'

She tried to get up but it was as if she were glued to the ground. 'Wait,' she thought. 'Don't panic. Breathe deeply. Relax.' But when she tried again she was lead. 'This has happened before. I'll be all right soon,' she told herself. But darkness was coming on very quickly. Some women passed on the road and she called to them. At first: 'Could you please . . . I'm so sorry to trouble you . . .' but the wind had got up and was blowing against her and no one heard. 'Help!' she called. Still no one heard.

Tightly buttoned up, carrying string bags, heads in headscarves, they passed and the road was empty.

With her back against the dustbin, shivering with cold, she prayed: 'God, don't leave me here. Dear God, let someone come. Let someone come!'

When she opened her eyes she was not at all surprised to see a figure leaning on her gate and to recognize Deena.

'Deena! Deena!' she called, trying to keep the hysterical relief out of her voice.

Deena advanced cautiously, stood a few yards off and contemplated Miss Verney lying near the dustbin with an expressionless face.

'Listen, Deena,' said Miss Verney, 'I'm afraid I'm not very well. Will you please ask your mother – your mum – to telephone to the doctor. He'll come, I think. And if only she could help me back into the house. I'm very cold . . .'

Deena said: 'It's no good asking my mum. She doesn't like you and she doesn't want anything to do with you. She hates stuck-up people. Everybody knows that you shut yourself up to get drunk. People can hear you falling about. "She ought to take more water with it," my mum says. Sleep it off lady,' said this horrible child skipping away.

Miss Verney didn't try to call her back or argue. She knew that it was useless. A numb weak feeling slowly took possession of her. Stronger than cold. Stronger than fear. It was a great unwillingness to do anything more at all – it was almost resignation. Even if someone else came would she call again for help? Could she? Fighting the cold numbness she made a last tremendous effort to move, at any rate to jerk the bread off her knee, for now her fear of the rat, forgotten all day, was starting to torment her.

It was impossible.

She strained her eyes to see into the corner where it would certainly appear – the corner with the old chair and carpet, the corner with the bundle of hay. Would it attack at once or would it wait until it was sure that she couldn't move? Sooner or later it would come. So Miss Verney waited in the darkness for the Super Rat.

It was the postman who found her. He had a parcel of books for her and he left them as usual in the passage. But he couldn't help noticing that all the lights were on and all the doors open. Miss Verney was certainly not in the cottage.

'I suppose she's gone out. But so early and such a cold morning?'

Uneasy, he looked back at the gate and saw the bundle of clothes near the shed.

He managed to lift her and got her into the kitchen armchair. There was an open bottle of whisky on the table and he tried to force her to drink some, but her teeth were tightly clenched and the whisky spilled all over her face.

He remembered that there was a telephone in the house where he was to deliver next. He must hurry.

In less time than you'd think, considering it was a remote village, the doctor appeared and shortly afterwards the ambulance.

Miss Verney died that evening in the nearest hospital without recovering consciousness. The doctor said she died of shock and cold. He was treating her for a heart condition he said.

'Very widespread now – a heart condition.'

June 1974

Kingsley Amis

———— CLIVE JAMES ————

'The process of writing a novel,' said Kingsley Amis while taking an aperitif at the Braganza in Soho, 'is not mystical but very complicated. And unknown. And so it should be. Put that in italic capitals.' I drew a ring around it instead, reserving italics for stage directions, voice-overs (*Your table is ready, Mr Amis*) and my own questions and asides. As we settled down to a working lunch, I was fully prepared to ply a quill with Boswellian fidelity. Amis talks a free yet shapely prose with no wasted words. The parts of it that are for publication are delivered politely, ready punctuated, at fast dictation speed. The parts of it that are strictly off the record are delivered at full tilt and with copious recourse to his famous reservoir of impersonations. Amis's mimicry is not quite in the same league with that of Peter Sellers as to accuracy, but the mind and invention behind it make it a feast for the gods. He is a brilliantly entertaining man. And as Philip Larkin recounts in the preface to the reissue of *Jill*, Amis at an early stage got plenty of practice at not being taken seriously for just that reason. His humour disqualified him.

This disqualification has been both his prison and his liberation. A prison in the sense that his realistic, independent mind, can, under the pressure of obtuse misrepresentation, be forced from realism into harshness and from independence towards crankiness. In that mood, he gives the trendy Lefties what they want: the Amis of everyday life would rather be taken seriously as a fire-breathing reactionary than trivialized as a clown. A liberation in the sense that the Amis of the novels and the poetry – the artist Amis – is enabled, as a licensed comic, to deal with awkward and often taboo topics under the cover of laughter. He is pre-eminently the *theme* novelist of his generation.

The immediate occasion for our interview was the forthcoming publication of *Ending Up*, which I had read in proof and enjoyed very much. The theme, old age, had declared itself straightforwardly. With Amis the theme always does, whether it is being your own man (*Lucky Jim*) or faithfulness (*That Uncertain Feeling/Only Two Can Play*) or Abroad (*I Like It Here*) or virginity (*Take A Girl Like You*) or swinishness (*One Fat Englishman*) or the necessity to kill (*The Anti-Death League*) or the limits of ambition (*I Want It Now*) or the reality of love and evil (*The Green Man*) or the responsibility of middle age (*Girl, 20*) or the innocence of youth (*The Riverside Villas Murder*).

Obviously each of these books deals with much more than the theme I have ascribed to it. But equally obviously each of them is *focused* on that theme. It is always possible with an Amis production to say what it is about. Each work deals with a specific moral area, and as you go on reading in his output you find the moral areas connecting up. The twin facts that he is so plainly a moralist, and yet has been 'dismissed' as a vulgarian by the chief moralist critic, Dr Leavis, seem to me to be comic in themselves – a jokey bonus, like two glazed cherries on top of an elaborate sundae of paradoxes. The humourless, the tin-eared, can't hear Amis. Amis impels the owls to declare themselves, which in an age stocked to the twigs with such creatures is a valuable function to perform.

'*Ending Up* incubated for about three years. You probably spotted when you were up at the house (*at Hadley Common, near High Barnet*) that we've got a species of commune going, with relations and people living in. Nobody in the book is anything like any of them, by the way. But the idea occurred, what would this sort of arrangement be like if one had a pack of characters who were all about 20 years older?'

The people of *Ending Up* are not only advanced in years, but critically short of meaningful experience. The book's considerable gruesomeness lies not so much in their dying – although no unwholesome aspect of death is fudged – as in their never having really lived. Adela is ugly; the dimension of love has never existed in her life. (In that respect, she is like Graham in *Take A Girl Like You*.) Marigold's brain is going. She is a frightening creation: an intelligent man's vision of what it will be like to lose control of one's own mind. If she has an ancestor, it is Lord Edgerstoune, also in *Take A Girl Like You*: the character who gives Patrick Standish an abrupt, gratuitous briefing on what it will be like when one's sexual desires cease to be accompanied by any degree of sexual prowess. Such glimpses into the toxic core of the reactor are an Amis speciality.

George, Emeritus Professor of Central European History, starts the book with nominal aphasia: he can't do nouns. Later on in the book he is cured, and can't do anything else. He is specifically a writer's vision of the insupportable (H.L. Mencken, it is worth recalling, spent his last years semantically aphasic) and he generates boredom on an epic scale. Without being boring for a moment, *Ending Up* is choc-a-bloc with boredom. A few young relatives are introduced to test the quality of the ennui the oldies generate. To do that, and to realize that they, too, must come to this.

The central character is Bernard Bastable, an archetypal Amis heavy right up there in a class with Roger Micheldene, the supershit of *One Fat Englishman*. Bernard keeps up a steady barrage of personality-assassination against his ex-lover, Shorty, an alcoholic ex-Army lurk-man, and all the other geriatric cases in the house. When, at the last, Bernard learns that he has cancer, his destructive effort escalates from the verbal to the actively mischievous. The bitterly funny scenes that ensue are comic writing of extraordinary boldness. They are in direct descent from, and on a par with, those scenes in Evelyn Waugh where you suddenly find yourself laughing helplessly at the idea of little Lord Tangent having his foot amputated. Finally *Ending Up* ends up, with a massacre of Forsterian comprehensiveness. The bodies are discovered by Bernard's putative son, Stanley, who gets one mention at the beginning of the book and makes one, functional, appearance at the finish.

'He's there at the start,' said Amis, 'because he had to be there at the end. Not that I knew that when I first put him in. A similar case is Brian Leonard. The security officer in *The Anti-Death League*, remember? I found myself asking, why discuss *him*? But instinct said leave him in. And later on he became important. Apparently Graham Greene is constantly finding he's written five thousand irrelevant words only to discover miles later that they were essential.'

Nominal aphasia scares me starry-eyed.

'A friend had it. He won't mind my using it. It's pure guesswork about the various stages of the disease, incidentally. But I'm now told that I fluked the right answers.'

Can we go back to the start?

'I started writing *Lucky Jim* in 1951, in Swansea. After years of no home, no study, nowhere to work, my then wife gets a small legacy. Two thousand quid. Enough for a house with a tiny study in Uplands, Swansea. Where I wrote the book. Finished it at the end of 1952.'

Somebody told me it did the rounds of all the publishers.

'A myth. It went straight to Gollancz and Hilary Rubinstein accepted it after some delay. It was published in January 1954 because Victor Gollancz said in January there are no books and everyone will review it. There *were* no books and everyone *did* review it. I think that really counted. But *Lucky Jim* isn't at all about Swansea: *That Uncertain Feeling* is, but *Lucky Jim* really started in 1946. I went to visit Larkin, who was in Leicester at the time. He took me into the Common Room there, and after about a quarter of an hour I said, "Christ, someone ought to do something about this lot." There was a dawning idea about being bored by powerful people. Before you enter the world of work, if people bore you you just move away. But when they've got power over you, you can't. My first father-in-law was a very genial old shag, now dead, who bored me like buggery. He was a folk-dancing buff. Used to tell me all about it. I didn't use that as such, although there is one reference to Jim almost attending a folk-dancing conference. But the main thrust had to be changed, and I made it madrigals.

'In fact I really enjoy madrigals. The idea that you only guy things you hate is of course false. You can guy things you like. "Filthy Mozart", for example. You have to consider Jim's situation. He's hung over; his enemy, Johns, is singing . . .

'You don't see themes when you're writing; they emerge. One theme of *Lucky Jim* was getting good things wrong.

Culture's good, but not the way the Welches did it. Education is good, but as Jim explains in one scene I put in especially for the purpose, it's self-defeating if it isn't done properly.

'*Lucky Jim* is about being bored by your boss. On top of that, it's about being bored by your girl, and you're too nice and/or cowardly – i.e., you're cowardly – to tell her to fuck off. And then, wrapped around all that, it's about that deadly provincial background.'

I like it when Bertrand says things like 'you Sam' and 'obviouslam'. People who can recite whole pages of the novel from memory do that 'Sam' stuff all the time.

'I picked it up from a brother officer in 1944. You store these things away. They await their moment.

'*That Uncertain Feeling* was already well over half way there when *Jim* was still in production: a procedure I've stuck to since. Always have another one going. Then, if the current one gets hammered, you've got something in reserve. Anyway, after I left Oxford I tried to become a university lecturer but there were no jobs. I came second for a British Council post in Prague, but that was about it. So there was no question of choosing to go to Swansea. Swansea chose me. It was the last job left that summer. That was 1948, before the big expansion of 1949 got under way. I finished Oxford Schools with a wife, two kids, and all I could teach was English. No cash, naturally. I would have had to schoolteach if I hadn't got that job.'

Vernon Gruffydd-Williams strikes me as the mature man to John Lewis's immature man. It's the same relationship as the one between Jim and Atkinson, or even Michie. I always think of them as the characters forecasting Julian Ormerod in Take A Girl Like You.

'Michie is just one of the people sent to persecute Jim. But I agree that Atkinson is a proto-Ormerod. So is Gore-Urquhart, in a way. I do admire people who aren't bothered.'

Some people connect your sceptical essays on Dylan Thomas with Gareth Probert.

'*Of course* Probert's not supposed to be Dylan Thomas. Probert is a generic third-rate Welsh poet.'

What did you think of the movie?

'On the whole not bad, but I was very disappointed that there was no fuck. Because it's vitally important, that fuck.

And not for sexual reasons alone. It terrifies you, what Lewis gets himself into as a result of it. He gets into a panic and basks fraudulently in a glow of moral principle about the job being fixed. What *I* didn't realize at the time of writing, so how could he, was that he was scared, and wanted out. The attack of principle gets him off the hook. In the film, where the screwing is cut out, all he has is an attack of principle, which makes him look priggish. I suspect Sidney Gilliatt (*producer: Bryan Forbes directed*) didn't like the decision either, but the heroes of romantic screen comedies didn't fuck in those days. Later on, in the film of *Take A Girl Like You*, it was all the other way: the producer, Hal Chester, kept saying, "Lemme see some tit". Jonathan (*Miller, who directed*) fought back, but it was a losing battle.'

Everybody thinks I Like It Here *is thin.*

'It was written in too much haste. It was 1955, and I was in Portugal on the Somerset Maugham Award money: if you don't travel, you can't have the money. I started to plan *Take A Girl Like You*, keeping the longest and most elaborate notebook I've ever kept on any novel. I put that aside to write *I Like It Here*. I know why now, though I didn't then: I just wasn't mature enough to do *Take A Girl Like You*.'

I think the Jenny Bunn character is in nearly all your novels – Christine in Lucky Jim, *Helene Bang in* One Fat Englishman *to take two examples – but in* Take A Girl Like You *she's the moral centre.*

'Jenny is one of my favourite types. Naïve yet shrewd like Peter in *The Riverside Villas Murder*. The line that redeemed the film version – I should have found a way of putting it into the book – was when Patrick says, "What's this virginity of yours *worth*? What's the *point*?" And Hayley Mills says, "It's the only thing I've got to give." I should have had that line, or something like it. Virginity is very hard to defend intellectually.'

Quite apart from the way you evoke her beauty by having bus-conductors lunge at her, you make her sound interesting to know. Her theory about the Stooge – things like that.

'Dick's a high-ranking Stooge because he keeps one finger hooked over the lid of his suitcase and keeps his change in a purse and files his copies of the *New Statesman* in chronological order. It fits Jenny's character. She's an observer. She's naturally a better mind than Patrick.'

I thought that Graham's aria about ugliness where he quotes the lines from Antony and Cleopatra *was an important formal extension of your range. I mean in the way you just let him rip. It was a development of Jim's complaint to Gore-Urquhart about boredom: a set speech, only this time genuinely tragic.*

'You don't plan it, but you feel . . . I don't say I got this from P. G. Wodehouse, but I immediately recognized and saluted the idea when I read *Performing Flea*. Wodehouse said, and I paraphrase, "Treat your cast of characters as if they were members of a repertory company. Everybody should get his bit of fat. The most minor character should dominate the action at some point, even if only for half a page." I agree with that.

'What Graham is saying is that his life and Jenny's don't connect, and that the division between the attractive and the unattractive is a decisive one. I think that idea got started when I was in the army, at the OCTU in Catterick. In the cookhouse there was one of the most amazingly ugly girls I've ever seen. Small, tank-like, repulsive. Her job was to welcome you in and say, "Good morning, Lieutenant Shagbag, the porridge is over there." I used to say, "Good morning" and, after a while, "How are you?" After a week of that she said, "You going to the dance on Friday, then?" I gabbled something at her, such as I wasn't going because I was going with someone else. And I thought (a) you poor little bugger, and (b) what disgraceful creatures men are. All I'd done was treat her like a lift-man, and look at the gratitude.

'That was probably the first instance I remember of consciously wondering what ugly people's lives were like. As for Graham himself, the original was someone I knew, but the minute he entered the novel he changed completely.'

Ormerod is so impressive that the reader might tend to think he was based on someone who impressed you.

'There was no prototype for him at all. What academics don't realize is that some characters don't start off from people, even fragmentarily: they just occur fully formed. Julian is much more of a dream figure than, say, Jim's Christine is. The importance of his background, all the Battle of Britain stuff . . .'

. . . and the stately home with cakes of soap like little rugger balls . . .

'Right, is to show that he's not a fraud or a crook. He's genuine. I didn't realize that when I started writing. I saw Isherwood say in a TV interview once that novelists are aware of no more than two-thirds of what they're doing.'

I've always been keen on the blonde that Patrick makes on the second attempt. The one who looks as if she's just written a thesis on Wittgenstein, or would look like that if it wasn't so obvious that she hasn't the slightest need to know anything about Wittgenstein.

'She was real! In the early days when one still bought tit mags, there was a model – isn't it incredible, I even remember her name – her name was Rosa Domaille. She had this amazing look of being sexy and intellectual as well. You know the look. Amazingly *thoughtful*. It's part of the impressiveness of really sexy women. They've thought a lot.'

I suppose you'd object if somebody suggested that characters like Atkinson and Ormerod were father-figures.

'Mildly. Admired elder-brother figures.'

But surely there can't be much argument about Jenny's father being an admirable type. Is there any connection between him and your own father as portrayed in your poem 'In Memoriam W.H.A.' and your essay 'A Memoir of my Father'?

'Can't say that I've spotted it. Although some of his anecdotes and habits are certainly family property. That bit about the sweet on the lavatory paper, for example. Happened to an uncle of mine. He cut his arse with an acid-drop. My grandmother was so mean that every piece of paper that came into the house would end up in the loo. When the maids came down at 5.00 A.M. to light the fire for the day the matchbox would have two matches in. A fail-safe ignition system.

'My father recounted anecdotes with full production (*here Amis erupted in a rapid flurry of miming*). Another of his brothers was invited to a bottle party where the invitation said bring a bottle of anything. He brought a bottle of OK sauce. A streak of naïvety, which I may have myself. It's important to be naïve. If you're not, you're always safe.'

With Patrick, are you separating charm and goodness?
'Yes, but don't forget that Patrick does know a few of the right things to do. Arranging Sheila's abortion, for example. But that's only costing him money.'
Will Patrick change?
'He'll marry her and bugger off.'
Several years ago in Cambridge I attended, as an undergraduate, one of Dr Leavis's famous lectures on Dickens. After delivering himself of the opinion that he doubted Edmund Wilson's capacity to talk about Dickens, or indeed about any literature whatsoever – an opinion which was gravely copied down by the hundreds of students crowding Lady Mitchell Hall – Dr Leavis then announced that 'Mr Kingsley Amis' did not share Dickens's concern with what constituted the behaviour of a gentleman. The statement about Wilson had seemed to me an abdication of intellectual responsibility amounting to criminal philistinism, but the crack about Amis was so obviously immaterial it aroused no anger – just a pang of regret. Dr Leavis was perfectly within his rights to be talking about what characterized a gentleman. It was a pity, however, that one of the writers he was 'dismissing' (for which majestic activity he inherits the talent of Canute) was a novelist – Amis – whose subject-matter might usefully be defined as concerning exactly that. Patrick Standish, like John Lewis and Jim Dixon before him, and like all the other heroes of the novels to come, is involved in the business of learning that it is what you do which matters. The gentleman is the man who knows what must be done. The Amis hero, then, is, in the strictest sense, a would-be gentleman. Usually, in Amis, it is only the heavies who don't care about becoming better. The central figure of the book usually cares very much, even if he can't quite make the grade. Only on two occasions is the hero himself a heavy. Bernard Bastable in the latest book, and Roger Micheldene in *One Fat Englishman*.
In the years (the early sixties) when Micheldene was germinating, Amis had done stints at Cambridge ('The flesh-pots. I had this insane idea that Cambridge would be full of bright and interesting people. It turned out to be, intellectually, socially and in every other way, markedly inferior to Swansea') and at Princeton. Micheldene is mainly a product of Amis's American

experience. To a large extent Micheldene's swinishness is a device, meant to discredit the opinions he holds. One of the opinions he holds is a strident anti-Americanism – a view that Amis was eager to contest at the time and indeed goes on contesting, although nowadays with rather less force, since he no longer credits American culture with much substance or any real existence.

'Roger is your idea of yourself if you pushed a bit of it to an extreme. But it would be too dull if the character's interests were (*a donnish chuckle*) *coterminous* with one's own. Until we get to Bernard Bastable, Roger is undoubtedly the most unpleasant of my leading characters. I like Roger.'

Cocking up his lecture is what changes Jim's life. Roger's lecture is cocked up before it even starts, when somebody steals his notes. Did anything like that ever happen in real life?

'To me. But my notes were pinched *after* the lecture. It was in Philadelphia, and the script was hidden in a fellow-Englishman's bowler hat. So I immediately thought, what if they were pinched *before* the lecture?'

You give two people ridiculous names like Ernst and Helene Bang, then later on it turns out that they are the people of moral substance. Do you consciously balance these things up before starting?

'A bit. You don't want to be predictable all the time. In *Girl, 20,* for instance, it would be easy if it were a matter of letting Beethoven down, because we're all against that. So it's a matter of letting Mahler down. Which consequently makes it a matter of not letting music in general down, and so of trying to prevent Roy Vandervane letting himself down. *One Fat Englishman*, incidentally, caused no end of trouble in Princeton. They were all busily trying to identify themselves.'

I find The Anti-Death League *the most condensed and difficult of your books.*

'It's my favourite of my own books. Partly because of being more ambitious than anything before. The fact that L. S. Caton finally gets bumped off in it is a signal that it's to be taken seriously.'

I miss Caton in the subsequent books.

'The original of him died recently. He was a vanity publisher who published an early book of my poems.'

*Do you mean he was the man who ran the Fortune Press, the outfit
that first published you and Larkin? That book must be worth a bomb
now.*

'Good. That'll keep its circulation nicely restricted. Anyway,
I'd have said that non-funniness was there from the beginning
in my books – there's nothing intrinsically amusing about
Margaret Peel's situation in *Lucky Jim*, for example – but in *The
Anti-Death League* it takes over.'

*Katherine is in the direct line of desirable women which includes
Christine and Jenny, but Lady Hazel is a new step. She's a good
nymphomaniac.*

'Here's plot being king a bit. I wanted that centre *away* from
the camp where characters could turn up. A nymphomaniac
was the ideal answer. Incidentally, the term nymphomaniac is
overused. She just likes it. Brian Leonard will end up getting
her. Brian is my favourite character in the book, because of his
naïvety. He is a chivalrous fool. One has an irrational fondness
for characters. Chivalry appeals to me because I haven't got
much. Magnanimity too. George Parrot in *I Want It Now* – he
can't have Simon, but he wants her to have the man she wants,
so he lends her his car to catch Ronnie before he gets to the
airport. Most men wouldn't.'

Were you ever a Communist?

'I had a brief flirtation with it, *after* the Hitler–Stalin pact. So
in the nature of things it couldn't have lasted very long. I
wasn't quite 17. It started looking impossible the moment I
joined the army, when I started finding out what life was all
about. It was all so theoretical. At Oxford it might have been
mildly on. In the army it was like trying to be a Scientologist
on an Antarctic expedition. By 1946 I was a bit anti. A
bit. Fairly neutral. Hungary turned me into a violent anti-
Communist. Anti-totalitarian.'

I ask because I think The Anti-Death League *raised the question
of what you believe politically. I think that without knowing anything
else about you I could tell from that book where you stand on Vietnam.*

'Oh, one had, and has, terrific reservations. Vietnam has
been one immense, prolonged balls-up. But it's more important
to oppose Communism even ineptly than not oppose it.'

On this line our conversation went no further. With Amis, as with Robert Conquest, one experiences no such thing as a generation gap, but there is what might be called a generation pot-hole on this particular topic. It seems to me that Amis and Conquest have learned the lessons of the forties and fifties (and indeed it has been Conquest who has outstandingly *taught* the lessons of the whole Soviet-dominated period in his capital work *The Great Terror*) but that neither writer is quite able to see that the intelligent men of the succeeding generation have learned a further lesson in the sixties – the lesson that the United States has been, on a world scale, just as eager as the Soviet Union to expunge independent liberal forces. To any small country caught between the hammer and the anvil it isn't a matter of deciding which system is the worse. The two systems compose *one* system.

Amis has always feared that names like Kolyma, Vorkuta and Karaganda would be blanks to the coming generation. To a large extent they probably are: whether an historical memory can be successfully transmitted is problematical. But just because the averagely intelligent member of my generation might not recognize many of those names doesn't necessarily mean that he attaches undue importance to a name like, say, Con Sohn. The process by which the United States always seems to end up backing the totalitarian Right has by now become one of those historical facts to which, as Amis and Conquest have so often complained, the Left tends to be blind. Only this time it's the Right which is blind.

The Anti-Death League is full of the old-fashioned virtues, which doesn't hurt it at all, but it deals with an old-fashioned problem, which does. Nobody intelligent quarrels with the supposition that the Chinese, like the Russians, would do anything that suited them. But the book's conclusion, that its hero, James Churchill, must therefore face up to the possibility of doing the unspeakable in return, is open to several kinds of objection – of which the most important, because the most damaging artistically, is one's doubt that the choice would be posed in quite that way. When the James Churchills spread poisons or drop terrible weapons, it is usually because they *don't* fully understand what these weapons are doing. To the extent that civilization depends on James Churchill at all, it depends on him criticizing such activities and even refusing to carry them out. There is always a plentiful supply of people ready to take up the burden. But the number of people ready to ask awkward questions – and to go on rejecting the answers – is very few.

In James Churchill's dilemma Amis has dramatized his own political choice, and because he is a fair-minded artist he has made the choice as difficult as possible. But finally the choice is made. And just as it is hard to imagine a man of James Churchill's sensitivity feeling bound to reach a conclusion on a question which must surely await events before it is properly posed, so it is hard to see why Amis is so committed – and determined to be *seen* to be committed – to one side in a conflict when the evidence increasingly demands that he should anathematize both. I should add here that I sympathize with him in his loathing of the trendy Left. But I can't sympathize with him at all in his supposedly hard-headed backing of a *realpolitik* which in almost every instance is not a tenth as fair-minded as he is. Not that anyone is immune, as time goes by, to mistaken allegiances. But in *The Anti-Death League* the personal struggle for conviction, through being simplistically resolved, disturbs the art. Some of the difficulty of *The Anti-Death League* is difficulty that no amount of re-reading can clear away. It is the work of an artist who is not content merely to understand. He wants to act. Amis himself, by the way, has no doubts.

'*The Anti-Death League* kept changing, and while working out that day's events I'd walk from Maida Vale, where I was living at the time, to Kilburn to buy a packet of cigars. Only a quarter of an hour's walk. I'd have the whole thing clear before I got back.'

Amis is unique among serious writers in having written an extended hymn to booze (*On Drink*) and intoxicating beverages are unarguably an important part of his creative life. It should be said that he handles them well. As he makes his stately way through the available stuff, you notice several clearly demarcated verbal stages of his imbibing. There is a wildly diverting stage when he becomes other people. There is a less hilarious but quietly amusing, and very informative, stage when he becomes eloquently himself. There is an apparently unproductive stage when he becomes no one. This, I now think, is the crucial part of the business, because it's when he wakes up from this psychological nowhere that he starts to work, and he works very hard.

His study is of a Balzacian chaos ('Books and bottles – that's the main thrust') with teetering heaps of magazines and papers and an old Manuel Toribio sherry-cask squatting in one corner, full (and later on, one is encouraged to believe, empty) of whisky. There is a *Britannica* and a 13-volume *OED* behind his desk, on which stands a big Adler typewriter. Norwegian and Japanese translations of his books lie scattered dustily about. Amis doesn't enshrine his own works; nowhere in the house can you find a neat row of what he has written.

You need only a glance at Amis's surroundings to realize that he couldn't possibly be much of a businessman – an assumption that turns out to be truer than true. A colour-supplement profile recently revealed that Elizabeth Jane Howard saved his financial hide from being removed and used as a rug by the tax-man. And that such a story appeared at all was yet a further indication of his engaging deficiency in guile. Any magazine anywhere will print anything by Amis sight unseen, but his price partly depends on his scarcity value. That his impecuniosity should be generally known is a situation calculated to give his agent the horrors. There are plenty of authors who say they don't care about money. But Amis genuinely doesn't. He likes spending the stuff, but money *per se* just doesn't interest him.

In I Want It Now *I like it when Robert Hamer tells the hire-car driver to stop making his 'pissy comments.' Is that wish-fulfilment?*

'Can't deny that it might well be so. Hamer enjoys the freedom of being a shit, and being *known* to be a shit. I thought he was only going to be in the book for one scene, but he grew.'

Will Ronnie and Simon make a go of it?

'You don't know. There's the question of her frigidity. It's like the question of Katherine's cancer in *The Anti-Death League.* The threat isn't withdrawn. All I had in mind, in both cases, was that the couples had decided to stay together. Which is less dramatic than a miracle cure but it's what you've got to do.'

You changed direction with The Green Man *and yet your critics accepted it without demur. Would you agree that you had a useful press on that book?*

'Yes, although it was already known that I was interested in genre fiction. *The Green Man* got started partly out of my love of genre writing. Every other day you say. "I must write a ghost story of my own some day." But you have to wait for a reason. The technical point was interesting: what happens when the man who sees ghosts is an alcoholic?'

Allington's love for his daughter is his only real love, isn't it?

'Yes. He uses his women all the time as objects and it doesn't work. Even his daughter is an object until late on in the book – just something that needs to be taken care of. But the *Waldteufel* brings them together.'

When he finally gets his wife and Diana into bed with him, they want each other and not him.

'When you think you've got everything set up for you, it doesn't happen.'

Anthony Powell, who admires *The Green Man* as much as I do, thinks Amis should have made it clearer that Allington's sexual shenanigans disturb Dr Thomas Underhill's malevolent spirit because they are so like – or are done in something of the same spirit as – the things Underhill used to get up to. I hadn't grasped the parallel at all until Powell mentioned it – and after he mentioned it I saw straight away that it must be so. How far Amis intended it (whether, that is, we are dealing with another case of the writer only being two-thirds aware of what he's doing) is an open question. Or, to put it another way, I stupidly didn't ask. Personally I think *The Green Man* benefits from being fully explicable.

Where did Girl, 20 *start?*

'It emerged one day when I was in Tottenham Court Road trying to get a taxi. A taxi swept past a small brown man and stopped for me. I thought, wouldn't it be funny if I said to the driver, "You racialist." Wait a second: not me, another man. And it would be better if there was a cock-hungry girl with him at the time, who wouldn't like him doing it – who wanted him to climb into the cab and shut up. Which leads you to a man of liberal sentiments who needs a young and awful girl. Which makes him a trendy Lefty.'

What was Roy's responsibility to his daughter?

'He should have fostered Penny's talent. He should have said, "Here is a violin and a piano. Get through these exercises by the end of the week." "Why, Dad?" "Never mind why. That's what you *do*." Permissiveness is irresponsibility.'

My wife loves the way Roy talks. We both do that 'tim peaches' routine all the time.

'I keep thinking of other Roy-isms and wishing like hell I could turn back time and put them in. I thought of a beauty the other day. Vogka. Roy would say that.'

As well as being a fond evocation of childhood, *The Riverside Villas Murder* is an excursion into a genre: the mystery story. (With the ghost story and the mystery story both successfully tackled, Amis still has the science-fiction story to go. Of that, more in a moment.) Amis is plainly more than somewhat fascinated with murder. The first time he showed me the big pond near his house he said, 'The police regularly drag it for weapons.' His glee was unmistakable. There was a frightful murder – people bashed and hacked to death – in a nearby house quite recently. Elizabeth Jane Howard says that Amis was thrilled when the police called to ask him what he had been doing that night, and for days afterwards cherished the notion that he might be under suspicion.

I'm a dedicated fan of The Egyptologists. *How did your connection with Conquest get started?*

'I had a poem in *New Poems 1951*. I had only a toehold in the London Literary World and would come from Swansea to London just for a party. There was a party for the publication of that book. I came down and met Bob. He told me 50 limericks and the whole of his sequel to *Eskimo Nell*, which is better than the original. I had to be put on the train afterwards. After that, I was in *New Lines*, the idea for which was all Bob's. We weren't consciously a group. One doesn't work that way: perish the thought. A style emerges a lot more gradually and a lot less wilfully than that. I started off writing crappy little poems for school awards, all based on terrible models. Then I went through a long period of writing utter nonsense. All most unsatisfactory. But you can't go to a doctor and say, "Doctor, I suffer from the lack of a personal style: can you help me to forge one?" With luck, you eventually find you're getting somewhere.

'Larkin helped. Auden helped, and also hindered, by suggesting that riddles were okay. The idea that you plan, let alone plot with others, is absurd. Empson came in, of course. He showed that strict forms were all right. Not only all right, but a great help. And that rhyming was all right. It all happened very gradually, and partly through remembering, at some level, that Housman and Tennyson had got marvellous results *clearly*. Which is not, of course, to say that the poem should be exhausted after one reading.

'And perhaps Maugham did the same sort of thing for me in fiction, just by showing it's all right to name the characters straight away, and say what's happening to them.'

It never fails to astonish when critics attack your tone of voice in a poem and it turns out on inspection that the tone of voice in question is one that you're attributing to a character and criticizing yourself. Doesn't that kind of deafness make you want to pack poetry in?

'If I was Robinson Crusoe I'd still do it.'

An Amis novel is usually reviewed thoughtfully but academic criticism of his writings tends to the ponderous and otiose. One of the few academic studies of his work which Amis himself values was written by Mme S. M. Haimart, an assistant lecturer at the Sorbonne, and published in *Études Anglaises*, Vol. XXV, No. 3 (1972). Amis sent Mme Haimart a long letter thanking her for her article, disagreeing with some of its points and amplifying others. In a PS he summed up, in condensed form, a topic which had been touched on several times in our conversation.

'In general, you tend to overestimate the part played in a novelist's career by planning, forethought, purpose (and, in the opposite direction, money and fame), while underestimating the role of chance, whim, laziness, excess of energy, boredom, desire to entertain oneself, wanting a change for change's sake. The novelist himself, of course, *over*estimates the role of these things.'

If I were asked to choose one of those impulses as the key to

Amis, I would pick 'desire to entertain oneself'. The self-delighting element in Amis is fundamental. He has no thought of the dignity of categories in writing – only of whether such-and-such a task would be interesting to do.

Was Colonel Sun *the last of James Bond? Will Robert Markham write again?*

'I'd like to have one more go and actually kill Bond off, but lots of 007 fans all over the world would lose interest in a hero who had become dead. Fleming's estate would not be best pleased. Also Bond might be hard to rub out, as Conan Doyle found Sherlock Holmes was. Their supposed last scenes might well be similar when you think about it. There's Rear-Admiral Bond pottering about in a hotel in Switzerland and a ravishing young girl comes up and pleads for help. "A man called Colonel-General Moriartski of the KGB is trying to kill my grandfather. Stop him and I'll do anything for you, anything." "Well, my dear," says Bond, "it's too late for that. Nevertheless . . ." And over the Reichenbach Falls go Bond and Moriartski, locked together. Leaving Bond plenty of opportunities to reappear.'

Are you working on a novel now?

'As always. It's a firm idea and I know just how it will go. I haven't written a word yet, but I've made a lot of notes. *Records and Recording* sent me two LPs to review: stuff from the EMI archives going back three-quarters of a century, with Alistair Cooke narrating. Half way through the first side you got to 1906. Cooke said, get ready for a strange sound. A piano starts going ba-ba-ba-ba-ba-ba and a soprano starts trilling *Ave Maria*. After 10 seconds they fade it down and Cooke says, you're listening to a 46-year-old man: Alessandro Moreschi, one of the last of the so-called castrati. (That "so-called" was very good.) Then we heard the rest of it. Musically very fine. High notes at the end well tackled. But the noise was indescribably depressing. You thought, this poor creature, singing away: big success, but no man at all. I was depressed for days. Jittery: it wasn't an inert depression. Can't tell you exactly how or why. Then I thought, someone – he or his father – must have *consented* to this operation. And that decision brings out everything of importance in human life. Your arguments for and against your duty to God, to sing his music. Your duty to art. Sex. Love. Marriage. Children. Fame. Money. Security.

'All right, which was it to be? A poem, or what? No, must be a story. But how do we do it? I thought of two obvious possibilities. (1) Historical novel in the 18th century. Research too boring. (2) Eccentric millionaire on Mediterranean island. The coward's way out. And so matters stood for some months. Then it dawned on me. (3) A kind of SF? I've always wanted to write an SF book, but as with the ghost story, you couldn't do it on purpose. You have to have a reason. And here was the reason. Because in SF you have a subgenre called (*American accent*) Alternate World. And by using Alternate World, I could have the castrato living here and now. All you have to do is go back and change history.'

How much would you have to change?

'Pretty well everything modern. And let me remind you (*a look of ill-suppressed mischief*) that modern history, as defined at Oxford and Cambridge, starts at about 1400.'

How does it end?

'Don't know yet. Have to write it to find out. Couldn't write it if I already knew the end.'

Are you already thinking about what to include in the Oxford Book of Light Verse?

'Yes, but you have to be careful. Editing a thing like that is an invitation to work at low pressure. You find yourself thinking, "I know what I'll do! I'll go off and read through Kipling again. Much more fun than working on the novel!"'

Do you ever lose faith in what you're doing?

'A lot of doubts about Whether It's All Worth While. You subject yourself to a lot of solitude. I consider myself gregarious to the nth degree. It would undoubtedly be nicer to be, say, the leader of a crack symphony orchestra – not the conductor, but the leader, the man who can make or break an orchestra. He is, as they say, working with people. That's *very* nice. Or if you're a singer, even more so. Not necessarily an international star, Shagbaghini or Tossoffetsi, just someone who's contributed a lot to society and will be remembered. You've got all these chaps around you. Colleagues. It would have been nice to be J. C. Higginbotham and his trombone. In the days when we were all using steel needles and swapping Vocalion deletions, I formed the theory that Higginbotham had shares in a steel needle factory. The needle would perform perfectly well through the Red Allen solo and then crack up on Higgy's entry. Colleagues. It must be a good feeling. If you got the *wrong* colleagues, of course, you'd be in terrible trouble.'

We left the Braganza and walked slowly along Frith Street to Old Compton Street. It was just after four o'clock: one of the best times of the day in Soho. Amis was in excellent condition and elegiac mood.

'I did a story,' he said thoughtfully, 'called "Dear Illusion". All about an old old poet who wondered if perhaps that long lifetime of effort hadn't been wasted. Wondered if he was really any good.'

We were standing on the corner where we would separate. Seeing that he had successfully drawn me into expressing, with a worried frown, an attitude of sympathy with his supposed turmoil of doubts and fears, Amis started shaking with laughter.

'And of course he *wasn't!*'

July 1974

Solid Geometry

───── IAN McEWAN ─────

In Melton Mowbray in 1875 at an auction of articles of 'curiosity and worth' my great grandfather, in the company of M his friend, bid for the penis of Captain Nicholls who died in Horsemonger jail in 1873. It was bottled in a glass 12 inches long and, noted my great grandfather in his diary that night, 'in a beautiful state of preservation'. Also for auction was 'the unnamed portion of the late Lady Barrymore. It went to Sam Israels for 50 guineas'. My great grandfather was keen on the idea of having the two items as a pair and M dissuaded him. This illustrates perfectly their friendship. My great grandfather the excitable theorist, M the man of action who knew when to bid at auctions. My great grandfather lived for 69 years. For 45 of them, at the end of every day, he sat down before going to bed and wrote his thoughts in a diary. These diaries are on my table now, 45 volumes bound in calf leather, and to the left sits Capt. Nicholls in the glass jar. My great grandfather lived on the income derived from the patent of an invention of his father, a handy fastener used by corset makers right up till the outbreak of the First World War. My great grandfather liked gossip, numbers and theories. He also liked tobacco, good port, jugged hare and, very occasionally, opium. He liked to think of himself as a mathematician, though he never had a job, and never published a book. Nor did he ever travel or get his name in *The Times*, even when he died. In 1869 he married Alice, only daughter of the Rev. Toby Shadwell, co-author of a not highly regarded book on English wild flowers. I believe my great grandfather to have been a very fine diarist and when I have finished editing the diaries and they are published I am certain he will receive the recognition due to him. When my work is over I will take a long holiday, travel somewhere cold and clean and treeless, Iceland or the Russian Steppes. I used to think that at the end of it all I would try, if it was possible, to divorce my wife Maisie, but now there is no need at all.

Often Maisie would shout in her sleep and I would have to wake her.

'Put your arm around me,' she would say. 'It was a horrible dream. I had it once before. I was in a plane flying over a desert. But it wasn't really a desert. I took the plane lower and I could see there were thousands of babies heaped up, stretching away into the horizon, all of them naked and climbing over each other. I was running out of fuel and I had to land the plane. I tried to find a space, I flew on and on looking for a space . . .'

'Go to sleep now,' I said through a yawn, 'it was only a dream.'

'No,' she cried, 'I mustn't go to sleep, not just yet.'

'Well *I* have to sleep now,' I told her. 'I have to be up early in the morning.' She shook my shoulder.

'Please don't go to sleep yet, don't leave me here.'

'I'm in the same bed,' I said. 'I won't leave you.'

'It makes no difference, don't leave me awake . . .' But my eyes were already closing.

Lately I have taken up my great grandfather's habit. Before going to bed I sit down for half an hour and think over the day. I have no mathematical whimsies or sexual theories to note down. Mostly I write out what Maisie has said to me and what I have said to Maisie. Sometimes, for complete privacy, I lock myself in the bathroom, sit on the toilet seat and balance the writing-pad on my knees. Apart from me there is occasionally a spider or two in the bathroom. They climb up the waste pipe and crouch perfectly still on the glaring white enamel. They must wonder where they have come to. After hours of crouching they turn back, puzzled or perhaps disappointed they could not learn more. As far as I can tell, my great grandfather made only one reference to spiders. On 8th May 1906 he wrote, 'Bismarck is a spider'.

In the afternoons Maisie used to bring me tea and tell me her nightmares. Usually I was going through old newspapers, compiling indexes, cataloguing items, putting down this volume, picking up another. Maisie said she was in a bad way. Recently she had been sitting around the house all day glancing at books on psychology and the occult, and almost every night she had bad dreams. Since the time we exchanged physical blows, lying in wait to hit each other with the same shoe outside the bathroom, I had had little sympathy for her. Part of her problem was jealousy. She was very jealous . . . of my great grandfather's 45-volume diary, and of my purpose and energy in editing it. She was doing nothing. I was putting down one volume and picking up another when Maisie came in with the tea.

'Can I tell you my dream?' she asked. 'I was flying this plane over a kind of desert . . .'

'Tell me later, Maisie,' I said. 'I'm in the middle of something here.'

After she had gone I stared at the wall in front of my desk and thought about M who came to talk and dine with my great grandfather regularly over a period of 15 years up until his sudden and unexplained departure one evening in 1898. M, whoever he might have been, was something of an academic, as well as a man of action. For example, on the evening of 9th August 1870 the two of them are talking about positions for lovemaking and M tells my great grandfather that copulation *a posteriori* is the most natural way owing to the position of the clitoris and because other anthropoids favour this method. My great grandfather, who copulated about half-a-dozen times in his entire life, and that with Alice during the first year of their marriage, wondered out loud what the Church's view was and straight away M is able to tell him that the seventh-century theologian Theodore considered copulation *a posteriori* a sin ranking with masturbation and therefore worthy of 40 penances. Later in the same evening my great grandfather produced mathematical evidence that the maximum number of positions cannot exceed the prime number 17. M scoffed at this and told him he had seen a collection of drawings by Romano, a pupil of Raphael's, in which 24 positions were shown. And he said he had heard of a Mr F. K. Forberg who had accounted for 90. By the time I remembered the tea Maisie had left by my elbow it was cold.

An important stage in the deterioration of our marriage was reached as follows. I was sitting in the bathroom one evening writing out a conversation Maisie and I had about the Tarot pack when suddenly she was outside, rapping on the door and rattling the door handle.

'Open the door,' she called out. 'I want to come in.'

I said to her, 'You'll have to wait a few minutes more. I've almost finished.'

'Let me in now,' she shouted. 'You're not using the toilet.'

'Wait,' I replied, and wrote another line or two. Now Maisie was kicking the door.

'My period has started and I need to get something.' I ignored her yells and finished my piece which I considered to be particularly important. If I left it till later certain details would be lost. There was no sound from Maisie now and I assumed she was in the bedroom. But when I opened the door she was standing right in my way with a shoe in her hand. She brought the heel of it sharply down on my head, and I only had time to move slightly to one side. The heel caught the top of my ear and cut it badly.

'There,' said Maisie, stepping round me to get to the bathroom, 'now we are both bleeding,' and she banged the door shut. I picked up the shoe and stood quietly and patiently outside the bathroom holding a handkerchief to my bleeding ear. Maisie was in the bathroom about ten minutes and as she came out I caught her neatly and squarely on the top of her head. I did not give her time to move. She stood perfectly still for a moment looking straight into my eyes.

'You worm,' she breathed, and went down to the kitchen to nurse her head out of my sight.

During supper yesterday Maisie claimed that a man locked in a cell with only Tarot cards would have access to all knowledge. She had been doing a reading that afternoon and the cards were still spread about the floor.

'Could he work out the street plan of Valparaiso from the cards?' I asked.

'You're being stupid,' she replied.

'Could it tell him the best way to start a laundry business, the best way to make an omelette or a kidney machine?'

'Your mind is so narrow,' she complained. 'You're so narrow, so predictable.'

'Could he,' I insisted, 'tell me who M is or why . . .'

'Those things don't matter,' she cried. 'They're not necessary.'

'They are still knowledge. Could he find them out?' She hesitated.

'Yes, he could.' I smiled and said nothing.

'What's so funny?' she said. I shrugged, and she began to get angry. She wanted to be disproved. 'Why did you ask all those pointless questions?' I shrugged again. 'I just wanted to know if you really meant *everything*.' Maisie banged the table and screamed.

'Damn you! Why are you always trying me out? Why don't you say something real?' And with that we both recognized we had reached the point where all our discussions led and we became bitterly silent.

Work on the diaries cannot proceed until I have cleared up the mystery surrounding M. After coming to dinner on and off for 15 years and supplying my great grandfather with a mass of material for his theories, M simply disappears from the pages of the diary. On Tuesday, 6th December, my great grandfather invited M to dine on the following Saturday, and although M came, my great grandfather in the entry for that day simply writes, 'M to dinner'. On any other day the conversation at these meals is recorded at great length. M had been to dinner on Monday the 5th of December and the conversation had been about geometry, and the entries for the rest of that week are entirely given over to the same subject. There is absolutely no hint of antagonism. Besides, my great grandfather *needed* M. M provided his material, M knew what was going on, he was familiar with London and he had been on the Continent a number of times. He knew all about socialism and Darwin, he had an acquaintance in the free love movement, a friend of James Hinton. M was *in* the world in a way which my great grandfather, who left Melton Mowbray only once in his lifetime to visit Nottingham, was not. Even as a young man my great grandfather preferred to theorize by the fireside; all he needed were the materials M supplied. For example, one evening in June 1884 M, who was just back from London, gave my great grandfather an account of how the streets of the town were fouled and clogged by horse dung. Now in the same week my great grandfather had been reading the essay by Malthus called 'On the Principle of Population'. That night he made an excited entry in the diary about a pamphlet he wanted to write and have published. It was to be called 'De Stercore Equorum'. The pamphlet was never published and probably never written, but there are detailed notes in the diary entries for the two weeks following that evening. In 'De Stercore Equorum' (Concerning Horseshit) he assumed a geometric growth in the horse population, and working from detailed street plans he predicted that the metropolis would be impassable by 1935. By impassable he took to mean an average thickness of one foot (compressed) in every major street. He described involved experiments outside his own stables to determine the compressibility of horse dung which he managed to express mathematically. It was all pure theory, of course. His results rested on the assumption that no dung would be shovelled aside in the 50 years to come. Very likely it was M who talked my great grandfather out of the project.

One morning, after a long dark night of Maisie's nightmares, we were lying side by side in bed and I said, 'What is it you really want? Why don't you go back to your job? These long walks, all this analysis, sitting around the house, lying in bed all morning, the Tarot pack, the nightmares . . . what is it you want?'

And she said, 'I want to get my head straight,' which she had said many times before.

I said, 'Your head, your mind, it's not like a hotel kitchen, you know, you can't throw stuff out like old tin cans. It's more like a river than a place, moving and changing all the time. You can't make rivers flow straight.'

'Don't go through all that again,' she said. 'I'm not trying to make rivers flow straight, I'm trying to get my head straight.'

'You've got to *do* something,' I told her. 'You can't do nothing. Why not go back to your job? You didn't have nightmares when you were working. You were never so unhappy when you were working.'

'I've got to stand back from all that,' she said. 'I'm not sure what any of it means.'

'Fashion,' I said, 'it's all fashion. Fashionable metaphors, fashionable malaise. What do you care about Jung, for example? You've read 12 pages in a month.'

'Don't go on,' she pleaded, 'You know it leads nowhere.'

But I went on.

'You've never been anywhere,' I told her, 'you've never done anything. You're a nice girl without even the blessing of an unhappy childhood. Your sentimental Buddhism, this junk shop mysticism, joss stick therapy, magazine astrology . . . none of it is yours, you've worked none of it out for yourself. You fell into it, you fell into a swamp of respectable intuitions. You haven't the originality or passion to intuit anything yourself beyond your own unhappiness. Why are you filling your mind with other people's mystic banalities and giving yourself nightmares?' I got out of bed, opened the curtains and began to get dressed.

'You talk like this was a fiction seminar,' Maisie said. 'Why are you trying to make things worse for me?' Self-pity began to well up from inside her, but she fought it down. 'When you are talking,' she went on, 'I can feel myself, you know, being screwed up like a piece of paper.'

'Perhaps we *are* in a fiction seminar,' I said grimly. Maisie sat up in bed staring at her lap. Suddenly her tone changed. She patted the pillow beside her and said softly:

'Come over here. Come and sit here. I want to touch you, I want you to touch me . . .' But I was sighing, and already on my way to the kitchen.

In the kitchen I made myself some coffee and took it through to my study. It had occurred to me in my night of broken sleep that a possible clue to the disappearance of M might be found in the pages of geometry. I had always skipped through them before because mathematics does not interest me. On the Monday, 5th December 1898, M and my great grandfather discussed the *vescia piscis*, which apparently is the subject of Euclid's first proposition and a profound influence on the groundplans of many ancient religious buildings. I read through the account of the conversation carefully, trying to understand as best I could the geometry of it. Then, turning the page, I found a lengthy anecdote which M told my great grandfather that same evening when the coffee had been brought in, and the cigars were lit. Just as I was beginning to read, Maisie came in.

'And what about you,' she said, as if there had not been an hour's break in our exchange, 'all you have is books. Crawling over the past like a fly on a turd.' I was angry, of course, but I smiled and said cheerfully:

'Crawling? Well at least I'm moving.'

'You don't speak to me anymore,' she said, 'you play me like a pin-ball machine, for points.'

'Good morning Hamlet,' I replied, and sat in my chair waiting patiently for what she had to say next. But she did not speak, she left, closing the study door softly behind her.

'In September 1870,' M began to tell my great grandfather, 'I came into the possession of certain documents which not only invalidate everything fundamental to our science of solid geometry but also undermine the whole canon of our physical laws and force one to redefine one's place in Nature's scheme. These papers outweigh in importance the combined work of Marx and Darwin. They were entrusted to me by a young American mathematician, and they are the work of David Hunter, a mathematician too and a Scotsman. The American's name was Goodman. I had corresponded with his father over a number of years in connection with his work on the cyclical theory of menstruation which, incredibly enough, is still widely discredited in this country. I met the young Goodman in Vienna where, along with Hunter and mathematicians from a dozen countries, he had been attending an international conference on mathematics. Goodman was pale and greatly disturbed when I met him, and planned to return to America the following day even though the conference was not yet half complete. He gave the papers into my care with instructions that I was to deliver them to David Hunter if I was ever to learn of his whereabouts. And then, only after much persuasion and insistence on my part, he told me what he had witnessed on the third day of the conference. The conference met every morning at nine-thirty when a paper was read and a general discussion ensued. At 11 o'clock refreshments were brought in and many of the mathematicians would get up from the long, highly polished table round which they were all gathered and stroll about the large, elegant room and engage in informal discussions with their colleagues. Now, the conference lasted two weeks, and by a long-standing arrangement the most eminent of the mathematicians read their papers first, followed by the slightly less eminent, and so on in a descending hierarchy throughout the two weeks, which caused, as it is wont to do among highly intelligent men, occasional but intense jealousies. Hunter, though a brilliant mathematician, was young and virtually unknown outside his university, which was Edinburgh. He had applied to deliver what he described as a very important paper on solid geometry, and since he was of little account in this pantheon he was assigned to read to the conference on the last day but one, by which time many of the most important figures would have returned to their respective countries. And so on the third morning, as the servants were bringing in the refreshments, Hunter stood up suddenly and addressed his colleagues just as they were rising from their seats. He was a large, shaggy man and, though young, he had about him a certain presence which reduced the hum of conversation to a complete silence.

'"Gentlemen," said Hunter, "I must ask you to forgive this improper form of address, but I have something to tell you of the utmost importance. I have discovered the plane without a surface." Amid derisive smiles and gentle, bemused laughter, Hunter picked up from the table a large white sheet of paper. With a pocket knife he made an incision along its surface about three inches long and slightly to one side of its centre. Then he made some rapid, complicated folds and, holding the paper aloft so all could see, he appeared to draw one corner of it through the incision and as he did so, it disappeared.

'"Behold, gentlemen," said Hunter, holding out his empty hands towards the company, "the plane without a surface."'

Maisie came into my room, washed now and smelling faintly

of perfumed soap. She came and stood behind my chair and placed her hands on my shoulders.

'What are you reading?' she said.

'Just bits of the diary which I haven't looked at before.' She began to massage me gently at the base of my neck. I would have found it soothing if it had still been the first year of our marriage. But it was the sixth year, and it generated a kind of tension which communicated itself the length of my spine. Maisie wanted something. To restrain her I placed my right hand on her left and, mistaking this for affection, she leaned forward and kissed under my ear. Her breath smelled of toothpaste and toast. She tugged at my shoulder.

'Let's go in the bedroom,' she whispered. 'We haven't made love for nearly two weeks now.'

'I know,' I replied. 'You know how it is . . . with my work.' I felt no desire for Maisie or any other woman. All I wanted to do was turn the next page of my great grandfather's diary. Maisie took her hands off my shoulders and stood by my side. There was such a sudden ferocity in her silence that I found myself tensing like a sprinter on the starting-line. She stretched forward and picked up the sealed jar containing Capt. Nicholls. As she lifted it his penis drifted dreamily from one end of the glass to the other.

'You're so COMPLACENT,' Maisie shrieked just before she hurled the glass bottle at the wall in front of my table. Instinctively I covered my face with my hands to shield off the shattering glass. As I opened my eyes I heard myself saying:

'Why did you do that? That belonged to my great grandfather.' Amid the broken glass and the rising stench of formaldehyde lay Capt. Nicholls, slouched across the leather covers of a volume of the diary, grey, limp and menacing, transformed from a treasured curiosity into a horrible obscenity.

'That was a terrible thing to do. Why did you do that?' I said again.

'I'm going for a walk,' Maisie replied and slammed the door this time as she left the room.

I did not move from my chair for a long time. Maisie had destroyed an object of great value to me. It had stood in his study while he lived, and then it stood in mine, linking my life with his. I picked a few splinters of glass from my lap and stared at the 160-year-old piece of another human on my table. I looked at it and thought of all the homunculae which had swarmed down its length, I thought of all the places it had been, Cape Town, Boston, Jerusalem, travelling in the dark, fetid inside of Capt. Nicholls's leather breeches, emerging occasionally into the dazzling sunlight to discharge urine in some jostling public place. I thought also of all the things it had touched, all the molecules, of Capt. Nicholls's exploring hands on lonely unrequited nights at sea, the sweating walls of cunts of young girls and old whores, their molecules must still exist today, a fine dust blowing from Cheapside to Leicestershire. Who knows how long it might have lasted in its glass jar? I began to clear up the mess. I brought the rubbish bucket in from the kitchen. I swept and picked up all the glass I could find and swabbed up the formaldehyde. Then, holding him by just one end, I tried to ease Capt. Nicholls on to a sheet of newspaper. My stomach heaved as the foreskin began to come away in my fingers. Finally, with my eyes closed, I succeeded, and wrapping him carefully in the newspaper, I carried him into the garden and buried him under the geraniums. All this time I tried to prevent my resentment towards Maisie filling my mind. I wanted to continue with M's story. Back in my chair I dabbed at a few spots of formaldehyde which had blotted the ink, and read on.

'For as long as a minute the room was frozen, and with each successive second it appeared to freeze harder. The first to speak was Dr Stanley Rose of Cambridge University, who had much to lose by Hunter's plane without a surface. His reputation, which was very considerable indeed, rested upon his "Principles of Solid Geometry".

'"How dare you, sir. How dare you insult the dignity of this assembly with a worthless conjuror's trick." And, bolstered by the rising murmur of concurrence behind him, he added, "You should be ashamed, young man, thoroughly ashamed." With that the room erupted like a volcano. With the exception of young Goodman, and of the servants who still stood by with the refreshments, the whole room turned on Hunter and directed at him an insensible babble of denunciation, invective and threat. Some thumped on the table in their fury, others waved their clenched fists. One very frail German gentleman fell to the floor in an apoplexy and had to be helped to a chair. And there stood Hunter, firm and outwardly unmoved, his head inclined slightly to one side, his fingers resting lightly on the surface of the long, polished table. That such an uproar should follow a worthless conjuror's trick clearly demonstrated the extent of the underlying unease, and Hunter surely appreciated this. Raising his hand and the company falling suddenly silent once more he said:

'"Gentlemen, your concern is understandable and I will effect another proof, the ultimate proof." This said, he sat down and removed his shoes, stood up and removed his jacket, and then called for a volunteer to assist him, at which Goodman came forward. Hunter strode through the crowd to a couch which stood along one of the walls and while he settled himself upon it he told the mystified Goodman that when he returned to England he should take with him Hunter's papers and keep them there until he came to collect them. When the mathematicians had gathered round the couch, Hunter rolled on to his stomach and clasped his hands behind his back in a strange posture to fashion a hoop with his arms. He asked Goodman to hold his arms in that position for him, and rolled on his side where he began a number of strenuous jerking movements which enabled him to pass one of his feet through the hoop. He asked his assistant to turn him on his other side where he performed the same movements again and succeeded in passing his other foot between his arms, at the same time bending his trunk in such a way that his head was able to pass through the hoop in the opposite direction to his feet. With the help of his assistant he began to pass his legs and head past each other through the hoop made by his arms. It was then that the distinguished assembly vented, as one man, a single yelp of incredulity. Hunter was beginning to disappear, and now, as his legs and head passed through his arms with greater facility, seemed even to be drawn through by some invisible power, he was almost gone. And now . . . he was gone, quite gone, and nothing remained.'

M's story put my great grandfather in a frenzy of excitement.

In his diary that night he recorded how he tried 'to prevail upon my guest to send for the papers upon the instant' even though it was by now two o'clock in the morning. M, however, was more sceptical about the whole thing. 'Americans,' he told my great grandfather, 'often indulge in fantastic tales.' But he agreed to bring along the papers the following day. As it turned out, M did not dine with my great grandfather that night because of another engagement, but he called round in the late afternoon with the papers. Before he left he told my great grandfather he had been through them a number of times and 'there was no sense to be had out of them'. He did not realize then how much he was under-estimating my great grandfather as an amateur mathematician. Over a glass of sherry in front of the drawing-room fire, the two men arranged to dine together again at the end of the week, on Saturday. For the next three days my great grandfather hardly paused from his reading of Hunter's theorems to eat or sleep. The diary is full of nothing else. The pages are covered with scribbles, diagrams and symbols. It seems that Hunter had to devise a new set of symbols, virtually a whole new language, to express his ideas. By the end of the second day my great grandfather had made his first breakthrough. At the bottom of a page of mathematical scribble he wrote, 'dimensionality is a function of consciousness'. Turning to the entry for the next day I read the words, 'It disappeared in my hands'. He had re-established the plane without a surface. And there, spread out in front of me, were step-by-step instructions on how to fold the piece of paper. Turning the next page I suddenly understood the mystery of M's disappearance. Undoubtedly encouraged by my great grandfather, he had taken part that evening in a scientific experiment, probably in a spirit of great scepticism. For here my great grandfather had drawn a series of small sketches illustrating what at first glance looked like yoga positions. Clearly they were the secret of Hunter's disappearing act.

My hands were trembling as I cleared a space on my desk. I selected a clean sheet of typing-paper and laid it in front of me. I fetched a razor blade from the bathroom. I rummaged in a drawer and found an old compass, sharpened a pencil and fitted it in. I searched through the house till I found an accurate steel ruler I had once used for fitting window panes, and then I was ready. First I had to cut the paper to size. The piece that Hunter had so casually picked up from the table had obviously been carefully prepared beforehand. The length of the sides had to express a specific ratio. Using the compass I found the centre of the paper and through this point I drew a line parallel to one of the sides and continued it right to the edge. Then I had to construct a rectangle whose measurements bore a particular relation to those of the sides of the paper. The centre of this rectangle occurred on the line in such a way as to dissect it by the Golden Mean. From the top of this rectangle I drew intersecting arcs, again of specified proportionate radii. This operation was repeated at the lower end of the rectangle, and when the two points of intersection were joined I had the line of incision. Then I started work on the folding lines. Each line seemed to express, in its length, angle of incline and point of intersection with other lines, some mysterious inner harmony of numbers. As I intersected arcs, drew lines and made folds, I felt I was blindly operating a system of the highest, most terrifying form of knowledge, the mathematics of the Absolute. By the time I had made the final fold, the piece of paper was the shape of a geometric flower with three concentric rings arranged round the incision at the centre. There was something so tranquil and perfect about this design, something so remote and compelling, that as I stared into it I felt myself going into a light trance and my mind becoming clear and inactive. I shook my head and glanced away. It was time now to turn the flower in on itself and pull it through the incision. This was a delicate operation and now my hands were trembling again. Only by staring into the centre of the design could I calm myself. With my thumbs I began to push the sides of the paper flower towards the centre, and as I did so I felt a numbness settle over the back of my skull. I pushed a little further, the paper glowed whiter for an instant and then it *seemed* to disappear. I say 'seemed', because at first I could not be sure whether I could feel it still in my hands and not see it, or see it but not feel it, or whether I could sense it had disappeared while its external properties remained. The numbness had spread right across my head and shoulders. My senses seemed inadequate to grasp what was happening. 'Dimensionality is a function of consciousness,' I thought. I brought my hands together and there was nothing between them, but even when I opened them again and saw nothing I could not be sure the paper flower had completely gone. An impression remained, an after-image not on the retina but in the mind itself. Just then the door opened behind me and Maisie said:

'What are you doing?'

I returned as if from a dream to the room and to the faint smell of formaldehyde. It was a long, long time ago now, the destruction of Capt. Nicholls, but the smell revived my resentment which spread through me like the numbness. Maisie slouched in the doorway muffled in a thick coat and woollen scarf. She seemed a long way off, and as I looked at her my resentment merged into a familiar weariness of our marriage. I thought, why did she break the glass? Because she wanted to make love? Because she wanted a penis? Because she was jealous of my work, and wanted to smash the connection I had with my great grandfather's life?

'Why did you do it?' I said out loud, involuntarily. Maisie snorted. She had opened the door and found me hunched over my table staring at my hands.

'Have you been sitting there all afternoon,' she asked, 'thinking about *that*?' She giggled. 'What happened to it, anyway? Did you suck it off?'

'I buried it,' I said, 'under the geraniums.' She came into the room a little way and said in a serious tone:

'I'm sorry about that, I really am. I just did it before I knew what was happening. Do you forgive me?' I hesitated and then, because my weariness had blossomed into sudden resolution, I said:

'Yes, of course I forgive you. It was only a prick in a pickle,' and we both laughed. Maisie came over to me and kissed me, and I returned the kiss, prising her lips with my tongue.

'Are you hungry?' she said when we were done with kissing. 'Shall I make some supper?'

'Yes,' I said. 'I would love that.' Maisie kissed me on the top of my head and left the room while I turned back to my studies, resolving to be as kind as I possibly could to Maisie that evening.

Later we sat in the kitchen eating the meal Maisie had cooked and getting mildly drunk on a bottle of wine. We smoked a joint, the first one we had had together in a very long time. Maisie told me how she was going to get a job with the Forestry Commission planting trees in Scotland next summer. And I told Maisie about the conversation M and my great grandfather had had about *a posteriori*, and about my great grandfather's theory that there could not be more than the prime number 17 positions for making love. We both laughed and Maisie squeezed my hand, and love-making hung in the air between us, in the warm fug of the kitchen. Then we put our coats on and went for a walk. It was almost a full moon. We walked along the main road which runs outside our house and then turned down a narrow street of tightly-packed houses with immaculate and minute front gardens. We did not talk much, but our arms were linked and Maisie told me how very stoned and happy she was. We came to a small park which was locked and we stood outside the gates looking up at the moon through the almost leafless branches. When we came home Maisie took a leisurely hot bath while I browsed in my study, checking on a few details. Our bedroom is a warm, comfortable room, luxurious in its way. The bed is seven foot by eight and I made it myself in the first year of our marriage. Maisie made the sheets, dyed them a deep, rich blue and embroidered the pillow-cases. The only light in the room shone through a rough old goatskin lampshade Maisie bought from a man who came to the door. It was a long time since I had taken an interest in the bedroom. We lay side by side in the tangle of sheets and rugs, Maisie voluptuous and drowsy after her bath and stretched full out, and I propped up on my elbow. Maisie said sleepily:

'I was walking along the river this afternoon. The trees are beautiful now, the oaks, the elms . . . there are two copper beeches about a mile past the footbridge, you should see them now . . . ahh that feels good.' I had eased her on to her belly and was caressing her back as she spoke. 'There are blackberries, the biggest ones I've ever seen, growing all along the path, and elderberries too. I'm going to make some wine this autumn

. . .' I leaned over her and kissed the nape of her neck and brought her arms behind her back. She liked to be manipulated in this way and she submitted warmly. 'And the river is really still,' she was saying. 'You know, reflecting the trees, and the leaves are dropping into the river. Before the winter comes we should go there together, by the river, in the leaves. I found this little place. No one goes there . . .' Holding Maisie's arms in position with one hand, I worked her legs towards the 'hoop' with the other. '. . . I sat in this place for half an hour without moving, like a tree. I saw a water rat running along the opposite bank and different kinds of duck landing on the river and taking off. I heard these plopping noises in the river but I didn't know what they were, and I saw two orange butterflies, they almost came on my hand.' When I had her legs in place Maisie said, 'Position number eighteen,' and we both laughed softly. 'Let's go there tomorrow, to the river,' said Maisie as I carefully eased her head towards her arms. 'Careful, careful, that hurts,' she suddenly shouted and tried to struggle. But it was too late now, her head and legs were in place in the hoop of her arms and I was beginning to push them through, past each other. 'What's happening?' cried Maisie. How the positioning of her limbs expressed the breathtaking beauty, the nobility of the human form and, as in the paper flower, there was a fascinating power in its symmetry. I felt the trance coming on again and the numbness settling over the back of my head. As I drew her arms and legs through, Maisie appeared to turn in on herself like a sock. 'Oh God,' she sighed, 'what's happening?' and her voice sounded very far away. Then she was gone . . . and not gone. Her voice was quite tiny, 'What's happening?' and all that remained was the echo of her question above the deep blue sheets.

July 1974

John Crowe Ransom
1888–1974

ROBERT LOWELL

He was born in 1888, my father's birthdate, and was the intellectual father I would have chosen. Twenty-five years ago, I wrote a short *festschrift* piece on Ransom's conversation. I thought his poetry was conversation as much as his criticism. Since then his accomplishment hasn't changed except for half a dozen fine elegiac essays, and eight poems curiously and dubiously revised. I have nothing new to offer but my wonder. My lasting, almost daily, picture of Ransom is slightly over-symbolic, and such as he couldn't have been. I was nineteen or twenty then, loud humoured, dirty and frayed – I needed to be encouraged to comb my hair, tie my shoes and say goodbye when leaving a house. I knew more about Dryden and Milton than most students, but had never read a word by a philosopher or Greek. I could not decode John's (none of us wished to call him this until after graduation) metaphysical terms, *ontology, catharsis*, with their homely Greek derivations and abstract, accurate English significations so unlike language. Ransom detested laurels and Byronic bravery, but his poetic calling showed in the fine fibre of his phrases, and in a convivial shyness. His recreations were games, all the brisk and precise ones, golf, croquet, crossword puzzles, bridge, charades, the Game. For someone so gracious, he was surprisingly put out by violations. An enemy charade-team once divided *Churchill* into *church* and *hill* instead of *church* and *ill*. This brought out his sustained aesthetic scoldings; so did the illegal moving of his croquet ball. He could live without cheating and within the rules of a game. His rather repelling and unwayward rows of flowers seemed laid out by tape-measure and flower-advertisements. 'I would fill rows of separate plots with flowers to my liking; and very congenial would be the well-clipped horizontal turfs between adjacent plots to walk upon. But I would replace the end-flowers of the two central plots with ten plants of Burpee's *Climax Marigold*, which bear blazing orange flowers; and the end-flowers of the upper and lower plots with *Wayside Gardens' Aster Frikarti*, whose blossoms are bright lavender . . . Think how the farmer and the visitors would be intrigued by the displacements of the sloping front border, which do not subtract a foot from its lawful length.' His parlours in three successive houses were the same room, bleak, comfortably barren, just-moved-into-looking; no games or students sipping a beer on the rug could injure it or alter. Most of Ransom's original paintings were loaned him by Kenyon's art instructor. They were coarse-textured and large, an affront to the instructor's rival, the Impressionist wife of the co-editor of the *Kenyon Review*. Ransom would say, 'Mr Mercer, like William Turner, is better at the sea than farmland.'

Ransom's mouth was large and always in slow perceptive motion, tight-drawn to deflect ignorant rudeness, giving an encouraging grimace, or relaxed, though busy, in season. It was a mouth more expressive than the small, beautiful mouths of the girls in his poems. He liked to be a poet, but not to be tagged as one; he preferred the manner of a country philosopher or classics professor – a man from his father's generation. He roughened his musical voice as with gravel, just as he revised to roughen metre. Once we watched my classmate, Mr Nerber, lope in his apricot corduroy suit across the Kenyon campus. 'Nerber is our only Kenyon man whose trousers match his coat.' Poor Nerber, nothing else in his whole life matched. Ransom could paraphrase a faculty meeting and make it interesting. He could make a sad comic masterpiece of a happening under his nose. My classics professor was a close friend of his and mine, and was a child-prodigy, who entered Harvard at thirteen, wrote the best Greek verse by an American in England, and later married another classics-child-prodigy – egregious people but fated for divorce and tragedy. They were plain and Socratic, yet their divorce was marked with violence and absurdity: a sheet wetted to cause pneumonia, a carving-knife left threateningly on a stairpost, a daughter held *incommunicado* by the Ransoms from both parents, insomnia, evidence, floods of persuasive, contradictory and retold debate. On the much adjourned day of trial, the presiding judge, the master of sarcasm, was kicked and incapacitated by a mule. Ransom told this story for a season as if possessed, and in an honest rococo style that left listening moralists pale and embarrassed. It was his version of the Southern tall-story – one of the strangest and most fascinating, though true. Ransom's natural conversation was abstract and soft-spoken, as if leading a slow actress.

There were moments in Ransom's ironic courtesies that reduced even Allen Tate to white-faced finger-twitching, so far had the conversation dropped from brave sublimity. In a letter just written me, Tate rightly boasts of being Ransom's oldest living student. But the relationship could never have been this, they were so near in genius, close in age, and different in character. Ransom affected fear, lest Tate, though matchless, prove too strong. He roamed in the danger areas, France, Rimbaud, Hart Crane, the *Waste Land*, was too eloquent, obscure, and menacing. Ransom liked to stand behind and later off from the Agrarian rush, an antislavery Southern commander with liberal connections in the East. I suppose I don't need to explain the decentralist provincial hopes of the Tennessee agrarians and neo-traditionalists, a utopia as impractical and permanent as socialism, though for now fallen away from the sunlight.

Ransom spent his last thirty-five years, over a third of his whole life, at an adopted college in Ohio. His affections warmed slightly to the bohemian; his politics grew less slashing and heroic. His Southern first-love levelled or dimmed into unoptimistic, though airy Northern reasonableness. The powerful Midwestern farms never became his soil, or harvest; not even a spot to sightsee. Who knows what was the choice? Did leaving Tennessee strengthen his health by derailing his inspiration? Health is the nurse of our functioning, according to the Stagirite, to use his ironic word.

Randall Jarrell said the gods who took away the poet's audience gave him students. No student was more brilliant than Jarrell, but Ransom had dozens, Allen Tate, Robert Penn Warren, Andrew Lytle, Peter Taylor, John Thompson, Robie Macauley, James Wright. We carried his academic brand, but were diverse, unsortable, ungroupable. Ransom's neatness fathered the haphazard. He was known throughout the English departments of America; in Southern universities, he is a cult, everyone has studied under him or under someone who has; any student can repeat scraps of Ransom dialogue, epigram and dogma, or laugh at his legendary defeat of some notable or boor. His classes were usually for a dozen or more students; they were home-made, methodical yet humdrum. For five years, he coolly taught the *Faerie Queene*; though he found Spenser's allegory without intellectual pith, it amused him like a crossword puzzle or a problem for his flowers. More brilliance and flare often came in his casual gossip. Sometimes classes would crackle with fire. Most often in Aesthetics. 'I must give Hegel's Triad an accurate terminology. When a teacher says that, he means his own.' He had a fairly rich though sketchy and out-of-vogue acquaintance with the old classical-romantic music. Once in Aesthetics, we were taken to hear a record of Beethoven's *Seventh Symphony*. It upset Ransom's spleen with the nineteenth century; he had discovered Shelleys everywhere in that unmetaphysical darkness. 'Beethoven is a romantic . . . he is too good.'

Ransom's Prose. He thought philosophy more intellectually stimulating than literary criticism; criticism more masculine than scholarship; scholarship more solid than criticism; poetry more intuitive than philosophy, though a florid and slipshod thinker. Technique was skeletal without intuition; intuition was soft. 'The minds of man and woman grow apart; and how shall we express their differentation? In this way, I think: man at his best is an intellectualized woman.' Or, 'The philosopher is apt to see a lot of wood and no trees, his theory is very general and his acquaintance with particulars is not persistent or intimate, especially his acquaintance with technical effects.' In the world of the sentiments and art's particularity, child, woman, art and creature are perfect, though they mostly fail before the verification – bodies without heads. All Ransom's thoughts are dialectical, games of pieces in opposition. None can be expelled, or manoeuvre without bumping. I hope I haven't suggested that everything is equal to everything in his aesthetic, that college course jars against college course without umpire or outcome. He could suffer breakage and bloodshed, he was a tough and untiring constructor.

Ransom received a low but passing grade for writing his final classics exam at Oxford in the Latin of Tacitus. No other Latin style seemed close and intelligent enough. He studied romantics with fear and pity, and never confused extravagance with sublimity. He himself, though, was a romantic, and had the underdog courage of someone always smaller, quicker and brighter. He was happier than us, though easily injured. My friend Jarrell was romantic in another style than Tate or Ransom. He was educated in the preoccupations of the thirties, Marx, Auden, Empson, Kafka, plane-design, anthropology since Frazer, the ideologies and news of the day. He knew everything, except Ransom's provincial world of Greek, Latin, Aristotle and England. His idiom was boyish, his clothes Southern collegiate. Our college President, Dr Chalmers, was a thoughtless disciple of the great American humanists, Paul Elmer More and Irving Babbit. Unlike Ransom, he believed in his anti-romanticism, and forever called out barbarously for measure, order, the inner check. For him, Socrates was a brand-new humanist professor at Harvard. He watched Randall going down a ski-crest in his unconventional, unlovely clothes, crying, 'I am like an angel.' Ransom suggested that Randall had shocked Dr Chalmers's belief. The Aristotelian schoolmen had known no such enthusiastic and inordinate angel. 'That boy needs a more generous vocabulary.' He knew that Randall had already *swallowed the dictionary*.

When Ransom wasn't playing games, golfing or taking us on hikers' discussions, or gardening in structured solitude, he was in his den. It was a compact, unwomanly room, the twin of last year's moved-out-of den – fresh and secure, though seasoned with pipesmoke, Greek, Latin, English, an infirm volume or two in French or German bought at college, a firm density of philosophy, criticism, a volume or two of Jane Austen, four by Faulkner, a fair spread of modern poetry, weakened by signed copies from friends. He talked metaphysics if he could, and poetry if he could, and gossip if he could. The strands were indistinguishable; one of his obsessive critical terms was *nostalgia*. Unlike the poets, he could write of women, and the fresh things of the sexes.

When he changed his poetry for criticism, everyone asked why he stopped writing. They discussed this behind his back, or studied him silently with a pained, consolatory eye. Perhaps the reverse question had only been put to him by himself. Why make pretty rhyming instead of an honest essay? Critics condescend to poets yet often must abase their own medium before poetry. Even so Ransom; but he was lucky to find criticism in his unoccupied hour, a more flexible and controlled sentence, and stricter sequence. No need to tinsel out syllogism and stories with metre; no passion to puff like balloons. Through criticism, Ransom discovered his *Review*, entered into correspondence with the first New Critics. He assembled critics annually each summer at Gambier, Ohio, to teach his School of Criticism. *O bel eta del oro*, when criticism had an air of winning! When Ransom's classical pessimism renounced its half-warning, 'They won't be content until the old work is done over.' Somehow in the next generation, the great analytical and philosophic project turned to wood, the formidable inertia of the pedagogue and follow-up man.

Ransom's poems, if anything, think more clearly than his prose. Yet the essays have the same language, and the same intent. His charming, biting criticism of Edna Millay is like one of his poems on Southern ladies. It has wit and flirtation yet skilfully avoids poetry. In his prose, Aristotle, Santayana and Sir Arthur Quiller-Couch breathe, though introduced as intellectual presences not portraits. His unruffled rhetoric and arguments against blur and enthusiasm once seemed to me perverse. They are medicine now.

Ransom wanted to go back to his poetry. Someone found an envelope he had scribbled with bizarre and hitherto unused off-rhymes. No other words. After the War, he published his first *Selected Poems*, with minor though magical revisions. Long after, he spent years rewriting and trying to perfect his old, almost perfect poems in a disastrously new style. I leave this insolent sentence as I wrote it. Not all of Ransom's changes are disastrous, some improve, almost all show surprising ways in which passages can be turned into variations. We are given a thousand opportunities to misrevise. A little ground is gained for the more that is lost. One new quatrain in 'Prelude to an

Evening' has the richness of lines from *Macbeth*. Ransom's prose *defences* of his new poetic versions are autobiographical and critical; they sometimes change the life-story. 'During the *Fugitive* days of my fourth decade I was at great pains to suppress my feelings in what I wrote. I was both sensitive and sentimental . . . My friends seemed to think I managed it. My third stanza, where chill replaces fever, is almost unutterably painful; but I was most intent upon it, and managed to the best of my ability. Lines two and three are the saddest perhaps in all my poems.' I hope these saddest lines were those of the first version, not those he ruined by revision.

His *Selected Poems* is no longer than single volumes by other poets; all his work is no longer than two such volumes. He made one or two debatable inclusions, and three or four omissions; these were missed and later restored. What he wrote could have come from knowing Hardy, E. A. Robinson, early Graves, Shakespeare, Milton, Mother Goose, ballads, Plato and Aristotle. His poems stick apart; and refuse to melt into their neighbours. They seem few until one tries to discover as many in some favourite, more voluminous author. Ransom's essays, even the most dazzling and strong, are like didactic poems (some of Auden's perhaps), a little monotonous and ill-jointed. The charm of his true poems seems to be first in their colours, people, beautiful, observant imagery, grace of rhyme and speed – his undefinable voice. They are short.

Ransom is able to like women, and the young, find them delightful, irritating, mortal, though not quite human. His women cannot be spoiled by abstraction, or impressed into drudgery. They are supporting figures; man stands in the middle, one unchangeable man wherever he is – troubled, gaunt, conscienced, philosophizing to no good, Quixote, Prufrock, too serious to see his own shadow or children . . . heavily unlike Ransom in life. Men and women court, quarrel, and whirl into disequilibrium, not tragic but pained. Nowhere a thoughtless happiness, a worldly innocence, places to 'hear the maiden pageant ever sing/of that far away time of gentleness'. Man goes creased and sometimes finds his puzzling joy.

In his art, too, Ransom discovered pain, or a harmony of disequilibrium. Why do we not come back, he asks, to a photograph for aesthetic pleasure, no matter how colourful and dramatic it is, not even if it is a picture of someone dead? We cannot feel, here, as in paintings, the artist's motherwork of hand and mind. I asked the master photographer Walker Evans how Vermeer's *View of Delft* (perhaps the first *trompe l'oeil* of landscape verisimilitude) differed from a photograph. He paused, staring, as if his eye could not give an answer. His solution was Ransom's – art is the intelligent pain or care behind each speck of brick and spot of paint.

Ransom made no case for a poetry of onomatopoeia, superior eeriness, passionate intensity. He liked his language to be elegant and unpainted, not far removed, except in its close texture, from written or spoken prose. He wished poetry to show its seams, and show the uncouthness caused by rhyming, compression, managing syntax. Out of pain, the art that can hide art. The poetic in the old sense was all to Ransom. He told me his poems came from brief, unevoked daydreams, a wisp of imagery, or a new fable. Many dreams, few poems. When the daydreams stopped or became inappropriate so did the muse.

I think of Ransom on a hill, as a student must see his loved master. Kenyon had a sentimental hill celebrated in student songs. I have left out my friend's personal life, his charming, healthy household, where with Jarrell I spent my second and key college year. I leave out too his wife, Rob Reavil, whose humour and particularity held him back from the ether of the metaphysics.

In his seventies, he confessed that he could not control his feeling when finishing two poems. 'But I must add that they are fictions.'

August 1974

Cat Gone

COLIN FALCK

They said it would be kinder to leave you there
But I could wish now that I had brought you home
For you to die in my arms, be buried in the garden – to become
The spirit of the house.
But you would have suffered longer.

Name? You did not have one, or not
One agreed. You were *Cat*, or *Get Off*, or for a joke
Pussy. The day you died they gave you a kind of identity card
That said Name: tabby cat.
What is a name but something to grow into?
(It is hard enough naming children.)
We wanted you to be what you were: tabby cat.

I have come to terms with death now
But still each day I see you
On the stairs, on the window-sill, on the table we wouldn't let
    you go on
And it is only a coat, or a bulb in a pot, or a loaf of bread.
I had not picked you up for three weeks when I first saw you
    were ill
But already you were fur and bones.
Too late for forgiveness.
Your dumb eyes reproach me from the corner you went to die
    in.
I do not know even if my tears are for you or for so many
Other loves and deaths.

Come back my love. Give me another chance.
I will protect you, play games with you, take you away for the
  weekend.
Who knows what might be possible?
We shall have a wonderful life together.
I will look after you till you die.

August 1974

The Beginning
of an Idea

──── JOHN McGAHERN ────

'*The word "oysters" was chalked on the waggon that carried Chekov's body to Moscow for burial. The coffin was carried in the oyster waggon because of the fierce heat of early July.*'

They were the first sentences in Eva Lindberg's loose notes, written in a large childish hand; and standing at the table in her small flat she read through the notes again while she waited for Arvo Meri to come. The same pair of sentences were repeated throughout the notes in a way which suggested that she leaned on them for inspiration. '*The word "oysters" was chalked on the waggon that carried Chekov's body to Moscow for burial. The coffin was carried in the oyster waggon because of the fierce heat of early July.*' There was also among the notes a description of Chekov's terrifying story called 'Oysters'.

The father and son were on the streets of Moscow again in that rainy autumn evening. They were both starving, the father having failed to find work after trudging about Moscow for five months, and he was trying to steel himself to beg. He had drawn the tops of a pair of old boots round his calves so that people wouldn't notice that his feet were bare under the galoshes. Above father and son was a blue signboard with the word *Restaurant* and on a white placard on the wall was written the word *oysters*. The boy had lived in the world eight years and three months and had never come across the word oysters before.

'What does oysters mean, father?'

The father had touched a passerby on the sleeve, but unable to beg and overcome with confusion stammered, 'I beg your pardon,' and staggered back. He did not hear.

'What does oysters mean, father?'

'It's an animal . . . it lives in the sea.'

The boy imagined it as something between a fish and a crab, delicious made into a hot fish soup flavoured with pepper and laurel or with crayfish sauce or served cold with horseradish. Brought from the market, quickly cleaned, quickly thrown into the pot, O quickly quickly, for everyone was starving. A smell of steaming fish and crayfish soup came from the kitchen. The boy started to work his jaws, oysters, blessed oysters, chewing and slugging them down. Overcome by this feeling of bliss he grabbed at his father's elbow to stop himself from falling, leaned against the wet summer overcoat. His father was shivering with the cold.

'Are oysters a lenten food, father?'

'They are eaten alive . . . They come in shells, like tortoise but . . . in two halves.'

'They sound horrible, father,' the boy shivered. A frog sat in a shell, staring out with great glittering eyes, its yellow throat moving, that was an oyster. A creature sat in a shell with claws, eyes that glittered like glass, slimy skin: the children hid under the table, while the cook lifted it by its claw, put it on a plate, and gave it to the grownups. It squealed and bit at their lips as they ate it alive, claws, eyes, teeth, skin and all. The boy's jaws still continued to move, up and down; the thing was disgusting but he still managed to swallow it, swallowed another one and then another, hurriedly, fearful of getting their taste. He ate everything in sight, his father's galoshes, the white placard, the table napkin, the plate. The eyes of the oysters glittered but he wanted to eat. Nothing but eating would drive this fever away.

'Oysters. Give me some oysters,' he cried and stretched out his hands.

'Help us, gentlemen. I am ashamed to ask but I can stand no more,' he heard his father's voice.

'Oysters,' the boy cried.

'Do you mean to say you eat oysters? As small a little bloke as you,' he heard laughter close. A pair of swells in top hats were standing over him. They were looking into his face and laughing. 'Do you really eat oysters, little man? This is too funny. Do you know how to eat them?' Strong hands drew him into the lighted restaurant. He was sat at a table. A crowd gathered round. He ate something slimy, it tasted of sea water and mould. He kept his eyes shut. If he opened them he'd see the glittering eyes and claws and teeth. And then he ate something hard, for it crunched.

'Good Lord. He's eating the bloody shells. This is too rich. Don't you know you can't eat the shells?'

The next thing he remembered was lying in bed with a terrible thirst, he could not sleep with heartburn, and there was a strange taste in his parched mouth. His father was walking up and down the small room and waving his arms about.

'I must have caught cold. My head is splitting. Maybe it's because I've eaten nothing today. I really am red rotten useless. Those gentlemen spent ten roubles on those oysters today and I stood there and did nothing. Why hadn't I the sense to go up to them and ask them, ask them to lend me something? They would have given me something.'

Towards evening the child fell asleep and dreamt of a frog sitting in a shell, moving its eyes. At noon he was woken by thirst and looked for his father. His father was still pacing up and down and waving his arms around.

'*The word "oysters" was chalked on the waggon that carried Chekov's body to Moscow for burial. The coffin was carried in the oyster waggon because of the fierce heat of early July,*' she found she'd written it down once more. Chekov was that boy outside the restaurant with his father in the autumn rain, was that starving boy crunching the oysters in the restaurant while they laughed, was the child in the bed woken by thirst at noon watching the father pace up and down the small room and wave his arms around. She wanted to write an imaginary life of Chekov from the day outside the restaurant to the day the body of the famous writer reached Moscow in the oyster waggon for burial. It'd begin with oysters and end with oysters, some of the oysters, after the coffin had been taken away for burial, going to the same restaurant in which the child Chekov had eaten shells. She wasn't yet sure whether it would take the form of a novel or a drama. The theatre was what she knew best but she was sure that it would probably never get written at all unless more order and calm entered her life than was in it now. She closed the folder very quietly on the notes and returned them to their drawer. Then she showered and changed into a blue woollen dress and waited for Arvo Meri to come.

That morning Arvo's wife had rung her at the theatre, where she was directing the rehearsals of Ostrovsky's *The Dragon*. Among other things, his wife had called her a whore before starting to sob hysterically into the telephone. She used the old defence of silence and put down the receiver and ordered the commissaire that no matter how urgent any call claimed to be she was not to be interrupted in rehearsal. She was having particular difficulty with one of her leads, an actress of some genius who needed directing with a hand of iron, since her instinct was to filch as much importance as possible for her own part regardless of what it had been allotted. Once she began to rehearse again she put the call out of her mind but it returned to trouble her during the midday break and she rang Arvo at his office. He was a journalist, with political ambitions on the Left, who had almost got into parliament at the last election and would almost certainly do so at the next. When he apologized for the call and blamed it on his wife's drinking she lost her temper.

'That makes a pair of you then,' and went on to say that she wanted a life of her own, preferably with him, but if not – without him. She had had enough of to-ing and fro-ing, what she called his Hamleting. This time he'd have to make up his mind, one way or the other. He countered by saying that over the phone was no way to discuss it and arranged to call at her flat at eight. As she waited for him in the blue woollen dress after showering, she more quietly determined to have that life of her own. The two sentences '*The word "oysters" was chalked on the waggon that carried Chekov's body to Moscow for burial. The coffin was carried in the oyster waggon because of the fierce heat of early July*' echoed like a revenant in her mind and would not stay still.

There was snow on Arvo Meri's coat and fur hat when he came and he carried a sheaf of yellow roses. Once she saw the flowers she knew nothing would change. She laid them across a sheepskin that covered a large trunk at the foot of the bed without removing their wrapping.

'Well?'

'I'm so sorry about this morning, Eva . . .'

'That doesn't matter,' she stopped him, 'but I do want to know what you propose to do?'

'I don't know what to do,' he said guiltily. 'You know I can't get a divorce.'

'I don't care about a divorce.'

'But what else is there to do?'

'I can take a larger flat than this. We can start to live seriously together,' she said and he put his head in his hands.

'Even though there's nothing left between us she still depends on the relationship. If I was to move out completely she'd just go to pieces.'

'That's not my problem.'

'Can't we wait a little longer?'

'More than two years seems long enough to me. You go to Moscow by going to Moscow. If you wait until all the conditions are right you can wait your whole life.'

'I've booked a table at the Mannerheim. Why don't we talk it out there?'

'Why not?' she shrugged with a bright sarcasm, and lifted the yellow roses from the sheepskin. 'I ask you for a life and you offer me yellow roses and a dinner at the Mannerheim,' but he did not answer as he had started to dial a taxi and she let the roses drop idly down on the sheepskin and pulled on her fur coat and boots and sealskin cap.

Charcoal was blazing in two braziers on tall iron stems on either side of the entrance to the Mannerheim. They hadn't spoken on the taxi drive and she remarked as she got out, 'They must have some important personage tonight.' She felt a sinking as in an aeroplane take-off as the lift went up. A uniformed attendant took their furs and they had a drink in the bar across from the restaurant while they gave their order to the waiter. The restaurant was half-empty: three older couples and a very large embassy party. They knew it was an embassy party because of a circle of toy flags that stood in the centre of the table. Through the uncurtained glass they could see out over the lights of the city to the darkness that covered the frozen harbour and sea. He had drunk a number of vodkas by the time the main course came and she was too tense to eat as she nibbled at the shrimp in the avocado and sipped at the red wine.

'You don't mind me drinking? I have a need of vodka tonight.'

'Of course not . . . but it won't be any use.'

'Why?' he looked at her.

'When I got pregnant you took me to the Mannerheim and said, "I don't know what to do. It's not the right time yet. That is all I know," and drank vodka and were silent for hours, except every now and then you'd say, "All I'm certain of is that it's not the right time yet for us to have a child." I had some hard thinking to do when I left the Mannerheim that night. And when I arranged and had the abortion without telling you and when I rang you up after coming out of the clinic you said how it was like walking round for you under a cloud all week but that I had made you so happy then. I was so understanding. One day we'd have a child when everything was right. And you came that evening with red roses and took me here to the Mannerheim and afterwards we danced all night in that place on the shore.'

She spoke very slowly. He didn't want to listen, it was too painful, but he didn't know what to say to stop her, and ordered more vodka.

'And now when we spend three days in a row together your wife rings up and calls me a whore. You bring me yellow roses and take me to the Mannerheim. No Arvo, the vodka won't do any good . . .'

'But what are we to do?'

'I've given my answer. I'll take a larger flat. We'll live together as two sexual people . . .'

'But can't we wait till after the elections?'

'No. It's always been wait and wait.'

'But I love you, Eva.'

'If you loved me enough you'd choose to live with me,' and he went silent. He had more vodka and she noticed the attendant's look of disapproval as he swayed into the lift. The tall braziers had been taken in and as they waited while the doorman hailed a taxi he asked, 'Can I come back with you tonight?' 'Why not? If you want,' she laughed in a voice that made him afraid. He was violently ill when he got to the flat and then fell at once into a drugged sleep sprawled all across the bed. She looked at him a moment with what she knew was the dangerous egotism of the maternal instinct before she made up a bed on the carpet and switched off the lights. He woke early with a raging thirst and she got him a glass of water. 'Was I sick last night?' 'Yes, but don't worry, in the bathroom.' 'Why didn't you sleep in the bed?' 'I'd have had to wake you, the way you were in the bed.' 'I'm sorry.' 'It doesn't matter.' 'Why don't you come in now?' 'All right,' she rose from the blankets on the floor. The night conversation seemed to her as dialogue from a play that had run for too long and the actors had gone stale. He drew her towards him in the bed, more, she knew, to try to escape through pleasure from the pain of the hangover than from desire. She grew impatient with his tired fumbling and pulled him on top of her, provoking him with her own body till he came. Afterwards they both slept. She shook her head in the morning when he asked her, 'When will we meet?' 'It's no use.' 'But I love you.' She still shook her head. 'I'm fond of you but you can't offer me what I want.' As he moved to speak she stopped him. 'No. I can't wait. I have work I want to do.' 'Is it that damned Chekov's body?' 'That's right.' 'It'll never come to anything,' he said in hatred. 'I don't care but I intend to try.' 'You're nothing but a selfish bitch.' 'I am selfish and I want you to go now.'

That morning there were several calls for her during rehearsals but she had left strict instructions that she wasn't to be disturbed and when she got home that evening she took the phone off the hook.

She was surprised in the next days how little she yearned for him back, it was as if a weight had lifted; she felt an affection for him that she felt for that part of her life that she had passed with him, but it was for her own life and not for his. As well him as any other. She would go on alone, and when he demanded to see her she met him with a calm that was indifference that roused him to fury. She had not built a life with him, she had built nothing: but out of these sentences '*The word "oysters" was chalked on the waggon that carried Chekov's body to Moscow for burial. The coffin was carried in the oyster waggon because of the fierce heat of early July*' she would build, and for that she had to be alone. She would leave this city that had so much of her past life, the theatre where she'd worked so long. She'd leave them like a pair of galoshes in the porch, and go indoors. She rang rich friends: was their offer of the house in Spain still open? It was. They only made use of it in July. They'd be delighted to loan it to her. She could be their cuckoo there till then. She went and offered her resignation to the old manager.

'But you can't leave in the middle of a production.'

'I'm sorry. I didn't explain properly. Of course I'll see the production through, but I won't be renewing my contract when it expires at the end of the year.'

'Is it salary?' he sat down behind his big desk and motioned to her to sit.

'No. I am leaving the theatre. I want to try to write,' she blurted out to save explanation.

'It's as precarious as the theatre, and now that you've made your way there why throw it over for something worse still?' he was old and kindly and wise, though he too must have had to be ruthless in his day.

'I must find out whether I can or not. I'll only find out by finding out. I'll come back if I fail.'

'You know contrary to the prodigal son story few professions welcome back their renegades?'

'I'll take that risk.'

'Well, I see you're determined,' he rose.

As soon as a production begins to take shape it devours everybody around it so that one has no need for company or friends or love or sex outside and in the evening you take a limp life home with no other idea but to restore it so that it can be devoured anew the next day. So as she went home on the tram two days before the dress rehearsal she hadn't enough strength to be angry when she saw her photo and read that she was leaving the theatre to write. She was leaving to *try* to write. She should have been more careful. Kind as he was she should have known the old manager would use any publicity in any way to fill the theatre. *To write* was better copy than the truthful *try to write*. She wondered tiredly if there was a photo too of the coffin being lifted out of the oyster waggon or of the starving man in his summer coat in the rain outside the restaurant while the boy crunched on the oyster shells within. And whether or not it was due to the kindness usually reserved for the dear departing no production of hers had ever before opened to such glowing notices, but she left on New Year's Eve for Spain, by boat and train, passing through Stockholm and Copenhagen and stopping five days in Paris, where she knew some people. She had with her the complete works of Chekov and the two sentences were more permanently engraved than ever in her mind: *'The word "oysters" was chalked on the waggon that carried Chekov's body to Moscow for burial. The coffin was carried in the oyster waggon because of the fierce heat of early July.'*

She stayed five days in the Hotel Celtik on the rue Odessa, and all her waking hours seemed taken up with meeting people she already knew. Most of them scraped a frugal living from translation or journalism or both and all of them wrote or wanted to be artists in some way or other. They lived in small rooms and went out a lot to cheap restaurants and movie houses. She saw that many of them were homesick and longed for some way to go back without injuring their self-esteem and thought her a fool for leaving. In their eyes she read contempt, 'So she too has got the bug. That's all we need. One more,' and she began to protect herself by denying that there was any foundation to the newspaper piece. On the evening before she took the train to Spain she had dinner in a Russian restaurant off the Boulevard St Michel with perhaps the cleverest of them all: the poet, Severi. He had published three books of poems and the previous year she had produced a play of his that was taken off after a week though it had been highly praised by the critics. His threadbare dark suit was spotless and the cuffs and collar of the white shirt shone, the black bow knotted with a studied carelessness. They were waited on by the owner, a little old hen of a Russian woman, who spoke heavily accented

French, and whose thinning hair was dyed a weird carrot. A wreck of a once powerful man played an accordion at the door.

'Well, Eva Lindberg, can you explain to me what you're doing haring off to Spain instead of staying up there to empty that old theatre of yours with my next play?' The clever mordant eyes looked at her through the unrimmed spectacles with ironic amusement.

'I was offered a loan of a house there,' she was careful.

'And they inform me you intend to write there. You know there's not room for the lot of us,' he did not let up.

'That's just a rumour that got into a newspaper.'

'What'll you do down there, a single woman among hordes of randy Spaniards?'

'For one thing I have a lot of reading to catch up on,' she was safe now, borrowing aggression from his aggression.

'And why did you leave the theatre?'

'I felt I was getting stale. I wasn't enjoying it anymore.'

'And have you money?'

'I have enough money. And what about your work?'

He started to describe what he was working on with an even more ferocious mockery than he reserved for the work of others. The accordion player came round the tables with a saucer and insulted everybody who offered him less than a franc. They had a second carafe of the red wine and finished with a peppered vodka. Warmed by the vodka he asked her to sleep with him, his face contorted into such a fury at having to leave himself open to rejection that she felt sorry for him.

'Why not?' he pushed, soon he would begin to mock his own desire.

'I've told you,' she said gently enough. 'I've had enough of sleeping with the Arvo business. I want to be alone for a time.'

She was left completely alone for the whole of the journey the next evening and night, going early to her sleeper, changing at the frontier the next morning into the wider Spanish train, which got into Barcelona just before noon. A taximan took her to the small Hotel New York in the Gothic Quarter and it proved as clean and cheap as he said it would be. She stayed five days in Barcelona and was happy. As an army in peacetime she was doing what she had to do by being idle and felt neither guilt nor need to strive to make the holiday, which kills any chance of actually enjoying it. She walked the narrow streets, went to a few museums and churches, bought a newspaper on the Ramblas, vivid with the flower stalls under the leafless trees in cold dry weather, and ate each evening in the Casa Agut, a Catalan restaurant a few minutes' walk from the hotel, sat where she could watch the kitchen, had always just a gazpacho and ensalada and small steak with a half bottle of red Rioja, enjoying the march of the *jefe* watching for the slightest careless-ness, the red and white towel on his shoulder like an epaulet. After five such days she took the train to Valencia, from where she got the express bus to Almería. She would get off at Vera and get a taxi to the empty house on the shore. It was on this bus that she made her first human contact since leaving Paris, a Swedish homosexual who must have identified her as Scandi-navian by her clothes and blonde hair and asked if he could sit beside her. 'How far are you going?' she asked when she saw she was stuck with him for the journey. 'I don't know. South. I can go as far as I want,' though the hair was dyed blonde the lines in the brittle feminine face told he was 60 or more. He spoke only his own language and some English, and was impressed by her facility in acquiring languages. She wondered if the homosexual love of foreignness was that having turned away from the mother or been turned away they needed to do likewise with their mother tongue. 'Aren't you a lucky girl to find languages so easy?' She resented the bitchiness that inferred a boast she hadn't made.

'It's no more than being able to run fast or jump. It means you can manage to say more inaccurately in several languages what you always can say better in your own. It's useful sometimes but it doesn't seem very much to me if that's all it achieves.'

'That's too deep for me,' he was resentful and impressed and a little scared. 'Are you on a holiday?'

'No. I'm going to live here for a time.'

'Do you have a house?'

'Yes. I've been loaned a house.'

'Will you be with people or alone?' his questioning was growing more eager and rapid.

'I'll be alone.'

'Do you think could I take a room in the house?'

She was grateful to be able to rest her eyes on the blue sea in the distance. At least it would not grow old. Its tides would ebb and flow, it would still yield up its oyster shells long after all the living had become the dead.

'I'm sorry. One of the conditions of the loan is that I'm not allowed to have people to stay,' she lied.

'I could market for you and cook.'

'It's impossible. I'm sorry,' he would cling to any raft to shut out of mind the grave ahead.

'You? Are you going far?' she diverted.

'The bus goes to Almería.'

'And then?'

'I don't know. I thought to Morocco.'

She escaped from him in Alicante, where they had a half-hour break and changed buses. She saw the shirt-sleeved porters pat the Swede's fur coat in amusement. 'Mucha fría. Mucha fría,' as they transferred it to the boot of the bus returning to Almería, and she waited till she saw him take the same seat in the new bus as on the bus they'd come on and took hers beside an old Spanish woman dressed all in black who she discovered smelled of garlic and had been seeing her daughter in hospital. She felt guilty at avoiding the Swede so pointedly but she knew, like in death or life, from either state the alternative was always worse and she did not look back when she got off at Vera.

The house was low and flatroofed and faced the sea. The mountain was behind, a mountain of the moon sparsely sprinkled with the green of farms that grew lemon trees and had often vine or olive on terraces of stone built on the mountain side. In the dried-up beds of rivers the cacti flourished. The village was a mile away, and had a covered market, built of stone and roofed with tiles the colour of sand. She was alarmed when the old women hissed at her when first she entered the market but then she saw it was only their way of trying to draw people to their stalls. Though there was a fridge in the house she went every day to the market and it became her daily outing. The house had four rooms but she arranged it so that she could live entirely in the main room.

She reread all of Chekov, ate and drank carefully, and in the solitude of her days felt her life for the first time in years was in order, and the morning came when she decided to face the solitary white page. She had an end, the coffin of the famous writer coming to Moscow for burial that hot July day; and a beginning, the boy crunching on the oyster shells in the restaurant while the man starved in his summer coat in the rain outside: what she had to do was to imagine the life in between. She wrote in a careful hand *'The word "oysters" was chalked on the waggon that carried Chekov's body to Moscow for burial. The coffin was carried in the oyster waggon because of the fierce heat of early July,'* and then became curiously agitated. She rose and looked at her face in the small silver-framed mirror. Yes, there were lines, but faint still, and natural. Her nails needed filing. She decided to change into a shirt and jeans and then to rearrange all her clothes and jewellery. A week, two weeks, passed in this way. She got nothing written. The early sense of calm and order left her.

She saw one person fairly constantly during that time, a local *guardia*, whose name was Manolo. He had first come to the house with a telegram from her old theatre, asking her if she'd do a translation of a play of Mayakovsky for them. She offered him a drink when he came with the telegram. He asked for water, and later he walked with her back to the village where she cabled her acceptance of the theatre's offer, wheeling his rattling bicycle, the thin glittering barrel of his rifle pointed skyward. The Russian manuscript of the play arrived by express delivery a few days afterwards and now she spent all her mornings working on the translation, and how easy it was, the good text solidly and reliably under her hand: it was play compared with the pain of trying to pluck the life of Chekov out of the unimaginable air.

Manolo began to come almost daily, in the hot lazy three or four of the afternoon. She'd hear his boots scrape noisily on the gravel to give her warning. He'd leave his bicycle against the wall of the house in the shade, his gun where the drinking-water dripped slowly from the porous clay jars into catching pails. They'd talk for an hour or more across the bare Scandinavian table and he'd smoke and drink wine or water. His talk turned often to the social ills of Spain and the impossibility of the natural division between men and women. She wondered how someone as intelligent as he could have become a *guardia* in the first instance. There was nothing else for it, he told her: he was one of the lucky ones in the village, he got a salary, it was that or Germany. And then he married and bang-bang, he said – two babies in less than two years. A third was now on its way. All his wife's time was taken up with the infants now. There was nothing left between them but babies, and that was the way it'd go on, without any money, seven or eleven or more . . .

'But that's criminal in this age,' she said.

'What is there to do?'

'There's contraception.'

'In Spain there's not.'

'They could be brought in.'

'Could you get some in? If you could get some in I'd pay you,' he said eagerly, and when she sent back the completed translation she asked the theatre's editor if he could send the contraceptives with the next commission; she explained why she wanted them, though she reflected that he'd think what he wanted anyhow. The contraceptives did get through with the next play they wanted done. They wanted a new translation of *The Seagull*, which delighted her, she felt it would bring her closer to her Chekov, and when she'd finished it she'd be able to begin what she'd come here to try to do in the first place. She was glad too that the editor didn't impute that she wanted the contraceptives 'to have a bit on the side', it was a favourite phrase of his, down in old Spain; but he did warn her for God's sake to be careful, it was against the law, and it was Spain, and policemen were as notorious as other people for wanting promotion. She thought Manolo was nervous and left her quickly after she handed him the package that afternoon, but she put it out of mind as natural embarrassment at having to take contraceptives from a woman, and went back to reading *The Seagull*. She was still happily reading it and making notes towards her translation on the margins when she heard boots and voices coming up the gravel and a loud knock with what sounded like a gun butt came on the door. She was frightened as she called out, 'Who's there?' and a voice she didn't know called back, 'Open. It's the police.' When she opened the door she saw Manolo and the *jefe* of the local *guardia*, a fat oily man she'd often seen lolling about the market, and he at once barged into the house. Manolo closed the door behind them as she instinctively got behind the table.

The *jefe* threw the package she'd given Manolo earlier in the day on to the table. 'You know this?' and as she nodded she noticed in growing fear that both of them were very drunk. 'You know it's against the law? You can go to prison for this,' he said, the small oily eyes glittering across the table, and she decided there was no use answering anymore.

'Still Manolo and myself have agreed to forget it if we can try them out here,' his eyes fell pointedly on the package on the table but the voice was hesitant. 'That's if you don't prefer it Spanish style,' he laughed back to Manolo for support and started to edge round the table.

They were drunk and excited. They'd probably take her anyhow. How often had she heard this problem debated at civilized gatherings. Mostly it was agreed that it was better to yield than to get hurt. Sex wasn't all it was cracked up to be. In Paris the butcher and the baker shook hands with the local whore when they met, as people simply plying different trades.

'All right. As long as you promise to leave as soon as it's done,' her voice stopped him, it had a calm she didn't feel.

'Okay, it's a promise,' they both nodded eagerly and they reminded her of mastered boys as they asked apprehensively, 'With the . . . or without?'

'With the condoms.'

The *jefe* followed her first into the room. 'All the clothes off,' was his one demand and she complied. She averted her face sideways while it took place. A few times after parties when she was younger had she not held almost total strangers in her arms. Then she fixed completely on the two sentences '*The word "oysters" was chalked on the waggon that carried Chekov's body to Moscow for burial. The coffin was carried in the oyster waggon because of the fierce heat of early July,*' her mind moving over

— 111 —

them from beginning to end and from beginning to end again and again. Manolo practically rushed out of the room when he'd finished. They kept their word and left then, very subdued and quiet. It had obviously not been as jolly as they had imagined it would be.

She showered and washed and changed into completely new clothes. She poured herself a large glass of cognac at the table, noticing that they must have taken the condoms with them, and then began to sob, dry and hard at first rising to a flood of rage against her own foolishness. 'There is only one real sin – stupidity. You always get punished for behaving stupidly,' the poet Severi was fond of repeating.

When she quietened she drank what was left of the cognac and then started to pack. She stayed up all night packing and putting the house in order for her departure. Numbed with tiredness she walked to the village the next morning. All the seats on the express that passed through Vera were booked for that day but she could take the *rápido* to Granada and go straight to Barcelona from there. She arranged for the one taxi to take her to the train. The taximan came and she made listless replies to his ebullient talk on the drive by the sea to meet the train. The *rápido* was full of peasants and as it crawled from station to small station she knew it'd be night before it reached Granada. She'd find some hotel close to the station. In the morning she'd see a doctor and then go to Barcelona. A woman in a black shawl on the wooden seat facing her offered her a sliver of sausage and a gourd of wine. She took the sausage but refused the wine as she wasn't confident that her hands were steady enough to direct the thin stream into her mouth. Then she nodded to sleep, and when she woke she thought the bitter taste of oysters was in her mouth and that an awful lot of people were pacing up and down and waving their arms around and she had a sudden desire to look out the window to see if the word 'oysters' was chalked on the waggon, but then she saw that the train had just stopped at a large station and that the woman in the black shawl was still there and was smiling on her.

August 1974

An Australian Garden

——— PETER PORTER ———

Here we enact the opening of the world
And everything that lives shall have a name
To show its heart; there shall be Migrants,
Old Believers, Sure Retainers; the cold rose
Exclaim perfection to the gangling weeds,
The path leads nowhere – this is like entering
One's self, to find the map of death
Laid out untidily, a satyr's grin
Signalling 'You are Here': tomorrow
They are replanting the old court,
Puss may be banished from the sun-warmed stone.

See how our once-lived lives stay on to haunt us,
The flayed limbs of childhood sculpted
In the bole and branches of a great angophora –
Here we can climb and sit on memory
And hear the words which death was making ready
From the start. Such talking as the trees attempt
Is a lesson in perfectibility. It stuns
The currawongs along the breaks of blue –
Their lookout cries have guarded Paradise
Since the expulsion of the heart, when man,
Bereft of joy, turned his red hands to gardens.

Spoiled Refugees nestle near Great Natives;
A Chorus of Winds stirs the pagoda'd stamens;
In this hierarchy of miniatures
Someone is always leaving for the mountains,

Civil servant ants are sure the universe
Stops at the hard hibiscus; the sun is drying
A beleagured snail and the hydra-headed
Sunflowers wave like lights. If God were to plant
Out all His hopes, He'd have to make two more
Unknown Lovers, ready to find themselves
In Innocence, under the weight of His green ban.

In the afternoon we change – an afterthought,
Those deeper greens which join the stalking shadows –
The lighter wattles look like men of taste
With a few well-tied leaves to brummel-up
Their poise. Berries dance in a southerly wind
And the garden tide has turned. Dark on dark.
Janus leaves are opening to the moon
Which makes its own grave roses. Old Man
Camellias root down to keep the sun intact,
The Act is canopied with stars. A green sea
Rages through the landscape all the night.

We will not die at once. Nondescript pinks
Survive the death of light and over-refined
Japanese petals bear the weight of dawn's first
Insect. An eye makes damask on the dew.
Time for strangers to accustom themselves
To habitat. What should it be but love?
The transformations have been all to help
Unmagical creatures find their proper skins,
The virgin or the leonine. The past's a warning
That the force of joy is quite unswervable –
'Out of this wood do not desire to go'.

In the sun, which is the garden's moon, the barefoot
Girl espies her monster, all his lovely specialty
Like hairs about his heart. The dream is always
Midday and the two inheritors are made
Proprietors. They have multiplied the sky.
Where is the water, where the terraces, the Tritons
And the cataracts of moss? This is Australia

And the villas are laid out inside their eyes:
It would be easy to unimagine everything,
Only the pressure made by love and death
Holds up the bodies which this Eden grows.

August 1974

Sleeping Out At
Gallt-y-Ceiliog

—— JOHN FULLER ——

Something, perhaps an idea, is again eluding me.
It belongs nowhere in particular but might
At any moment appear and surprise me.

It's not part of the usual epiphanies.
It has no colour, or even night-colour, since
Lying awake half the night will not fix it.

The trees are alive, the candle flame gusty
And flattened. We lie in our quilted chrysalises
With still heads, like ancient funeral masks.

The moon at our backs rises over the mountains:
An understudy, practising with silent lips,
Sharing the sky with one star above the holly tree.

Nothing is spoken. The precise text of leaf
And crag is not known, or has been quite forgotten.
We're happy with what is offered, like visitors.

Perhaps after all there is nothing to remember
But this simplicity. The grass is grey
At dawn. It is the earth awakes, not I.

October 1974

Just a Smack at

——— GAVIN EWART ———

The Fathers found this last pain for the damned.
('This last pain for the damned the Fathers found'
suggests poetic mechanisms jammed,

not sense colloquially and surely rammed
home; but inverted – the ejected round.)
'The Fathers found this last pain for the damned'

is not a perfect line, but not so hammed
and actorly; to get it off the ground
you sweetened it, the bread was over-jammed,

old-fashioned word-order, so promise-crammed
and Marvellous in its archaic sound.
'The Fathers found this last pain for the damned'

at least is horse/cart right, with nothing shammed.
Do I disturb a lying, sleeping hound
or close escaped-from doors, long open-jammed?

It's long ago that Auden smack was slammed
and with his bliss, you might say, he is crowned.
The Fathers found this last pain for the damned:
they got poetic mechanisms jammed.

November 1974

He Said, She Said

A. ALVAREZ

Abruptly, the smell of flowers, sharp, far, delicate,
The old heart beating sweetly, eyes
Fresh as an apple, all the wrinkles gone.
Who would have thought it? Not her, not him.

Something passed through the room and didn't linger
'Did you see its face?' she said. He said,
'What was it saying?' '"Gone",'
She replied, 'Or that's what I thought it said.'
He answered, 'Not so. "Come." I'm sure it was "come".
It beckoned,' he said, 'We should follow. It won't come back.'
'Hawthorn in autumn,' she said, 'Don't make me laugh.
"Gone" was the word, and it's gone. Don't be a fool.'

'Hawthorn,' he said, 'Mayflower, the late smell of spring.
Everything's opening up, just like it was.
Won't you come with me?' he said, 'We've still
Got a chance. Listen. Smell it,' he said,
'We've been reprieved.' Slowly, idly,
She shook her heavy head and turned away.
'I won't be waiting,' she said, 'Don't think I will.'

The hair dark round her face, her eyes shrouded.
'Never,' she said, 'I've waited enough already.'
He answered, 'Listen. It's calling. It's our last chance.'
Like food, like rain, like mist. Mouth open, heart open.
'All that blossom,' he said, 'Like when we were young.'
'When *were* we young?' she asked, 'I don't remember.'

A flicker of gold, a smile, a far voice calling
Confusedly, 'Come', 'Gone', 'Come'. The jumbled scents
Of spring on the autumn night. 'Our last chance,' he said.
And she answered, 'You take it without me.'

December 1974

Down With Dons

───── JOHN CAREY ─────

From the viewpoint of non-dons, probably the most obnoxious
thing about dons is their uppishness. Of course, many dons are
quite tolerable people. But if you ask a layman to imagine a
don the idea will come into his head of something with a loud,
affected voice, airing its knowledge, and as anyone who has
lived much among dons will testify, this picture has a fair
degree of accuracy. The reasons are not far to seek. For one
thing, knowledge – and, in the main, useless knowledge – is the
don's *raison d'être*. For another, he spends his working life in the
company of young people who, though highly gifted, can be
counted on to know less than he does. Such conditions might
warp the humblest after a while, and dons are seldom humble
even in their early years. Overgrown schoolboy professors,
they are likely to acquire, from parents and pedagogues, a high
opinion of their own abilities. By the time they are fully fledged
this sense of their intellectual superiority will have gone very
deep and, because of the snob-value attached to learning and
the older universities, it will almost certainly issue in a sense of
social superiority as well. Modern young dons sometimes feel
guilty on this score, and break out in jeans, sweat-shirts and
other casual wear, in the forlorn hope that they will be taken
for persons of the working class. However, the very deliberate-
ness of their disguise is an earnest of their real aloofness.

Anyone wishing for a whiff of the more old-world,
unashamed brand of donnish uppishness could scarcely do
better than thumb through *Maurice Bowra* (Duckworth, £3.25),
a sheaf of tributes which, besides giving a complete anatomical
rundown of Sir Maurice from his 'curiously twisted navel' to

his private parts (resembling, Francis King bafflingly reports, 'Delphi in microcosm'), casts some telling light on the social assumptions of its contributors and subject. The editor is Hugh Lloyd-Jones, Regius Professor of Greek at Oxford. His is a name that sticks in my mind because of a contribution he made, two or three years back, to some correspondence in *The Times* about dons' pay. It was at a time when the miners or the power-workers or some other vital body were having one of their strikes, and an English tutor at University College called Peter Bayley wrote in suggesting that, by comparison with such people, dons were perhaps paid too much. Professor Lloyd-Jones replied that, if Bayley thought that, he could never have done any worthwhile teaching or research. The discourtesy of this retort was, I suppose, calculated: a reminder of professorial eminence. But what struck me as weird was that Professor Lloyd-Jones should apparently have no inkling that, as against a miner or a power-worker, his own contribution to the community was of uncommonly little consequence, and that what he deemed worthwhile teaching or research would impress most of the people whose taxes went towards paying his salary as a frivolous hobby. Humility, it seemed to me, was the only becoming attitude for academics in the debate about pay, since their avocations, and their maintenance at the public expense are, if they don't happen to be nuclear physicists or doctors, notoriously difficult to justify. How these aspects of the matter could have escaped Professor Lloyd-Jones puzzled me for a goodish while. In the end I attributed it to the insulating effect of donnish uppishness. Years of self-esteem had, as it were, blinded the Professor to his true economic value.

Bumptiousness and insolence are the quite natural outcome of such a condition, and the Bowra volume has some excellent examples of both. When holidaying abroad, we are told, Sir Maurice would size up other tourists and, though they were perfect strangers to him, 'pronounce with shameless clarity on their social origins: "English LMC"' We learn, too, of his behaviour at a Greek play to which he was taken:

He drew attention, shortly after the rise of the curtain, to the knees of the Chorus, and engaged those on either side in such brisk conversation that a cold message was delivered to me during the interval to keep him quiet or get out.

Behind such conduct can be detected the unhesitating donnish assumption that the comfort and pleasure of ordinary people are of no account when set against the need to advertise one's superiority.

Don-fanciers love this rudeness, of course, and suck up those who dole it out. The kind of people who work as secretaries and dogsbodies in the various Faculties, for instance, can often be heard relating, with many a titter, the latest offensive outburst of Professor This or Dr That. Dons' children, too, are likely to admire and imitate their parents' ways, and this can make them peculiarly detestable. A good many Oxford (and, I suppose, Cambridge) citizens must have bitter memories that would bear this out, but an experience of my own will serve as an illustration of the general truth. For a while I lived opposite a don's family. The father, a philosopher, was a shambling, abstracted figure, whom one would glimpse from time to time perambulating the neighbourhood, leering at the milkbottles left on doorsteps and talking to himself. If he had any contact with the outside world, or any control over his numerous children, it certainly wasn't apparent. To make matters worse, the mother was a don too, and the house was regularly left in the children's sole charge. The result was bedlam. The din of recorded music resounded from the place at all hours, and it never seemed to occur to anyone to shut a window or moderate the volume. One summer afternoon, when I was doggedly trying to mark a batch of A-level papers, my patience gave out, and I crossed the street to protest. As usual, every gaping window blared: it was like knocking at the door of a reverberating three-storey transistor set. Not surprisingly I had to pound away at the knocker for a good while before anyone heard. Eventually a teenage girl, one of the daughters, answered, and – with the familiar upsetting mixture of outrage and humiliation that one feels on such occasions – I asked if she would mind playing the music a little more quietly. The girl gave a supercilious smile. 'Oh,' she said, 'it's no good your complaining about that. The whole street got up a petition about us once, but it didn't have any effect.' And with that she shut the door.

I withdrew, trembling with impotent rage, and quite unfit, needless to say, to mark any more scripts that day, even if the row across the street had abated – which it didn't. For a while after that I got into the way of asking after this girl whenever I was talking to anyone who knew the family, in hopes that I would hear she had been run over or otherwise incapacitated. Unfortunately she never was, so far as I know. But it was through one of these conversations that I came to hear of another of her escapades. My interlocutor on this occasion was a Professor of Moral Philosophy, and he explained that the girl had caused considerable consternation at her school because she had discovered how to manufacture (using clay, All Bran and other ingredients) a compound which closely resembled human excrement, and had left quantities of this in little heaps around the classrooms. How they found out it was her, I don't know, but apparently they did. My informant was immensely tickled by the affair, and shook with laughter when relating the discomfiture it had caused to the school staff.

In a moral philosopher that might seem a surprising reaction to such foulmindedness. But in fact he was illustrating another common donnish attribute, namely, contempt for authority, particularly the authority of those whom, like schoolteachers or policemen, the don feels to be in a lowly position compared to himself. Dons' children are notoriously arrogant at school, and it's hardly to be wondered at since they find that their elders, like my moral philosopher, greet their misdemeanours with asinine hilarity. The donnish cult of liberty extends further than this, of course. One frequently encounters letters in the press, for instance, with strings of academic signatories, gravely informing some foreign government that the way it deals with its refractory minorities does not tally with donnish notions of freedom. No doubt those who put their names to these documents get a pleasurable feeling of importance, but in fact a don is about as well placed to start clamouring for liberty as a budgerigar. Like the bird, he lives in a highly artificial, protected environment, in which all his wants are catered for. Any appreciable degree of liberty conceded to his fellow beings would quickly put an end to his existence. For it cannot be supposed that the ignorant, philistine majority would go on supporting the universities financially if it had freedom of choice in the matter, since it receives no benefit from these institutions, or none that it could be brought to appreciate, beyond, I suppose, the annual Oxford and Cambridge Boat Race, and even that is less popular than it used to be.

In the Bowra volume much hearty commendation is given to Sir Maurice's lifelong sympathy with those who 'desired to resist authority', and his support for 'all libertarian causes'. In his youth, one gathers, the causes he mostly spoke out in favour of were buggery and masturbation, though he also encouraged:

> open snobbishness, success worship, personal vendettas, unprovoked malice, disloyalty to friends, reading other people's letters (if not lying about, to be sought in unlocked drawers) – the whole bag of tricks of what most people think and feel and often act on, yet are themselves ashamed of admitting they do and feel and think.

The commentator on human nature here is Anthony Powell. He does not record whether smearing erastz excrement on school furniture would count as 'unprovoked malice' and therefore as a libertarian cause in the Bowra code. However, it seems much on a par with the rest.

But though Sir Maurice continued, apparently, to decry authority long after youth had passed, he himself represented authority for the greater part of his life. He became a Fellow of Wadham in 1922, Warden in 1938, and Vice-Chancellor of Oxford in 1951, and he was an inveterate university politician, adept at imposing his will on committees and at bulldozing himself and his protégés into positions of power. One need go to no hostile account to discover this domineering side to his nature, for his friends who contribute to the memorial volume are effusive about it. For a man so constituted, supporting 'libertarian causes' would plainly entail constant and self-deluding doublethink. Not that Sir Maurice was, in that respect, an untypical don. Dons are inalienably responsible for the government of the colleges and the university, so when they indulge in anti-authoritarian polemics it always involves a lie.

Regrettably undergraduates cannot be counted on to realize this. In their trusting way, they believe that dons are perfectly sincere when they prate of revolution and liberty. It is a misunderstanding that can lead to painful disappointment, for the young tend to carry their beliefs into action, and they then find that the dons, who had seemed such pals, have suddenly turned nasty. Bowra, it appears, was in his early days one of those dons who curry favour by hobnobbing with the undergraduates, and Anthony Powell tells of an occasion on which the conviviality wore thin.

> I remember the unexpectedness of a sudden reminder of his own professional status, sense of what was academically correct, when, after a noisy dinner-party at Wadham, someone (not myself) wandering round Bowra's sitting-room suddenly asked:
> 'Why, Maurice, what are these?'
> Bowra jumped up as if dynamited.
> 'Put those down at once. They're Schools papers. No, indeed. . .'
> A moment later he was locking away in a drawer the candidates' answers to their examination, laughing, but, for a second, he had been angry. The astonishment I felt at the time in this (very justifiable) call to order shows how skilfully Bowra normally handled his parties of young men.

Quite so. And his skill consisted in concealing from them the truth, which was that his comfortable job depended on keeping them under. Young Powell's astonishment was, surely, quite reasonable. For had not the libertarian Bowra positively recommended the reading of other people's private papers?

The chagrin and surprise undergraduates feel when they come up against reality in this way was recently demonstrated, on a larger scale, at the trial of 18 students before the Oxford University Disciplinary Court. They were accused (and eventually found guilty) of having staged a sit-in at the University Registry. In fact they had been ejected from the building, after a short occupation, by irate Registry staff, who got in through a window. This brush with ordinary, hard-working citizens, who wanted to get on with their jobs, was in itself a disillusioning experience for youngsters intent upon organized idleness, and elicited howls of protest from the undergraduate press. But worse was to follow. Brought to trial, the defendants at first treated the court-room as an arena for libertarian high-jinks, volubly aided by their friends who packed the public gallery. The proceedings were adjourned in uproar. But the court was then reconvened in a smaller room; the revolutionary claque was excluded; and the trial went ahead. Defendants who continued to rant and sermonize and interrupt were first warned, then asked to leave, then, after they had refused, forcibly removed.

As it happened, I was on duty as an usher, so I had a ringside seat. The undergraduates linked arms to form a tight bunch against one wall. The barristers and solicitors, clutching armfuls of papers, huddled against another wall to avoid the mêlée. Eventually a squad of specially conscripted university police, decked out in ill-fitting bowler hats for the occasion, marched in, methodically dragged each offender from his clinging companions, and carried him, kicking and shouting, from the room. There was, I suppose, little violence – much less, say, than you could see on the rugby fields round the university any afternoon of the week. But in the elegantly panelled court-room the panting and scuffling and the bellows of rage from the undergraduates seemed crude and debasing. The defendants who remained behind were stunned. It had plainly never dawned on them that the university would actually enforce discipline. Several wept. I remember particularly a graduate student, who must have been in his early 20s, and whom no one had laid a finger on, blubbing tempestuously in the middle of the court-room. Nor could the students be blamed for this reaction. They had been led astray by their upbringing – by the unquestioning approval of liberty which modern education encourages from nursery school on, as well as by the revolutionary attitudinising of a few leftist dons who, it should be noted, did not appear before the court to take any part of the blame, but retained their lucrative posts after the undergraduates they had beguiled had been sent down.

Bowra, of course, had died a couple of years before any of this took place. One can be pretty sure that he would have felt nothing but regret at the recurrent sit-ins, protest-marches and other diversions by means of which students who have no academic motivation try to justify being at university. However, the support for 'all libertarian causes' celebrated by his obituarists exemplifies, as I have suggested, a widespread donnish cast of mind which inevitably provokes student indiscipline. His response to what he saw of undergraduate militancy was tolerant and lacking in foresight.

> When, in 1968, some undergraduates wanted to have their objections to the proctorial system heard by the Privy Council, Bowra was the first to give them public support, and in answer to the objection 'Why should they?' answered simply 'Because they are entitled to and because they want to'.

To anyone less filled with the notion of the special importance of Oxford and its doings, it might surely have occurred to enquire why these already highly privileged youngsters should be 'entitled' to occupy eminent public men with their little upsets, any more than the pupils at any polytechnic or training college or kindergarten throughout the land. Bowra's assumption here partly reflects the Oxford of his youth, adorned with gilded sprigs from the foremost families who would naturally deem it their right to be heard before the highest tribunal. But it also represents a grandiose and typically donnish sense of the university's place in the scheme of things. This, incidentally, is something dons share with militant students, who invariably believe that their grouses are of national importance. In placards and graffiti around Oxford the disciplinary court was referred to as a 'show trial', and the defendants were labelled 'The Oxford Eighteen', as if they were at least on a level with the Tolpuddle Martyrs.

The relative insignificance of Oxford, and of universities in general, Bowra, like most dons, did not care to think about. Anthony Powell tells of how, in his undergraduate days, he once confessed to Bowra, then a rising star in the Oxford firmament, his own impatience with the university, how little he liked being there, and how he longed to get it over and go down. Bowra was so put out that it took 35 years for their relationship to recover. Jobs within the university, and who got them, mattered terribly to him. He fought and intrigued, on and off committees, to get his candidates in. He revelled in the bickering and gossip that surrounded contested elections to academic posts: they brought drama to his life, exercised his quick brain, and gratified his malicious sense of humour. 'To anyone outside a university,' Lord Annan condoningly remarks, 'the frenzy which elections and appointments produce seems petty and absurd.' To some inside, too, one would hope. The kind of scholar who is absorbed enough in learning and teaching to reckon every hour spent on administration and committees wasted may, it is true, leave the field clear for the hardened business-fixers, and is to that extent a liability. Still, he is and must be the life-blood of any university worth the name. He will have something larger and more permanent in view than inter-departmental wrangling or the pursuit of his career, and will consequently be exempt from the degradations attendant on ambition. Bowra's craving for honours, on the other hand, was voracious. When E. R. Dodds, rather than himself, succeeded Gilbert Murray as Regius Professor of Greek, he was bitterly disappointed and, it appears, purposely made things difficult for the new professor. Small-mindedness isn't something one easily associates with Bowra, but it is hard to see his reaction here as the outcome of anything else, and the species of small-mindedness involved is persistently if not uniquely nurtured by universities.

From the academic angle, of course, the chief danger is that the don who bothers himself with administration will get so tied up in it that he will have no time for the subject he's supposed to be studying. The disastrous improvement in modern techniques of photo-copying and duplication has greatly added to this peril. Bushels of paper nowadays debouch from university and college offices every week and, as a result of the cry for 'participation', even the undergraduates have been sucked into the papery maelstrom. Some of them sit on committees almost full-time, and the busybodies in their ranks are agitating for sabbatical years, during which they will not have to study at all, but may devote themselves undistracted to needless circulars and memoranda. They will then be indistinguishable from the administrative dons. Even when administration doesn't oust learning (and it didn't in Bowra's case), there's a likelihood that the don who becomes attached to the idea of the university, as distinct from the culture which the university exists to serve, will apprehend that culture in a form which is processed and ordered for university consumption. What were originally great endeavours of the human spirit, the offspring of passion and inspiration, will decline for him into the material of lectures and syllabuses, of examinations and career-furthering books. The flat, pedestrian feel of much of Bowra's writing about Greek literature, which is rather harped on by contributors to this volume, may be relevant here. So may the awful donnishness of jokes on the subject of art and literature. Traipsing round galleries and churches abroad, he would award points to the paintings on show. When you had totted up 50, you were entitled to a drink. Another game was classing the poets, as if in the Final Honour School: 'Goethe,' we are told, 'notably failed to get a First: "No: the Higher Bogus", "Maurice, we've forgotten Eliot." "Aegrotat."' And so on.

If this carries a warning for present-day dons, the social set-up at Oxford in Bowra's era may seem too remote to have much relevance. Most undergraduates came from public schools. Often they had been friends at prep school or Eton or Winchester before they came up. It was a tiny, ingrown world. The public-school atmosphere of the memorial volume is appropriately heavy, several contributors debating, as if it were a matter of genuine concern, whether Bowra's explosive mode of speech should be traced to Winchester, via New College, or to his own old school, Cheltenham. As a matter of fact one is probably over-optimistic if one assumes that all this is a thing of the past. The public-school element in the Oxford and Cambridge intake has never dropped much below a half, and is bound to increase over the next few years. This is because the Socialist policy of converting the country's non-fee-paying grammar schools into massive comprehensives, in which the clever and the cretinous are jumbled together, means, in effect, that the non-public-school university entrance candidate will receive less individual attention from the teaching staff than formerly. The more crackbrained type of educational theorist will actually defend this, arguing that teachers should devote their time to the dullards, whose need is greater. But the result is that a candidate whose parents haven't the cash to pay public-school fees is no longer able to compete with his intensively coached public-school counterpart. Thus a policy which was, in concept, egalitarian, is now in the process of turning the older universities back into public-school enclaves, as they were before the First World War. As the dons are, by and large, recruited from among the undergraduates, they too will revert to being exclusively public school before very long. This seems a pity, because the influx of grammar-school dons into Oxford common rooms over the last 20 years or so has brought a good deal of sense to the place, and they usually turn out to be uninfected by the donnish follies and foibles I've been outlining. However, the Oxford of the future will not contain them.

Presumably because of the preponderance of public-school boys, there was a fair amount of dandified sodomy around in Bowra's Oxford, and one gathers that he was a participant. Lord Annan says that he regarded sex as something 'to be luxuriously indulged with either boys or girls', and Isaiah Berlin connects his love of pleasure, 'uninhibited by a Manichean sense of guilt', with his enthusiasm for Mediterranean culture. But his homosexuality seems to have been furtive and saddening rather than blithely Hellenic. He was terrified of blackmail. One of his friends, Adrian Bishop, had lost his job in an oil company because of his homosexual escapades, and Bowra dreaded similar exposure. When Gide came to Oxford to collect his honorary degree, he refused to put him up in the Warden's Lodgings for fear of scandal. To commemorate Bishop, he wrote a homosexual parody of the *Waste Land* entitled *Old Croaker*, enough of which is printed here to show that he, like Forster, had only to touch on this topic for his literary sense to desert him. He wasn't, of course, at all like the popular notion of the donnish fairy queen. On the contrary, he was robustly masculine, and seems to have coveted a stable heterosexual relationship. He dallied with the idea of marriage more than once. 'Buggers can't be choosers,' he retorted, when someone deplored the plainness of a girl he was wooing. But he never married, and his aloneness was recurrently a misery. When a woman friend referred to him in his hearing as a 'carefree bachelor', he flared up: 'Never, *never*, use that term of me again.' He loved children, and the thought of him having to make do with kindness to other people's is not a happy one.

It seems arguable that his homosexuality did not satisfy the deeper demands of his nature, and maybe it should be regarded as something foisted on him by his education rather than an inherent trait. The Oxford he grew up in was unrelievedly male, so the undergraduates, especially the outgoing and social ones, almost inevitably drifted into flirtations with members of their own sex. In these conditions it was hard to learn how to get on, or off, with girls, and Bowra didn't. He never developed much instinct for what they were thinking or feeling, a friend recalls. His bitterest jokes seem to have been about love and marriage. Given all this, it's rather staggering to consider that, half a century later, most of Oxford's colleges are still single sex, and many dons are determined to keep them that way. Their reasons, when you bother to enquire, never boil down to anything but the obtusest male prejudice. However, they are aided by the fact that the women's colleges also oppose co-education, fearing that mixed colleges, though they would give girls a fairer chance of getting to Oxford, might have an adverse effect on their own class-lists – an ordering of priorities which shows that women, in an emergency, can be just as donnish as men.

Perhaps Bowra's profound interest in eating and drinking was a kind of compensation for the lack of sexual satisfaction in his life. His hospitality was 'gargantuan', we learn, 'his digestion and head ironclad'. The friends who commemorate him plainly regard these as entirely fitting attributes for the successful academic. Indeed *The Times* obituary recorded, as if it were one of his signal achievements, that he had 'greatly raised the standard of hospitality' shown to honorands at Oxford. But to an impartial observer it may perhaps admit of question whether scholarship necessarily entails passing large quantities of rich food and fermented liquor through the gut. True, it is a traditional part of Oxford life. But even Oxford's traditions need reconsideration from time to time, and with Britain rapidly dwindling into a small, unimportant, hungry nation, it seems unlikely that corporate gluttony will flourish in its universities for much longer. Nor need its disappearance be greatly lamented. The spectacle of a bevy of dons reeling away from one of their mammoth tuck-ins is distinctly unappealing, and would be even if there were no such thing as famine in the world. Nevertheless one may be sure that dons will hotly defend their right to swill and guzzle. Their feelings of social superiority, earlier referred to, unfailingly come into play when this issue is raised, and I have known quite young dons seriously contend that college feasts should not be discontinued because, if they were, they would have nowhere to entertain their grand friends. The question is not a minor óne but reflects on the way in which university shapes the personality, and therefore on the justification for having universities at all. If it can be shown that the effect of higher education is to stimulate greed and self-indulgence, the public, whose money keeps universities open, may be excused for feeling that these attributes could be picked up more cheaply elsewhere.

Reading about Bowra and his Oxford teaches you, of course, not only what to avoid but also what to imitate, or try to. His positive qualities were immense. Above all, the breadth of his learning offers a challenge and a reproach to modern dons with their increasingly narrow specializations. He had travelled across Russia as a schoolboy, before the revolution, and this gave him a lifelong interest in Russian poetry. He also read French, German, Italian, Spanish, Greek and Chinese. World literature to him was not a set of linguistic cupboards, mostly closed, but a warm and welcoming ocean in which he splashed about freely. He spanned time as well as space. From Homer, Pindar and Sophacles his love and knowledge extended to Yeats, Valéry, Rilke, George, Blok, Cavafy, Apollinaire, Mayakovsky and Lorca. Pasternak, Quasimodo, Neruda and Seferis were his personal friends. Set against these riches, the burrowings of the typical modern researcher shrivel into absurdity. The things that pass for education in graduate departments – hunting for subjects sufficiently devoid of interest not to have been researched before, manufacturing unneeded theses on unread-able authors – would have filled Bowra with horror and disbelief. He characterized the graduate student as a dinosaur, sinking into a bog undér the weight of his erudition.

Another aspect of his approach to literature which looks pretty healthy in retrospect was his indifference to the Cambridge emphasis on 'evaluation' which was all the rage in the thirties. Encouraging youths scarcely out of short trousers to deliver judgment on the masterpieces of the past was not at all what he went in for. He made his pupils aware of literature as a wealth they had still to inherit, rather than as a terrain of fallen idols and soured hopes into which it would be foolish to venture.

The range of his reading challenged your own provinciality and sloth. In the post-war years he was always suggesting that one should read poets whom the new orthodoxy had dismissed as negligible or harmful – Tennyson, Swinburne and Kipling . . . He was a traveller forever suggesting that if only you would journey further some new and life-enhancing experience was yours for the asking.

He enlarged the imagination of his undergraduates, too, by becoming a legend long before his death. Like all legends, he was partly make-believe. People added to him bits and pieces from their own fancy, so that by the end he was not so much a man as a joint fictional venture. This is plain enough from the memorial volume, for we encounter there several different Bowras, according to the writer. He is variously likened to Yeats, Hardy, Swift, the *Royal Soverign*, one of Napoleon's marshals, and the Heracles of the metope at Olympia. Cyril Connolly's Bowra 'rode high above academic honours' – quite unlike the envious careerist other contributors knew. There is disagreement, too, about his eyes. To Connolly they were *'gli occhi onesti e tardi*, eyes of a platoon commander in the First World War'. Lord Annan remembers them as 'pig's eyes', while for Susan Gardiner it was their 'passion and piercing intensity' that impressed. A passionate pig? Even the story about Bowra and Gide, which one would have imagined was readily verifiable, exists in two versions: the second, also printed here, has it that it was the Vice-Chancellor, not Bowra, who refused to entertain Gide at Oxford, and that Gide was looked after by Bowra and Enid Starkie instead. Far from mattering, the contradictions are proof of Bowra's success. Whatever else may seem obsolete about him, he inspired others to creativity, which is any teacher's most important job.

January 1975

Fishbowl

—— DAVID HARSENT ——

1

A couple are stepping out on platform four;
his campaign ribbons gleam, her breasts
roll beneath the satin. Nests
of tourists spread their maps out on the floor.
The patterns alter. There's a law
that governs departures, and one that governs murders.
In the gloom of the roof, workmen are welding girders.

2

A 'northern airstream' puckers the parkside trees.
The animals in the zoo lean on their bars
or pace in heady circles. No one sees.
The rich arrive, downy in perfect furs,
at theatres with neon-etched marquees.
The wind that killed the Brontës. Iron spears
ring the wolf enclosure. There are pleas
for one more encore from the velvet tiers.

3

The bald man mutters across the rim of his glass
to the girl in the stetson; she has brought her dog.
They're nothing special. Except for the sunny gloss
on his skull, they'd be lost in the multicoloured clog
of drinkers and talkers. The neatly bevelled fosse,
that drains into the river, froths with ale
and scraps of muddied bunting from the farce

(the players have left, taking their cash-on-the-nail).
The party revolves like a slowly sinking wreck.
'Perfection . . .' he whispers, resting a hand on her neck.

4

Couple by couple, they find their place in the dark.
The girls know how to glide beneath a touch:
sleek and unevolving, like the shark.
The piano-player downstairs knows too much
about the gritty business of the skin;
even so, he likes to leave his mark.
Angling her knees, she reaches to guide him in.
He yelps as his spreading fingers brush her fin.

5

Sheep nudge and nibble the pallid downs. The hare
circles, in a frenzy, back to where
women in bowlers and breeches are crossing a stream,
flexing their thighs as they hear the quarry scream.
The bank is pocked with the marks of paws and studs
that will garner scabs of ice from the freezing air.
The season is right for worshipping cruel gods.
On a mattress of coats, acting a part from a dream,
Wednesday's child is screwing his girl in the woods.

6

She smiles and smiles at his raw, grogblossomed face.
Smiling makes the good times come.
Dance-floor partners stall and change the pace,
their stomachs touching, and their heads in space.
His dampened finger tamps a crumb:
he licks it, gives his empty plate a shove,
and looks up, smiling. All we know of love
is pain and the response to pain.
They waltz in the old-fashioned way, with impulsive grace;
he leans back to speak, and she smiles again.

7

They are slender-waisted, blonde, with eyes like glass.
Lodged in the grass, they watch for rival styles.
She smiles as he gets up on his knees to piss.
Crook a finger at bliss and music storms
between the tents where, adorned in pretty rags
she sighs and sags against his bony chest,
rumpling a nest amid their tangled rugs.
Sometimes he begs; she sometimes flirts with theft.
His pinkie browses the cleft between her legs.

8

Laughter in the wendy-house, a ghost
of someone's face reflected in the pane.
Love provides the terrors that we hide,
then seek . . . the party's nerveless host.
The scents that gather in the gathering rain
bleed off from the garden like a tide,
spilling across the pavement. Parents ride
in convoy to the house; insane
visions make them shudder as they coast
along the driveway: lights through a seepage of fog.
The children hoard their secrets, safe and smug.

March 1975

In Isfahan

——— WILLIAM TREVOR ———

They met in the most casual way, in the upstairs office of
Chaharbagh Tours Inc. In the downstairs office a boy asked
Normanton to go upstairs and wait: the tour would start a little
late because they were having trouble with the engine of the
minibus.

The upstairs office was more like a tiny waiting room than
an office, with chairs lined against two walls. The chairs were
rudimentary: metal frames and red plastic over foam rubber.
There was a counter stacked with free guides to Isfahan in
French and German, and guides to Shiraz and Persepolis in
English as well. The walls had posters on them, issued by the
Iranian Tourist Board: Mount Damavand, the Chalus road,
native dancers from the Southern tribes, club-swinging, the
Apadana Palace at Persepolis, the Theological School in Isfahan.
The fees and conditions of Chaharbagh Tours were clearly
stated: *Tours by De Lux microbus. Each Person Rls. 375 ($5).
Tours in French and English language. Microbus comes to Hotel
otherwise you'll come to Office. All Entrance Fees. No Shopping.
Chaharbagh Tours Inc. wishes you the best.*

She was writing an air-mail letter with a ballpoint pen,
leaning on a brochure which she'd spread out on her handbag.
It was an awkward arrangement, but she didn't seem to mind.
She wrote steadily, not looking up when he entered, not
pausing to think about what each sentence might contain. There
was no one else in the upstairs office.

He took some leaflets from the racks on the counter. *Isfahan
était capitale de l'Iran sous les Seldjoukides et les Safavides. Sous le
règne de ces deux dynasties l'art islamique de l'Iran avait atteint son
apogée.*

'Are you going on the tour?'

He turned to look at her, surprised that she was English. She was thin and would probably not be very tall when she stood up, a woman in her thirties, without a wedding ring. In a pale face her eyes were hidden behind huge round sun-glasses. Her mouth was sensuous, the lips rather thick, her hair soft and black. She was wearing a pink dress and white high-heeled sandals. Nothing about her was smart.

In turn she saw a man who seemed to her to be typically English. He was middle-aged and greying, dressed in a linen suit and carrying a linen hat that matched it. There were lines and wrinkles in his face, about the eyes especially, and the mouth. When he smiled more lines and wrinkles gathered. His skin was tanned, but with the look of skin that usually wasn't: he'd been in Persia only a few weeks, she reckoned.

'Yes, I'm going on the tour,' he said. 'They're having trouble with the minibus.'

'Are we the only two?'

He said he thought not. The minibus would go round the hotels collecting the people who'd bought tickets for the tour. He pointed at the notice on the wall.

She took her dark glasses off. Her eyes were her startling feature: brown, beautiful orbs, with endless depth, mysterious in her more ordinary face. Without the dark glasses she had an Indian look: lips, hair and eyes combined to give her that. But her voice was purely English, slow and nasal, made uglier than it might have been by attempts to disguise a Cockney twang.

'I've been writing to my mother,' she said.

He smiled at her and nodded. She put her dark glasses on again and licked the edges of the air-mail letter-form.

'Microbus ready,' the boy from downstairs said. He was a smiling youth of about fifteen with thick, black-rimmed spectacles and very white teeth. He wore a white shirt with tidily rolled-up sleeves, and brown cotton trousers. 'Tour commence please,' he said. 'I am Guide Hafez.'

He led them to the minibus. 'You German two?' he enquired, and when they replied that they were English he said that not many English came to Persia. 'American,' he said. 'French. German people often.'

They got into the minibus. The driver turned his head to nod and smile at them. He spoke in Persian to Hafez, and laughed.

'He commences a joke,' Hafez said. 'He wishes me the best. This is the first tour I make. Excuse me, please.' He perused leaflets and guide-books, uneasily licking his lips.

'My name's Iris Smith,' she said.

His, he revealed, was Normanton.

They drove through blue Isfahan, past domes and minarets, and tourist shops in the Avenue Chaharbagh, and blue mosaic on surfaces everywhere, and blue taxi-cabs. Trees and grass had a precious look because of the arid earth. The sky was pale with the promise of heat.

The minibus called at the Park Hotel and at the Intercontinental and the Shah Abbas, where Normanton was staying. It didn't call at the Old Atlantic, which Iris Smith had been told at Teheran Airport was cheap and clean. It collected a French party, and a German couple who were having trouble with sunburn, and two wholesome-faced American girls. Hafez continued to speak in English, explaining that it was the only foreign language he knew. 'Ladies-gentlemen, I am a student from Teheran,' he announced with pride, and then confessed: 'I do not know Isfahan well.'

The leader of the French party, a testy-looking man whom Normanton put down as a university professor, had already protested at their guide's inability to speak French. He protested again when Hafez said he didn't know Isfahan well, complaining that he had been considerably deceived.

'No, no,' Hafez replied. 'That is not my fault, sir, I am poor Persian student, sir. Last night I arrive in Isfahan the first time only. It is impossible my father send me to Isfahan before.' He smiled at the testy Frenchman. 'So listen please, ladies-gentlemen. This morning we commence happy tour, we see many curious scenes.' Again his smile flashed. He read in English from an Iran Air leaflet: *'Isfahan is the showpiece of Islamic Persia, but founded at least two thousand years ago!* Here we are, ladies-gentlemen, at the Chehel Sotun. This is pavilion of lyric beauty, palace of forty columns, where Shah Abbas II entertain all royal guests. All please leave microbus.'

Normanton wandered alone among the forty columns of the palace. The American girls took photographs and the German couple did the same. A member of the French party operated a moving camera, although only tourists and their guides were moving. The girl called Iris Smith seemed out of place, Normanton thought, teetering on her high-heeled sandals.

'So now Masjed-e-Shah,' Hafez cried, clapping his hands to collect his party together. The testy Frenchman continued to expostulate, complaining that time had been wasted in the Chehel Sotun. Hafez smiled at him.

'*Masjed-e-Shah,*' he read from a leaflet as the minibus began again, '*is most outstanding and impressive mosque built by Shah Abbas the Great in early seventeenth century.*'

But when the minibus drew up outside the Masjed-e-Shah it was discovered that the Masjed-e-Shah was closed to tourists because of renovations. So, unfortunately, was the Chehel Lotfollah.

'So commence to carpet-weaving,' Hafez said, smiling and shaking his head at the protestations of the French professor.

The cameras moved among the carpet-weavers, women of all ages, producing at speed Isfahan carpets for export. 'Look now at once,' Hafez commanded, pointing at a carpet that incorporated the features of the late President Kennedy. 'Look please on this skill, ladies-gentlemen.'

In the minibus he announced that the tour was now on its way to the Masjed-e-Jamé, the Friday Mosque. This, he reported after a consultation of his leaflets, displayed Persian architecture of the ninth to the eighteenth century. '*Oldest and largest in Isfahan,*' he read. '*Don't miss it! Many minarets in narrow lanes!* All leave microbus, ladies-gentlemen. All return to microbus in one hour.'

At this there was chatter from the French party. The tour was scheduled to be conducted, points of interest were scheduled to be indicated. The tour was costing three hundred and seventy-five rials.

'OK, ladies-gentlemen,' Hafez said. 'Ladies-gentlemen come by me to commence informations. Other ladies-gentlemen come to microbus in one hour.'

An hour was a long time in the Friday Mosque. Normanton

wandered away from it, through dusty crowded lanes, into market-places where letter-writers slept on their stools, waiting for illiterates with troubles. In hot, bright sunshine peasants with produce to sell bargained with deft-witted shopkeepers. Crouched on the dust, cobblers made shoes; on a wooden chair a man was shaved beneath a tree. Other men drank sherbet, arguing as vigorously as the heat allowed. Veiled women hurried, pausing to prod entrails at butchers' stall or to finger rice.

'You're off the tourist track, Mr Normanton.'

Her white high-heeled sandals were covered with dust. She looked tired.

'So are you,' he said.

'I'm glad I ran into you. I wanted to ask how much that dress was.'

She pointed at a limp blue dress hanging on a stall. It was difficult when a woman on her own asked the price of something in this part of the world, she explained. She knew about that from living in Bombay.

He asked the stall-holder how much the dress was, but it turned out to be too expensive, although to Normanton it seemed cheap. The stall-holder followed them along the street offering to reduce the price, saying he had other goods, bags, lengths of cotton, pictures on ivory, all beautiful workmanship, all cheap bargains. Normanton told him to go away.

'Do you live in Bombay?' He wondered if she perhaps was Indian, brought up in London, or half-caste.

'Yes, I live in Bombay. And sometimes in England.'

It was the statement of a woman not at all like Iris Smith: it suggested a grandeur, a certain style, beauty, and some riches.

'I've never been in Bombay,' he said.

'Life can be good enough there. The social life's not bad.'

They had arrived back at the Friday Mosque.

'You've seen all this?' He gestured towards it.

She said she had, but he had the feeling that she hadn't bothered much with the mosque. He couldn't think what had drawn her to Isfahan.

'I love travelling,' she said.

The French party were already established again in the

— 141 —

minibus, all except the man with the moving camera. They were talking loudly among themselves, complaining about Hafez and Chaharbagh Tours. The German couple arrived, their sunburn pinker after their exertions. Hafez arrived with the two American girls. He was laughing, beginning to flirt with them.

'So,' he said in the minibus, 'we commence the Shaking Minarets. *Two minarets able to shake*,' he read, '*eight kilometres outside the city*. Very famous, ladies-gentlemen, very curious.'

The driver started the bus, but the French party shrilly protested, declaring that the man with the moving camera had been left behind. '*Où est-ce qu'il est?*' a woman in red cried.

'I will tell you a Persian joke,' Hafez said to the American girls. 'A Persian student commences at a party – '

'*Attention!*' the woman in red cried.

'*Imbecile!*' the professor shouted at Hafez.

Hafez smiled at them. He did not understand their trouble, he said, while they continued to shout at him. Slowly he took his spectacles off and wiped a sheen of dust from them. 'So a Persian student commences at a party,' he began again.

'I think you've left someone behind,' Normanton said. 'The man with the moving camera.'

The driver of the minibus laughed and then Hafez realizing his error, laughed also. He sat down on a seat beside the American girls and laughed unrestrainedly, beating his knees with a fist and flashing his very white teeth. The driver reversed the minibus, with his finger on the horn. 'Bad man!' Hafez said to the Frenchman when he climbed into the bus, laughing again. 'Heh, heh, heh,' he cried, and the driver and the American girls laughed also.

'*Il est fou!*' one of the French party muttered crossly. '*Incroyable!*'

Normanton glanced across the minibus and discovered that Iris Smith, amused by all this foreign emotion, was already glancing at him. He smiled at her and she smiled back.

Hafez paid two men to climb into the shaking minarets and shake them. The Frenchman took moving pictures of this motion. Hafez announced that the mausoleum of a hermit was located nearby. He pointed at the view from the roof where they stood. He read slowly from one of his leaflets, informing them that the view was fantastic. 'At the party,' he said to the American girls, 'the student watches an aeroplane on the breast of a beautiful girl. "Why watch you my aeroplane?" the girl commences. "Is it you like my aeroplane?" "It is not the aeroplane which I like," the student commences. "It is the aeroplane's airport which I like." That is a Persian joke.'

It was excessively hot on the roof with the shaking minarets. Normanton had put on his linen hat. Iris Smith tied a black chiffon scarf around her head.

'We commence to offices,' Hafez said. 'This afternoon we visit Vank Church. Also curious Fire Temple.' He consulted his leaflets. 'An Armenian Museum. *Here you can see a nice collection of old manuscripts and paintings.*'

When the minibus drew up outside the offices of Chaharbagh Tours Hafez said it was important for everyone to come inside. He led the way, through the downstairs office and up to the upstairs office. Tea was served. Hafez handed round a basket of sweets, wrapped pieces of candy locally manufactured, very curious taste, he said. Several men in lightweight suits, the principals of Chaharbagh Tours, drank tea also. When the French professor complained that the tour was not satisfactory, the men smiled, denying that they understood either French or English and in no way betraying that they could recognize any difference when the professor changed from one language to the other. It was likely, Normanton guessed, that they were fluent in both.

'Shall you continue after lunch?' he asked Iris Smith. 'The Vank Church, an Armenian museum? There's also the Theological School, which really is the most beautiful of all. No tour is complete without that.'

'You've been on the tour before?'

'I've walked about. I've got to know Isfahan.'

'Then why – '

'It's something to do. Tours are always rewarding. For a start, there are the other people on them.'

'I shall rest this afternoon.'

'The Theological School is easy to find. It's not far from the Shah Abbas Hotel.'

'Are you staying there?'

'Yes.'

She was curious about him. He could see it in her eyes, for she'd taken off her dark glasses. Yet he couldn't believe that he presented as puzzling an exterior as she did herself.

'I've heard it's beautiful,' she said. 'The hotel.'

'Yes, it is.'

'I think everything in Isfahan is beautiful.'

'Are you staying here for long?'

'Until tomorrow morning, the five o'clock bus back to Teheran. I came last night.'

'From London?'

'Yes.'

The tea-party came to an end. The men in the lightweight suits bowed. Hafez told the American girls that he was looking forward to seeing them in the afternoon, at two o'clock. In the evening, if they were doing nothing else, they might meet again. He smiled at everyone else. They would continue to have a happy tour, he promised, at two o'clock. He would be honoured to give them the information they desired.

Normanton said goodbye to Iris Smith. He wouldn't, he said, be on the afternoon tour either. The people of a morning tour, he did not add, were never amusing in the afternoon: it wouldn't be funny if the Frenchman with the moving camera got left behind again, the professor's testiness and Hafez's pidgin English might easily become wearisome as the day wore on.

He advised her again not to miss the Theological School. There was a tourist bazaar beside it, with boutiques, where she might find a dress. But prices would be higher there. She shook her head: she liked collecting bargains.

He walked to the Shah Abbas. He forgot about Iris Smith.

She took a mild sleeping-pill and slept on her bed in the Old Atlantic. When she woke it was a quarter to seven.

The room was almost dark because she'd pulled over the curtains. She'd taken off her pink dress and hung it up. She lay in her petticoat, staring sleepily at a ceiling she couldn't see. For a few moments before she'd slept her eyes had traversed its network of cracks and flaking paint. There'd been enough light then, even though the curtains had been drawn.

She slipped from the bed and crossed to the window. It was twilight outside, a light that seemed more than ordinarily different from the bright sunshine of the afternoon. Last night, at midnight when she'd arrived, it had been sharply different, too: as black as pitch, totally silent in Isfahan.

It wasn't silent now. The blue taxis raced their motors as they paused in a traffic-jam outside the Old Atlantic. Tourists chattered in different languages. Bunches of children, returning from afternoon school, called out to one another on the pavements. Policemen blew their traffic whistles.

Neon lights were winking in the twilight, and in the far distance she could see the massive illuminated dome of the Theological School, a fat blue jewel that dominated everything.

She washed herself and dressed, opening a suitcase to find a black and white dress her mother had made her and a black frilled shawl that went with it. She rubbed the dust from her high-heeled sandals with a Kleenex tissue. It would be nicer to wear a different pair of shoes, more suitable for the evening, but that would mean more unpacking and anyway who was there to notice? She took some medicine because for months she'd had a nagging little cough, which usually came on in the evenings. It was always the same: whenever she returned to England she got a cough.

In his room he read that the Shah was in Moscow, negotiating a deal with the Russians. He closed his eyes, letting the newspaper fall on to the carpet.

At seven o'clock he would go downstairs and sit in the bar and watch the tourist parties. They knew him in the bar now. As soon as he entered one of the barmen would raise a finger and nod. A moment later he would receive his vodka-lime, with crushed ice. 'You have good day, sir?' the barman would say to him, whichever barman it was.

Since the Chaharbagh tour of the morning he had eaten a chicken sandwich and walked, he estimated, ten miles. Exhausted, he had had a bath, delighting in the flow of warm water over his body, becoming drowsy until the water cooled and began to chill him. He'd stretched himself on his bed and then had slowly dressed, in a different linen suit.

His room in the Shah Abbas Hotel was enormous, with a balcony and blown-up photographs of domes and minarets, and a double bed as big as a nightclub dance-floor. Ever since he'd first seen it he'd kept thinking that his bed was as big as a dance-floor. The room itself was large enough for a quite substantial family to live in.

He went downstairs at seven o'clock, using the staircase because he hated lifts and because, in any case, it was pleasant to walk through the luxurious hotel. In the hall a group of forty or so Swiss had arrived. He stood by a pillar for a moment, watching them. Their leader made arrangements at the desk, porters carried their luggage from the airport bus. Their faces looked happier when the luggage was identified. Swiss archaeologists, Normanton conjectured, a group tour of some Geneva society. And then, instead of going straight to the bar, he walked out of the hotel into the dusk.

They met in the tourist bazaar. She had bought a brooch, a square of coloured cotton, a canvas carrier-bag. When he saw her, he knew at once that he'd gone to the tourist bazaar because she might be there. They walked together, comparing the prices of ivory miniatures, the traditional polo-playing scene, variously interpreted. It was curiosity, nothing else, that made him want to renew their acquaintanceship.

'The Theological School is closed,' she said.

'You can get in.'

He led her from the bazaar and rang a bell outside the school. He gave the porter a few rials. He said they wouldn't be long.

She marvelled at the peace, the silence of the open courtyards, the blue mosaic walls, the blue water, men silently praying. She called it a grotto of heaven. She heard a sound which she said was a nightingale, and he said it might have been, although Shiraz was where the nightingales were. 'Wine and roses and nightingales,' he said because he knew it would please her: Shiraz was beautiful too, but not as beautiful as Isfahan. The grass in the courtyards of the Theological School was not like ordinary grass, she said. Even the paving stones and the water gained a dimension in all the blueness. Blue was the colour of holiness: you could feel the holiness here.

'It's nicer than the Taj Mahal. It's pure enchantment.'

'Would you like a drink, Miss Smith? I could show you the enchantments of the Shah Abbas Hotel.'

'I'd love a drink.'

She wasn't wearing her dark glasses. The nasal twang of her voice continued to grate on him whenever she spoke, but her eyes seemed even more sumptuous than they'd been in the bright light of day. It was a shame he couldn't say to her that her eyes were just as beautiful as the architecture of the Theological School, but such a remark would naturally be misunderstood.

'What would you like?' he asked in the bar of the hotel. All around them the Swiss party spoke in French. A group of Texan oilmen and their wives, who had been in the bar the night before, were there again, occupying the same corner. The sunburnt German couple of the Chaharbagh tour were there, with other Germans they'd made friends with.

'I'd like some whisky,' she said. 'With soda. It's very kind of you.'

When their drinks came he suggested that he should bring her on a conducted tour of the hotel. They could drink their way around it, he said. 'I shall be Guide Hafez.'

He enjoyed showing her because all the time she made marvelling noises, catching her breath in marble corridors and fingering the endless mosaic of the walls, sinking her high-heeled sandals into the pile of carpets. Everything made it enchantment, she said: the gleam of gold and mirror-glass among the blues and reds of the mosaic, the beautifully finished furniture, the staircase, the chandeliers.

'This is my room,' he said, turning the key in the lock of a polished mahogany door.

'Gosh!'

'Sit down, Miss Smith.'

They sat and sipped at their drinks. They talked about the room. She walked out on to the balcony and then came and sat down again. It had become quite cold, she remarked, shivering a little. She coughed.

'You've a cold.'

'England always gives me a cold.'

They sat in two dark, tweed-covered armchairs with a glass-topped table between them. A maid had been to turn down the bed. His green pyjamas lay ready for him on the pillow.

They talked about the people on the tour, Hafez and the testy professor, and the Frenchman with the moving camera. She had seen Hafez and the American girls in the tourist bazaar and in the teashop. The minibus had broken down that afternoon: he'd seen it outside the Armenian Museum, the driver and Hafez examining its plugs.

'My mother would love that place,' she said.

'The Theological School?'

'My mother would feel its spirit. And its holiness.'

'Your mother is in England?'

'In Bournemouth.'

'And you yourself – '

'I have been on holiday with her. I came for six weeks and stayed a year. My husband is in Bombay.'

He glanced down at her left hand, thinking he'd made a mistake.

'I haven't been wearing my wedding ring. I shall again, in Bombay.'

'Would you like to have dinner?'

She hesitated. She began to shake her head, then changed her mind. 'Are you sure?' she said. 'Here, in the hotel?'

'The food is the least impressive part.'

He'd asked her because, quite suddenly, he didn't like being in this enormous bedroom with her. It was pleasant showing her around, but he didn't want misunderstandings.

'Let's go downstairs,' he said.

In the bar they had another drink. The Swiss party had gone, so had the Germans. The Texans were noisier than they had been. 'Again, please,' he requested the barman, tapping their two glasses.

In Bournemouth she had worked as a shorthand typist for the year. In the past she had been a shorthand typist when she and her mother lived in London, before her marriage. 'My married name is Mrs Azann,' she said.

— 148 —

'When I saw you first I thought you had an Indian look.'

'Perhaps you get that when you marry an Indian.'

'And you're entirely English?'

'I've always felt drawn to the East. It's a spiritual affinity.'

Her conversation was like the conversation in a novelette. There was that and her voice, and her unsuitable shoes, and her cough, and not wearing enough for the chilly evening air: all of it went together, only her eyes remained different. And the more she talked about herself, the more her eyes appeared to belong to another person.

'I admire my husband very much,' she said. 'He's very fine. He's most intelligent. He's twenty-two years older than I am.'

She told the story then, while they were still in the bar. She had, although she did not say it, married for money. And though she clearly spoke the truth when she said she admired her husband, the marriage was not entirely happy. She could not, for one thing, have children, which neither of them had known at the time of the wedding and which displeased her husband when it was established as a fact. She had been displeased herself to descover that her husband was not as rich as he had appeared to be. He owned a furniture business, he'd said in the Regent Palace Hotel, where they'd met by chance when she was waiting for someone else: this was true, but he had omitted to add that the furniture business was doing badly. She had also been displeased to discover on the first night of her marriage that she disliked being touched by him. And there was yet another problem: in their bungalow in Bombay there lived, as well as her husband and herself, his mother and an aunt, his brother and his business manager. For a girl not used to such communal life, it was difficult in the bungalow in Bombay.

'It sounds more than difficult.'

'Sometimes.'

'He married you because you have an Indian look. While being the opposite of Indian in other ways. Your pale English skin. Your – your English voice.'

'In Bombay I give elocution lessons.'

He blinked, and then smiled to cover the rudeness that might have shown in his face.

'To Indian women,' she said, 'who come to the Club. My husband and I belong to a club. It's the best part of Bombay life, the social side.'

'It's strange to think of you in Bombay.'

'I thought I mightn't return. I thought I'd maybe stay on with my mother. But there's nothing much in England now.'

'I'm fond of England.'

'I thought you might be.' She coughed again, and took her medicine from her handbag and poured a little into her whisky. She drank a mouthful of the mixture, and then apologized, saying she wasn't being very ladylike. Such behaviour would be frowned upon in the Club.

'You should wear a cardigan with that cough.' He gestured at the barman and ordered further drinks.

'I'll be drunk,' she said, giggling.

He felt he'd been right to be curious. Her story was strange. He imagined the Indian women of the Club speaking English with her nasal intonation, twisting their lips to form the distorted sounds, dropping 'h's' because it was the thing to do. He imagined her in the bungalow with her elderly husband who wasn't rich, and his relations and his business manager. It was a sour little fairy-story, a tale of Cinderella and a prince who wasn't a prince, and the carriage turned into an ice-cold pumpkin. Uneasiness overtook his curiosity, and he wondered again why she had come to Isfahan.

'Let's have dinner now,' he suggested in a slightly hasty voice.

But Mrs Azann, looking at him with her sumptuous eyes, said she couldn't eat a thing.

He would be married, she speculated. There was pain in the lines of his face, even though he smiled a lot and seemed light-hearted. She wondered if he'd once had a serious illness. When he'd brought her into his bedroom she wondered as they sat there if he was going to make a pass at her. But she knew a bit about people making passes, and he didn't seem the type. He was too attractive to have to make a pass. His manners were too elegant; he was too nice.

'I'll watch you having dinner,' she said. 'I don't mind in the least watching you if you're hungry. I couldn't deprive you of your dinner.'

'Well, I am rather hungry.'

His mouth curved when he said things like that, because of his smile. She wondered if he could be an architect. From the moment she'd had the idea of coming to Isfahan she'd known that it wasn't just an idea. She believed in destiny and always had.

They went to the restaurant, which was huge and luxurious like everywhere else in the hotel, dimly lit, with oil lamps on each table. She liked the way he explained to the waiters that she didn't wish to eat anything. For himself, he ordered a chicken kebab and salad.

'You'd like some wine?' he suggested, smiling in that same way. 'Persian wine's very pleasant.'

'I'd love a glass.'

He ordered the wine. She said:

'Do you always travel alone?'

'Yes.'

'But you're married?'

'Yes, I am.'

'And your wife's a home bird?'

'It's a *modus vivendi*.'

She imagined him in a house in a village, near Midhurst possibly, or Sevenoaks. She imagined his wife, a capable woman, good in the garden and on committees. She saw his wife quite clearly, a little on the heavy side but nice, cutting sweet-peas.

'You've told me nothing about yourself,' she said.

'There's very little to tell. I'm afraid I haven't a story like yours.'

'Why are you in Isfahan?'

'On holiday.'

'Is it always on your own?'

'I like being on my own. I like hotels. I like looking at people and walking about.'

'You're like me. You like travel.'

'Yes, I do.'

'I imagine you in a village house, in the Home Counties somewhere.'

'That's clever of you.'

'I can clearly see your wife.' She described the woman she could clearly see, without mentioning about her being on the heavy side. He nodded. She had second sight, he said with his smile.

'People have said I'm a little psychic. I'm glad I met you.'

'It's been a pleasure meeting you. Stories like yours are rare enough.'

'It's all true. Every word.'

'Oh, I know it is.'

'Are you an architect?'

'You're quite remarkable,' he said.

He finished his meal and between them they finished the wine. They had coffee and then she asked if he would kindly order more. The Swiss party had left the restaurant, and so had the German couple and their friends. Other diners had been and gone. The Texans were leaving just as Mrs Azann suggested more coffee. No other table was occupied.

'Of course,' he said.

He wished she'd go now. They had killed an evening together. Not for a long time would he forget either her ugly voice or her beautiful eyes. Nor would he easily forget the fairy-story that had gone sour on her. But that was that: the evening was over now.

The waiter brought their coffee, seeming greatly fatigued by the chore.

'D'you think,' she said, 'we should have another drink? D'you think they have cigarettes here?'

He had brandy and she more whisky. The waiter brought her American cigarettes.

'I don't really want to go back to Bombay,' she said.

'I'm sorry about that.'

'I'd like to stay in Isfahan for ever.'

'You'd be very bored. There's no club. No social life of any kind for an English person, I should think.'

'I do like a little social life.' She smiled at him, broadening her sensuous mouth. 'My father was a counter-hand,' she said. 'In a Co-op. You wouldn't think it, would you?'

'Not at all,' he lied.

'It's my little secret. If I told the women in the Club that, or my husband's mother or his aunt, they'd have a fit. I've never even told my husband. Only my mother and I share that secret.'

'I see.'

'And now you.'

'Secrets are safe with strangers.'

'Why do you think I told you that secret?'

'Because we are ships that pass in the night.'

'Because you are sympathetic.'

The waiter hovered close and then approached them boldly. The bar was open for as long as they wished it to be. There were lots of other drinks in the bar. Cleverly, he removed the coffee-pot and their cups.

'He's like a magician,' she said. 'Everything in Isfahan is magical.'

'You're glad you came?'

'It's where I met you.'

He rose. He had to stand for a moment because she continued to sit there, her handbag on the table, her black frilled shawl on top of it. She hadn't finished her whisky, but he expected that she'd lift the glass to her lips and drink what she wanted of it, or just leave it there. She rose and walked with him from the restaurant, taking her glass with her. Her other hand slipped beneath his arm.

'There's a discotheque downstairs,' she said.

'Oh, I'm afraid that's not really me.'

'Nor me, neither. Let's go back to our bar.'

She handed him her glass, saying she had to pay a visit. She'd love another whisky and soda, she said, even though she hadn't quite finished the one in her glass. Without ice, she said.

The bar was empty except for a single barman. Normanton ordered more brandy for himself and whisky for Mrs Azann. He much preferred her as Iris Smith, in her tatty pink dress and the dark glasses that hid her eyes: she could have been any little

— 153 —

typist except that she'd married Mr Azann and had a story to tell.

'It's nice in spite of things,' she explained as she sat down. 'It's nice in spite of him wanting to you-know-what, and the women in the bungalow, and his brother and the business manager. They all disapprove because I'm English, especially his mother and his aunt. He doesn't disapprove because he's mad about me. The business manager doesn't much mind, I suppose. The dogs don't mind. D'you understand? In spite of everything, it's nice to have someone mad about you. And the Club, the social life. Even though we're short of the ready, it's better than England for a woman. There's servants, for a start.'

The whisky was affecting the way she put things. An hour ago she wouldn't have said 'wanting to you-know-what' or 'short of the ready'. It was odd that she had an awareness in this direction and yet could not hear the twang in her voice which instantly gave her away.

'But you don't love your husband.'

'I respect him. It's only that I hate having to you-know-what with him. I really do hate that. I've never actually loved him.'

He regretted saying she didn't love her husband: the remark had slipped out, and it was regrettable because it involved him in the conversation in a way he didn't wish to be.

'Maybe things will work out better when you get back.'

'I know what I'm going back to.' She paused, searching for his eyes with hers. 'I'll never till I die forget Isfahan.'

'It's very beautiful.'

'I'll never forget the Chaharbagh Tours, or Hafez. I'll never forget that place you brought me. Or the Shah Abbas Hotel.'

'I think it's time I saw you back to your own hotel.'

'I could sit in this bar for ever.'

'I'm afraid I'm not at all one for night-life.'

'I shall visualize you when I'm back in Bombay. I shall think of you in your village, with your wife, happy in England. I shall think of you working at your architectural plans. I shall often wonder about you travelling alone because your wife doesn't care for it. Your *modus*.'

'I hope it's better in Bombay. Sometimes things are, when you least expect them to be.'

'It's been like a tonic. You've made me very happy.'

'It's kind of you to say that.'

'There's much that's unsaid between us. Will you remember me?'

'Oh yes, of course.'

Reluctantly, she drank the dregs of her whisky. She took her medicine from her handbag and poured a little into the glass and drank that, too. It helped the tickle in her throat, she said. She always had a tickle when the wretched cough came.

'Shall we walk back?'

They left the bar. She clung to him again, walking very slowly between the mosaiced columns. All the way back to the Old Atlantic Hotel she talked about the evening they had spent and how delightful it had been. Not for the world would she have missed Isfahan, she repeated several times.

When they said goodbye she kissed his cheek. Her beautiful eyes swallowed him up, and for a moment he had a feeling that her eyes were the real thing about her, reflecting her as she should be.

He woke at half-past two and could not sleep. Dawn was already beginning to break. He lay there, watching the light increase in the gap he'd left between the curtains so that there'd be fresh air in the room. Another day had passed: he went through it piece by piece, from his early-morning walk to the moment when he'd put his green pyjamas on and got into bed. It was a regular night-time exercise with him. He closed his eyes, remembering in detail.

He turned again into the offices of Chaharbagh Tours and was told by Hafez to go to the upstairs office. He saw her sitting there writing to her mother, and heard her voice asking him if he was going on the tour. He saw again the sunburnt faces of the German couple and the wholesome faces of the American girls and faces in the French party. He went again on his afternoon walk, and after that there was his bath. She came towards him in the bazaar, with her dark glasses and her small purchases. There was her story as she had told it.

For his part, he had told her nothing. He had agreed with her novelette picture of him, living in a Home Counties village, a well-to-do architect married to a wife who gardened. Architects had become as romantic as doctors, there'd been no reason to disillusion her. She would for ever imagine him travelling to exotic places, on his own because he enjoyed it, because his wife was a home bird.

Why could he not have told her? Why could he not have exchanged one story for another? She had made a mess of things and did not seek to hide it. Life had let her down, she'd let herself down. Ridiculously, she gave elocution lessons to Indian women and did not see it as ridiculous. She had told him her secret, and he knew it was true that he shared it only with her mother and herself.

The hours went by. He should be lying with her in this bed, the size of a dance-floor. In the dawn he should be staring into her sumptuous eyes, in love with the mystery there. He should be telling her and asking for her sympathy, as she had asked for his. He should be telling her that he had walked into a room, not in a Home Counties village, but in harsh, ugly Hampstead, to find his second wife, as once he had found his first, in his bed with another man. He should in humility have asked her why it was that he was naturally a cuckold, why two women of different temperaments and characters had been inspired to have lovers at his expense. He should be telling her, with the warmth of her body warming his, that his second wife had confessed to greater sexual pleasure when she remembered that she was deceiving him.

It was a story no better than hers, certainly as unpleasant. Yet he hadn't had the courage to tell it because it cast him in a certain light. He travelled easily, moving over surfaces and revealing only surfaces himself. He was acceptable as a stranger: in two marriages he had not been forgiven for turning out to be different from what he seemed. To be a cuckold once was the luck of the game, but his cuckoldry twice had a whiff of revenge. In all humility he might have asked her about that.

At half-past four he stood by the window, looking out at the empty street below. She would be on her way to the bus station, to catch the five o'clock bus to Teheran. He could dress, he could even shave and still be there in time. He could pay, on her behalf, the extra air fare that would accrue. He could tell her his story and they could spend a few days. They could go together to Shiraz, city of wine and roses and nightingales.

He stood by the window, watching nothing happening in the street, knowing that if he stood there for ever he wouldn't find the courage. She had met a sympathetic man, more marvellous to her than all the marvels of Isfahan. She would carry that memory to the bungalow in Bombay, knowing nothing about a pettiness which brought out cruelty in people. And he would remember a woman who possessed, deep beneath her unprepossessing surface, the distinction that her eyes mysteriously claimed for her. In different circumstances, with a less unfortunate story to tell, it would have emerged: he could sense that in retrospect. But in the early morning there was another truth, too. He was the stuff of fantasy. She had quality, he had none.

June 1975

The Cargo

NEIL RENNIE

Part II: From Business to Pidgin

Tess Again

Paper flags are strung around the airfield.
On each your face is the same.
Its zig-zag lines, still faltering
across the background pattern of a cushion,
are flying now for leaves of thatch
and painted bark: for 'planes as thick as bush'.

The Story So Far

On this, the day of the Sunday page, John comes,
trailing speed lines, by instalments to the islands.
For you and me, at the end of the Customs wharf
on Rue Higginson, it's a single page affair:
the story so far, then, later the same day,
a row of sunsets in a sky of Ben Day dots.

The Silent Trade

The bush is solid yellow with blue dots
as regular as dimes and noughts.
The kanakas wind past in rolls of calico,
mission fashion, on their way to the store.
They form a line to take the flash 'Good evening!'
that slides along their slicked-down hair.

Dick, Reading

'Okay, boy,' he said. 'Me savy.
Allsame German.' He shook as he read
and brightly coloured croton leaves
like flowers, overblossoming in the 'office',
fell around him where he sat,
underneath a lightbulb, slightly blurred.

The Steamer of the Dead

The head-he-go-round men are up late,
hardboiled, listening to the flagpole.
The dogs have risen and walk the shore,
among the traces of the European boots.
Cane flashlights show the steamer's there.
Its rails are lined with John's white boys.

January 1976 (since revised)

An Upstairs Kitchen

— SUSANNAH AMOORE —

It is strange that I used to think
The summers were best in this kitchen
High in the back of the house:
A time when thick greens
From the trees and the park beyond
Smother the windows
And enter the room.

A time when I easily leave the peeling
Or cleaning to drift and lean
On cool glass, drawn
By the astonishing pink of the jay.
By short bare legs which distantly
Lift the swings, by the dog
Racing the trains.

Strange, because now is clearly the time
I like best. The Bank Holiday fairs
Crammed close round the oaks
Have all gone; old ginger leaves
Are heaped soaking and deep in their place,
And the footballers' turkey-red shirts
Flare through the branches.

And some days, on the top edge of the far
Distance, through bare trees,
I can see the tower of the riverside
Church, where a mother lies buried

With six of her children, three
Distressingly drowned
At different times.

How surprised she might be to know
That more than a century later
I worry in winters
Over her carelessness and pain,
While the iron gently noses its way
Between buttons and pleats,
With soft steam sighs.

March 1976

Are You
Distraining Me?

———— KARL MILLER ————

The jazz musician Sandy Brown died in 1975. I was a friend of
his for many years, but I never knew that he was half-Hindu,
or that there were two of him, in the persons of Sandy Brown
and Alistair Babb. These persons he identifies and names in an
autobiography which is due to be published, and I had to wait
until I read that work before I made the discoveries I'm referring
to. I want to show that they are substantially the same discovery.
It is an interesting discovery, to my mind, and I hope it will
become clear why I also say that it will remain an interesting
discovery even if some of his statements are discovered to be a
put-on on Sandy's part, and fictional.

We both went to the Royal High School of Edinburgh, he
being slightly older and already a notorious Mephistophelean
playground presence before I got to the Temple of Theseus.
Built in the 1820s as a further monument lavished on the city's
Classical New Town, the school was a copy of the Athenian
edifice of that name. It has recently, and disgracefully, been
stripped of the schoolboys for whom it was built, and is soon
to house the unSandyish devolved deliberations of the Scottish
Assembly. Its glooms, colonnades and fine proportions were
not inhospitable: an impressive building, but pre-Victorian in
the sense that it was scaled to accommodate human behaviour
rather than to overwhelm or sneer at it. Ankle-breaking steep
staircases – not very accommodating, I admit – seemed to
descend into a 19th century where martinet Classics masters
equipped their students to be public-spirited Scottish Whigs
and to fight for and draft the Reform Bill. In the classrooms
were roaring fires, large enough for suttee or the stake. I

remember the hearth of Room Three, with one boy inadvertently toasting a standing penis which had slipped out of his shorts in the heat of the moment – as if to poke the past, or salute the embers and old flames of the Athens of the North.

The boys wore elegant black jackets and caps, which displayed the school badge, a white castle, and a motto on a scroll: *Musis respublica floret.* A civic place, the High School, now civically betrayed. But Sandy would have nothing to do with these sables and insignia. He wore what I remember as a yellow bow-tie, and what he remembered as a brown velvet bow-tie: whatever it was, it hung out, and fell about, in a very mocking way. He was bald, and bold, and bad. And he was a jazz musician. At the Royal High, 'musical' was a word which described those who belonged to the choir and orchestra, which performed to applause in spotless white on the platforms of concert halls, and were drilled and fretted over by a red-haired elderly Englishman (the name, Mellalieu, was euphony itself, and comprised, he said, all the vowels used in vocal music). In that world, Sandy was an outcast, and on occasion an outlaw – as he had already recognized himself to be in the world of Willowbrae Avenue, the district where he lived with his mother. Sandy was late for school, comical, hostile, friendly, formidable. I was a swot, less late for school, and we could not be pally. But I was keenly conscious of him, and would watch him, and perhaps I had already glimpsed that it was Sandy, rather than the swots and concert artistes, who was in touch with the muses. And in the playground there were others like him in that respect. The Royal High helped to make the British jazz of the forties and fifties the best in Europe, and yet at the school itself it was an extra-curricular activity – rated low and dirty by the authorities. Education is a wonderful thing.

For a number of years after we left school we met only once or twice, in the thick of jazz-band balls, where I was a fish out of water and he was Moby Dick, blowing his clarinet. Then, in London, we became pals. For some six years I edited the *Listener*, and he used to write about jazz in that journal, leading, meanwhile, two lives – that of a jazz musician and that of an acoustician-architect. In the second capacity he worked as a BBC employee, before quitting to start his own firm, and as a

BBC employee he may be said to have found his only rival for awkwardness and intransigence in the straight musician Hans Keller. His jazz pieces would often tax the Corporation with a failure to take jazz seriously and treat it decently, and with a policy which led to the destruction of important tapes. His pieces were full of character and invention: full, too, of knots and congestions, and not the easiest copy in the world to edit. But they bore the stamp of the talent, style and wit which never failed him, and of that excellent pride of his. It was very like him to answer as he did when he was asked, in a BBC Television interview recorded in his last days, whether he'd prefer to be, if he had to choose, an architect or the world's best jazz clarinettist. Sandy said: 'You must excuse my arrogance, but do you really suppose that I'm not?' His pieces were the pieces of the man who made that reply.

An outsider might wonder whether the combativeness of his articles, the insistent claims made on behalf of the musicians he felt closest to, were affected by the resentments of a jazz musician whose standing, and hearing, had been attacked by the explosive arrival, in the sixties, of pop music and the groups – of all that jazz which was not his jazz. This gave him trouble, but did not make him bitter, though the acoustician in him counted the decibels of the new sounds, and the cost in eardrums. I'm sure he never doubted that his own music had kept its virtue. There were later times when an evening of that music among his friends was like a gathering of brave spirits, a blessed remnant, surrounded by their fit audience though few. But they came to play, not to complain or commiserate, and I did not notice any of the rancour which you get with writers who feel cheated of celebrity.

I was curious to read his posthumous autobiography, and I think it a remarkable document, a convincing picture of an artist's life, of the pleasures and pains, fantasies and phantasmagorias, which the practice of an art brings with it, and on which it ensues. I also discovered that the autobiography had a special interest for me, and it may be worth explaining what that interest is.

Not long ago I published a book called *Cockburn's Millennium*. The Cockburn in question was an Edinburgh man, and a High

School man, and the book is an account of his life and times. Henry Cockburn was a Whig historian and lawyer who helped to draft the Scottish Reform Bill of 1832, and who wrote beautiful autobiographies, of which his *Memorials* is the best-known. In the course of the book I discussed the theme of double identity as it is manifested in the Gothic or Romantic literature which appeared in Britain, Germany and elsewhere during Cockburn's lifetime. Scotsmen have been thought to have been more than usually exercised by the theme, and have been responsible for some of the most compelling treatments of the theme, such as Hogg's *Confessions of a Justified Sinner* and Stevenson's *The Strange Case of Dr Jekyll and Mr Hyde*. I didn't want it to be supposed that Cockburn was some kind of split personality or Gothic personage, or a subscriber to the Gothic account of human nature, which increasingly insisted on its essential duality. But he could employ the Gothic vocabulary of duality, and could do so in order to describe his own behaviour. Furthermore, his tastes were both classical and romantic, as became the inhabitant of a town that was two towns, offering the rival attractions of a surviving medieval enclave and a Neoclassical utopia. He was in certain respects a divided man, whose divisions could appear to re-enact, and also to precede, the quarrel with his father over politics which took place in his youth.

It struck me as reasonable, therefore, to ask whether he might have been influenced by whatever compulsions of the period gave rise to the distinctive Scottish preoccupation with double lives and second selves. These possibilities were studied with frequent reference to hitherto unpublished writings by Cockburn which were included in the book – above all, the poems which he wrote in private. Critics who suggested that he had been wickedly Gothicized, and who suggested, in effect, that the standing interpretation of his career as that of a hard-headed Whig lawyer who relaxed by writing classical commentaries and civic gossip needed to be reaffirmed, were inclined to ignore the manuscript writings, together with the sensitivity to new outlooks, and the evidence of divided loyalties, which these and other writings of his embody.

It was an effort to get the arguments and affinities satisfac-
torily sorted out. I wanted to present a picture of Cockburn's
experience which would make him look like a human being,
and which would keep its distance from the sensationalism of
the early, and the latterday, Gothic literary modes: I didn't want
him looking like some precursor of that tribe of gentlemen, real
and imaginary, who stole through the twilights of the Victorian
Babylon, and who were conceived of in terms of their shameful
secrets, and of their willingness to confess such secrets.

For every person who is excited by the talk of double and
divided selves which has never ceased since Cockburn's time,
there are two who will hard-headedly assert that such things are
just a fashion or fad, a convenient high-flown way for writers
to talk about certain of the ordinary human difficulties and
recourses – to talk, for instance, about role-playing and hypocrisy. Scholarship knows for a fact that doubles are a dream.
While I was writing the book, I used to wonder what it might
be like to feel divided, to feel that it wasn't nonsense to say that
you had more than one self. John Stonehouse has claimed that
an established personality was supplanted by another, and in
Gothic style, in order to lead a new life, he pretended that he
had died. But then many might be suspicious of these claims. I
had known what it was to experience contradictory desires, but
the self I was conscious of – for all that I could be conscious of
it – had always appeared the same: without imagining that I
was ever likely to be mistaken for James Callaghan, I had
always felt myself sole and undivided – *e pluribus unum*, like the
United States of America. And yet it seemed conceivable that
you didn't have to be subject to chemically-induced hallucinations, or clinically mad, in order to be beside yourself, in
order to consign part of your pleasures and ambitions to a
separate self which could be experienced as something other
than a hypothesis, as something other than romantic hyperbole.

In the course of the book, a scheme was worked out for the
attitudes and compulsions which might have helped to shape
the response to the idea of duality during Cockburn's lifetime.
The scheme laid stress on repressive religion and authoritarian
parenthood; on rebellious conduct in relation to family codes,
and to the customs of the country as these were enjoined within

the family; on the doubting, double or contradictory character which such conduct could assume; on the interest in orphans which is evident in the literature of the first half of the 19th century, and on the role of the self-constituted orphan which certain mutineers could adopt. The role of the self-constituted orphan could be enacted by a second self, and could therefore form part of a 'double life' (I am using this last expression in a sense broader than the one which is now colloquial, and which makes it mean very little more than 'delinquency'). The recourse to fantasies of duality and bereavement could sometimes seem to be related to a son's quarrel with his father, and could also seem to include elements of the oedipal experience predicated by Freud.

By these and other features of the scheme I was worried at the time. But I feel less bashful about them now, and I am bound to say that Sandy's memoir has enabled me to take heart. Here is a man who was both a real and imaginary orphan. Here is a double life, confessed – as has rarely happened – in terms of autobiography rather than fiction. Here, we might hope, are duality's very words.

Confessions, fantasies and affectations of duality are largely restricted to the literature of the subject. But the literature of the subject may well have promoted a disposition to feel split, to affect to feel split, and to behave in Gothic ways. It may well have encouraged Mr Stonehouse to inform the House of Commons, on 21 October last year, that a 'parallel personality took over, separate and apart from the original man'. And it may equally well have encouraged the psychiatrist referred to in that statement to instruct Stonehouse to use this language, to speak of his 'psychiatric suicide'. The arrival of this parallel personality, we are to think, caused him to simulate a drowning in Miami, and to disappear. While writing the book, I had classed this as a Gothic act: then, late in the day, I came across a manuscript letter of Cockburn's in which an Edinburgh youth, oppressed by the feats expected of him at the school Cockburn helped to found, Edinburgh Academy, feigned a drowning in the Danube, and disappeared. Seized by 'a sudden Germanizing of the noddle', supposed Cockburn. Was Stonehouse's noddle Germanized at any point? Whether or not he was ever impressed by a reading of E. T. A. Hoffmann, Hogg, Stevenson and company, it is hard to suppose him unaffected by the impact of the Gothic tradition, by the correspondence between its doctrine of duality and the ordinary understanding of tensions and dilemmas which appear to have persisted in the society, and by the translation of that doctrine into the doctrines of some of our current psychologies. And I believe that the same could be said of Sandy Brown, alias Alistair Babb.

Stonehouse's 'Confessions', entitled *Death of an Idealist*, are by no means forthcoming about this aspect of the affair, among others. The book has in common with the overcharged public record of his breakdown that it does not allow one to guess how far he has controlled, and how far he has been controlled by, his impersonations and performances. As I write, he is in court facing criminal charges, and the prosecuting counsel has been speaking in such a way as to persuade people that the psychiatric explanation of his pretended drowning, the talk about a new self or leaf, was really an alibi of a kind for the conduct he is charged with. I doubt whether the question of his sincerity will be settled by the verdict of the court, any more than it was settled by his autobiography. Literature has pronounced, and we needn't flatly disbelieve, that indictable offences are highly compatible with some kind of first-hand experience of duality, while also being compatible, of course, with elaborate excuses. And if we do decide that Stonehouse's account is fictional, it would be as well to remember that fiction can be interesting and instructive.

Death of an Idealist is very much a politicians' book, as we can see when, during his troubles, Stonehouse feels the truth of the saying: 'I can deal with my enemies but heaven save me from my friends.' Cockburn once wrote: 'Enemies are easily managed, but wrong-headed friends are the very devil.' This statement is linked, in the book, to the quarrel with his kindred, but it is also the kind of thing that politicians say, and think. As well as idealists. It is worth adding that those who share an interest in duality – or an involvement in politics – need not be very like one another, any more than duality has to lead to larceny. Cockburn's 'wrong-headed friends are the very devil' is like a precis of those Gothic tales where such friends were a

— 168 —

way of talking about someone's capacity to prove his own worst enemy, in the days when heaven and hell were thought to care about plights of that sort. Cockburn has accidentally described what happens in Hogg's *Confessions*.

I don't remember whether Sandy ever spoke to me about the 19th-century fictions of duality, but he needn't have read them in order to have been aware that double lives of one kind or another were especially Scottish. He was once friendly, in a special sort of way, with the Scotsman who is duality's leading authority in the modern world, and who is known for his polemical concern with the self-protective powers which duality can bring to bear in relation to the family, and with the sufferings to which it may be a response: this is R. D. Laing. How far Sandy's autobiography derives from an influential literature, how far it copies the fictions it may be thought to corroborate, is unclear. But it is likely that it owes something to Laing, who owes something to Scotland. At any rate, it is plain from the autobiography that an intelligent and in some respects hard-headed man could feel himself to be double – to the extent of enlisting the old confessional metaphor of the second self in order to evoke his experience and account for it. In order to make sense of what had become of him, lying in a hospital bed at the end of his days, with, perhaps, a consequent freedom to pick and choose his metaphors, he chose to be someone with two selves at least, the second of which, roughly speaking, was an orphan.

These memoirs of his could not readily be broken down to form an item in the *Dictionary of National Biography*. A few early episodes are dwelt on to the complete exclusion of a very great deal. It is as if they were the matrix from which issued almost everything of importance that he ever was, though this would have to be called a false impression: the memoirs are family-free, for instance, as far as his wife and children are concerned, which was certainly not true of his life. They open with a meditation on colours which have obsessed him, and this serves to introduce a strain of phantasmagoria. For the purposes of his autobiography, family is parents. His upbringing in India is sketched: there are words about a father – of whom Sandy may have been very much the son – who cuts himself off from the Raj by marrying a woman who was coloured. As the offspring of a mixed marriage, Sandy suffers an ostracism and orphaning of his own. Then he is bereaved by his father's death, which shook and distressed him, launching, amid his fantasies, like a ship of death, the yellow submarine of a coffin. Masturbation and girls put those fantasies to brisk work. He breaks a leg, and evokes operations at the Edinburgh Royal Infirmary (the odysseys of those born in that city will often be a royal road).

The operations are traumatic, conveying the sense of an agony of birth mingled with one of bereavement. The acid, threatening colours of before recur as the colours of birth, the brightest imaginable, with the wave-machine at Portobello Pool delivering an additional element of threat. Out of all this travail – born, bereaved, cast out and of doubtful caste, operated on, threatened, sobbing, ejaculating – emerges an orphan lad, a fellow who is two fellows, as Stevenson expressed it: Alistair Babb and Sandy Brown, his real name scarcely less apt than his pseudonym. If the first of these two fellows, whose name is Americanized at times as Al Babb, took that name from the well-known oriental Ali Baba, this might indicate that the early sufferings gave birth to the clarinettist whose career another self went on to manage. But I'd prefer to be tentative about the principle which governed the separation of his two selves, which governed his self-administered Siamesing (Cockburn's word, and Stonehouse's), and about the 'ligature' which bound these selves together. This strange operation, in which the Royal Infirmary played its involuntary part, cannot be said to be carefully explained in Sandy's Memorials, though it is made to seem vividly authentic. The invented name, incidentally, may allude, not only to Ali Baba, but to the word 'alibi'.

Those people who knew Sandy–Alistair might object that he wasn't *like* an orphan: no one could have been less plaintive. I agree. The orphan was, as it were, internal, historical. He was not like any Victorian orphan of the storm, on the wrong side of the window-pane in his nightie, while the thunder pealed loud and long. In point of appearance, he was not unlike some fierce sailor – say, Captain Haddock of the Tintin books. In point of style, a style in which that broken leg had not been forgotten, he was much more like a Captain Hook than a Peter Pan, as much Captain Ahab as the white whale. Or, to return to the *dramatis personae* of Gothic duality, he was more of a princely tempter than any of the outcasts tempted by such princes, though he was occasionally tempted and occasionally fell.

It was like him to tempt me to give up playing football, on grounds of old age: he told me at lunch, over the escalope Milanese, that when he'd come to watch me play, as he'd stealthily done the previous weekend, he'd found that I was past it. You don't say that lightly even to a Sunday footballer. The untouchable was uttering the unspeakable. The untouchable didn't seem to mind that Rodney Marsh of Queen's Park Rangers was quite old. Sandy rightly admired the brilliance of Marsh's individualism, his eccentric or orphan style.

He was both of each pair of opposites or opponents that could be detected in him. Such were his united states. Nevertheless (Muriel Spark once observed that this is *the* Edinburgh word, pronounced 'niverthelace'), the ophan in him seems to have mattered, and his autobiography sets out to say so – to expose the self that might not have been taken for granted, that might not even have been detected, and wasn't by me, amid the activities of the outlaw. We have his word for it that his behaviour incorporated the fears of an outcast, bewildered by the country to which he had come to be cast away for a further term, a country which threatened him, and was to threaten his music.

On the face of it, his double life was that of a romantic, hairy jazzman, off to Ronnie Scott's or rattling in his van to places like Craigellachie, who was also a business executive with his auditoria in Iboland. But there was more to it than that: it seems to have amounted to a complex of double, or to several, lives. Just as a new leaf may turn out to proliferate in fresh identities, duality is easily seen now as multiplicity. And to see it as that is to wonder who can be free of it – to wonder who isn't *e pluribus*, who isn't the polity of multifarious denizens which Stevenson predicated. It would not be surprising if in recent years, when the subject has often been wondered about, and when Marilyn Monroe was able to declare that there were

700 Arthur Millers, the single life has looked meagre and insufficient.

Sandy was dual or plural to the extent that he could call himself by two names, and could behave as a victim who was also an outlaw or pirate. In other words, there was an isolation in him, never outgrown, which accompanied his being masterful, ambitious. Here we have what is probably the least superficial aspect of his double life, though it does not do much to correct or qualify what we have been accustomed to think of outlaws or pirates. His autobiography, as I've said, may provide duality's very words. These words could well be taken to mean that his two or several selves were hypothetical or figurative, and they do not allow one to know for certain whether he considered himself more divided than most people are. At the same time, they suggest that the hypothesis was believed, and experienced, that it could be experienced with the force of hallucination, and that it was best described in the language of hallucination.

Among the symptoms of his condition was the way he had of making you feel both liked and disliked, of attacking his friends with ironies. In my own case, memories of school may have sharpened his ironies, and fetched him to the touchline. He could see in me the swot who played second fiddle in the raucous royal, high school orchestra. This enabled him to discover that I couldn't play football.

I mentioned Edinburgh words a moment ago, and Sandy's autobiography is eloquent about the part played by language in his life. In India and afterwards, his father's isolation and death were referred to by the family in embarrassed words which seemed to be surrounded by invisible inverted commas, and in Edinburgh at large, words were used in a distinctive way which could also invite inverted commas. Edinburgh has two languages – Scots and posh English. A lot of the first survived in Sandy till the end of his life – the voice rather than the vocabulary. This situation is no impediment to the double life, but it causes quaintness, and a precarious aplomb. Double-tongued schoolboys have a tendency to be a bit pedantic and scholarly, and are drawn to jargon and the higher gibberish in a manner that may be less common among one-tongued Southerners, as Cockburn called them, of the same age.

On one occasion in Sandy's youth, the manager of Edinburgh's West End Cafe, where jazz was played, refused to let him in after closing-time. Out in the cold, Sandy enquired: 'Are you distraining me?' The last brown-and-cream tram – with its little lurching alternative spiral staircases at either end, like the two parts of a double life – had long gone to Joppa or Corstorphine. There he was, lost in the dark and stormy night of Shandwick Place and Prince's Street, frowned at by Binn's department store, cast out by the Caledonian Station: there was Caledonia's orphan, whose word for his own plight, 'distraining', was a practical, legal word signifying bankruptcy and the surrender of worldly goods, a word of doubtful application here, you could say, and yet the *mot juste*. When I read it in his memoirs, that word brought back Edinburgh and Midlothian to me as nothing else could have done. Having hurt my leg at my village school, I told the teachers, with the air of a James Callaghan: 'I collidded with another boy.' The teachers laughed at the mispronunciation, and I was aware that there were two sorts of word. Scots words could be low and bad, apparently, and big English words could be dangerous: from both sorts, schoolboys stood distrained, or strained.

Words mattered to Sandy because he was a wit. Humour was his element, almost as much as music. His wit discharged itself, not so much in repartee and epigram, as in stories and fantasies, and in the letters he wrote, which were seldom grave. Once he was showing his mother-in-law the sights of London. They were travelling by bus, and the bus was making its way along Fleet Street. 'And this,' said Sandy of a recently excavated temple, 'is where they found the Roman remains.' Round-eyed, in the accents of Edinburgh, his mother-in-law cried: 'Terrible!' Or rather: 'Tairrible!' Once, when he'd come to visit me at the *Listener*, he asked permission to leave with the commissionaire the monstrous Martian sky-blue crash-helmet which he sometimes wore. Sorry, it was more than the commissionaire's job was worth. Sandy explained to me that this man belonged to a class with which jazz musicians were familiar, and for which they had a name. Like many another janitor, custodian and sky-high official, he was a Job's Worth.

Sandy, single-mindedly, was the opposite of a Job's Worth,

and he was seldom sorry. He liked to play with words. His blue bonnet or helmet buzzed with verbal bees, with coinages and christenings. There were words for the disease that killed him: malignant hypertension. It sounds like a grim name, and could be a name for what happens to artists – to jazzmen, whose lives tend to be short. He used to point out that, after 40, he was living on borrowed time, statistically speaking. But he did not speak statistically when he gave news of his illness. He spoke humorously. And I was too stupidly self-absorbed at the time to take in that he was done for. He died a Roman death. He wouldn't go into intensive care after a heart attack, and waited at home instead with a glass of whisky – watching a Scotland–England rugby game, in which Scotland could have triumphed and didn't, suffering one of its fiascos or Floddens – for its successor, which did not keep him waiting very long.

In the last two years or so, three of my dearest friends have died in middle age. The others were the critic Marius Bewley and Tony White. All three were of divided nationality: Tony was literally half-French, Marius spiritually Anglo-American. Marius died in the loathing of Nixon's America, but his great wit could signal how much he enjoyed some other Americas, to the point of patriotism. As for Sandy, he was half-Hindu and an Anglo–Indian who was also an intensely Scottish Anglo-Scot. It might have been said of Tony what the boxing Brando, whom he resembled, said in *On the Waterfront:* 'I could have been a contender.' By this I mean that he had it in him to be a very good actor, and in fact proved himself one in his early days at Cambridge. But he gave it up, and devoted himself to football, to friendship, to solitude, to reading, writing, working as a builder, and to building himself a house in the wilds of Ireland. When he broke his leg colliding on the football field, the junior hospital doctors were on strike, so that he was discharged from hospital straight away after the leg was set, and he had a great deal of trouble getting attention from hospitals when complications came: no doubt it was more than their jobs were worth. A blood clot produced an embolism. I'm told that he would have died anyway – even if these doctors and hospital officials had behaved like human beings. Some people would say that it was wrong for a grown man to go on playing football and caring about it, and painfully ridiculous to die of it: that it could only have made sense, this zeal, if he had been signed by Queen's Park Rangers. Well, I think he felt that it was better to play football than to do what most of his contemporaries were doing, and I am not exaggerating when I say that he would have thought it rich, and a rich joke, to die like this.

Each of the three died before his time, at a time when this had begun to seem like quite a good idea, and their deaths have made their friends feel like orphans. I loved them very much, and am glad of the chance to write in their praise. It might have been advisable to talk less about duality in doing so: an unreal world, and a subject on which it is hard to trust your perceptions. Equally, the experience of the colliding and distrained, in their infirmary of broken legs and divided selves, can often seem like an unreal world, though it is one of which few people are ignorant. Niverthelace, I can trust what I felt about these men, and I hoped that this would help me to write about Sandy's Confessions, in which two lives, or nine, are darkly revealed.

May 1976

A Bad Day
for Eton

——————— JAMES FOX ———————

Richard John Bingham, 7th Earl of Lucan, has been missing since 7th November 1974. The Metropolitan Police have a warrant out for his arrest on a double charge of murder and attempted murder. A London inquest in June last year named him as the man who had killed his children's nanny. His estranged wife, Veronica, gave a vivid description of his attempts that night to murder her as well.

Since the 39-year-old peer vanished into the night from Belgrave Square, the search has moved from the UK, through the USA, South America, Swaziland, Mozambique, South Africa, the Caribbean, France, Germany and Portugal. Fresh 'sightings' are still reported to Scotland Yard every week, and followed up in vain. In the first 48 hours after the incident, Lucan escaped the police traps despite two telephone calls to his mother who was sitting with police officers. Then there are two hotly contested theories whose interest, as in all great unsolved mysteries, will never wane: is he alive, or is he dead and if so was his suicide so exceptional as to leave no trace of his corpse?

The Lucan murder, however, has an extra fascination which puts it beyond the range of British suburban wife slaying. In the case of Lucan, the light was thrown on the English upper class, and therefore on the whole waterlogged English class system itself. It showed them with their backs to the wall, ultra sensitive to exposure, with political views far to the right. When the police began questioning the several hundred people in Lucan's three address books, and came up against that world united on foundations of class, privilege and wealth, they were oddly unfamiliar with it, and were taken by surprise. So were readers of the *Sunday Times Magazine* – where their utterances were quoted at length, much to their irritation.

I wrote the story in question. I took weeks to collect the information, and in the end became involved as a piece of the drama which unfolded throughout 1975 – one of the longest-running topics of obsessive gossip in the last decade.

The proof of the role that class played in the tragedy itself is to be found in the awesome probability that given their different backgrounds, and the secret damage it did them both, 'Lucky' Lucan and his wife Veronica were embarked on a course of tragedy from the moment they met. When it happened, Lady Lucan, the victim of an attempted murder, was subjected to an almost hysterical degree of misogynistic abuse, from men and women alike.

Veronica Lucan had married into a family that commanded, if nothing else, a certain genealogical respect. The Binghams were an old West of England family. Robert de Bingham became Bishop of Salisbury in 1229, and the tomb of Richard Bingham, a distinguished Elizabethan soldier, is in Westminster Abbey. In the eighteenth century they bought vast estates in Ireland and joined the ranks of the Anglo Irish. The Earldom of Lucan was granted in 1795.

Lucan's great great grandfather, who first sullied the family's reputation at Crimea, succeeded to the title in 1839, while he was managing the Irish estates. These were in even worse condition than those owned by the English absentee landlords, although Lucan too was absent a great deal. John Harris, author of *The Gallant Six Hundred*, a writer who strains to excuse such behaviour, wrote nevertheless: 'For the most part the peasants lived in huts which they shared with their animals and their rents were rarely paid, and the country, dependent only on the potato, had been tottering on the edge of famine for generations.' Lucan decided to consolidate and evicted hundreds of tenants in a spectacularly ruthless fashion. When the crop failures of 1845 and 1846 led up to the appalling human disaster of the great famine in Ireland, Lucan was hauled over the coals in Parliament as one of the worst instigators of those conditions.

He was an arrogant, quick-tempered man, without the slightest hint of self-doubt.

Having, some years earlier, bought command of the 17th Lancers for £25,000, it was he who unquestioningly carried out the illegible order from Lord Raglan to charge insanely with cavalry against a battery of Russian guns at the end of a narrow valley, at Balaclava in 1854 – thus wiping out a cavalry brigade, two whole regiments, in twenty minutes.

Lucan survived the Charge – he was bringing up reinforcements – and lived to the age of 89. Sir William Fraser in a book published in 1893 wrote: 'Lord Lucan was pleasant enough as a companion; but not one whom I should like to serve under: in argument his temper seemed to get the better of him: I should say it was a naturally violent one.'

The family traditions of 'military expertise' lasted until the Second World War, when the present Lord Lucan's father, Pat Lucan, brother of Lady Alexander of Tunis, commanded the Coldstream Guards from 1942 to 1945.

After the war he became a socialist, which was viewed by some members of his family as a tragedy almost on a par with the Light Brigade fiasco. Indeed he became Labour Chief Whip in the House of Lords. Asked once why he had become a socialist, he replied that after the war it had struck him, on his visits to London, that a few people – notably his fellow officers – 'seem to have all the champagne and the girls – and others don't have anything.'

The Dowager Countess of Lucan, who survives him, is still Secretary of the St John's Wood Labour Party – a grey-haired, bony lady, typical of Hampstead between the wars, well-supplied with para-medical knowledge and a fondness for the sciences. Her allegiance to the Labour Party prompted one of Lucan's right-wing friends to say that she is 'to all intents and purposes a communist', and another to say that he believes she was 'trained in Moscow'.

Like the rest of his class, however, Lucan's education, despite socialist parents, was very classical. But before he had even reached his preparatory school, he had been sent, as were many children of his background, to America for the duration of the war. He lived from the age of five to eight with a woman he had never met before, Mrs Marcia Tucker, in grand houses in New York and Connecticut. When he returned to St Arnold's School, his behaviour was odd enough for his parents to consider psycho-analysis. He was totally silent, could not eat his food, would have fits of hysterical rage, etc. Eventually analysis was thought to be too drastic and Lucan submitted instead to the varying repressions of the English public-school system.

A contemporary at St Arnold's, Jonathan Miller, remembers going to the Lucans' house in London, near Regent's Park. 'I dimly remember a huge neglected ballroom, and his parents sitting stiffly around in the sitting room, with regimental drums everywhere. There were lots of dressing-up trunks with sabres and uniforms and so on. I am fascinated by what happened to him. I could never equate the photographs you see now as a thickened, sullen, moustachioed figure, flushed and water-logged, joylessly playing cards, with my memory of him as a rather wiry and mischievous boy at school.'

In the early fifties Eton, where Lucan was sent next, was fundamentally unchanged from the pattern set by some of its great Victorian teachers, or from the Eton described by Cyril Connolly in *Enemies of Promise*. It was an Eton of athlete worship, a temple to the philistinism that Connolly, among others, repeatedly pointed to as characteristic of the English upper class. Boys who had large fortunes and prospects of secure futures made it 'hot' for those who did not. It was divided into scholars – those boys who had gained scholarships into the school and lived in cloisters and wore different clothes – and the 'oppidans' who sneered at them and who lived in houses outside the old buildings. The harsh discipline meted out was still largely in the hands of senior boys, who as a reward for conformity had enormous powers and privileges which they never forgot in later life – unless strength of character saved them. The headmaster in Lucan's time, Robert Birley, was known as 'red Robert', for the sole reason that he had once spoken against apartheid.

Lucan, who was of medium intelligence and no great athlete, moved through the school like hundreds of other rich and unambitious boys – doing little work and concentrating all their efforts on the richly ornamented social life of the school.

His housemaster, Fred Coleridge, now the Vice Provost of Eton, and descendant of the poet Samuel Taylor Coleridge, said: 'He took an average middle of the road course and ended up as Captain of the House over about 47 other boys in his last half ["half" in Eton parlance means term]. He did quite well and went off to the Army for his National Service. I always expected him to end up as something in the City.'

In February 1953, as Lord Bingham, he joined the Army, and passed out of officer training school as a second lieutenant in October 1953. Michael Langley, a fellow officer, says of Bingham: 'He was neither painfully stupid nor brilliantly resourceful, fitting into that no-man's land of mediocrity from which no sensible cadet obtruded. I do not recall that he was an outstanding leader of men, except that he may, by virtue of birth, have appeared so to awestruck guardsmen.'

He was commissioned as an officer in his father's regiment, the Coldstream Guards. 'We served in London and Germany,' a brother officer told the *Daily Express*. 'John was just like all other officers, played bridge quite well and enjoyed the odd drink.'

London in the fifties was a drab period, stagnating in the cold war and under the real fear of the bomb. Nothing was changing for the upper class. Lacking any fresh impetus they made the fifties into a decadent and more corrupt version of the thirties. Gossip ruled the space in the newspapers. The 'Princess Margaret set' was chic. Below that you dropped through to the more or less fashionable drinking clubs of Soho – the Gargoyle, the Mandrake, the Blue Angel, and, still, the 400 club. The sixties, when they came, caused nothing but resentment in Lucan's world – whose style was rigidly backward looking. The permissive society was no longer the prerogative of the ruling classes.

There was also in the fifties a big industry in gambling, which was illegal off the racecourse. The London scene revolved around one man, John Aspinall, who set up private games at private addresses in London. Under the watchful eye of his mother, Lady Osborne, known as 'Al Capone with a shopping bag', the young heirs would be softened up and drawn into the big games. Aspinall finally bought the Clermont Club in Berkeley Square, and made it the most fashionable of the London gambling houses. Aspinall, who likes to be called 'Aspers', was a curious mixture, for a casino proprietor. With his 'bruiser's' face, he used to hang around the fringes of the literary world, at Oxford, his intellectual pretensions, say contemporaries, getting the better of his tact. He left with a fund of literary quotations which he plays to death, feudal views and romantic obsessions, especially with Saxon lore, and above all, genetics.

When he met Lucan in 1955 or thereabouts, Aspinall responded immediately. For Lucan, Aspinall always remained a central figure in his life. 'I saw in him,' said Aspinall, 'a figure like myself, born out of his own time. Lucan was a model that would have been better exposed in the early nineteenth century. That of course applies to myself. Such a remark should of course be taken more as an indictment of the times we live in than of Lucan. His qualities, as they appeared to me, were the old-fashioned qualities, like loyalty, honesty, reliability. Lucan had the *dignitas* of an aristocrat without any of the impertinences that go with a great name or possessions. He was really a leader of men . . . in fact he wasn't, but in more rigorous times Lucan could have found a better role in life. In other words in a state of war Lucan would have been a valuable acquisition to a country. He wouldn't have had any difficulty getting loyalty from his men. He was a warrior, a Roman. He was genetically endowed as a warrior and, you see, there's not much upside in being an army officer today – there's nobody to fight except the Ulstermen, or whatever it is, the IRA.'

Since he left the Army Lucan had been racing bobsleighs on the Cresta Run, with a friend from the Coldstream Guards, William Shand Kydd, an eligible heir to a wallpaper fortune. He had also been racing powerboats, and, almost incidentally, working for William Brandt's, a merchant bank in the City of London. He joined as a management trainee, earning £500 a year. A colleague in that bank remembers Lucan well: 'His intelligence may not have been too bad but as far as education was concerned he was a very limited fellow. He had no economic training whatsoever. But then, of course, there was some pretty low grade thinking in the City. Even in those days his horizons stopped at Jules Bar [a smart bar in Jermyn Street]. He was a bar fascist – which is something above a saloon bar fascist. And he believed that through eugenics he must somehow naturally be a success. In fact he was rather a failure.'

Lucan also owned a greyhound and used to go to the dog track dressed in a dinner jacket. Later he bought a racehorse called, rather appropriately, 'Stress Signal'. He played in the bank's bridge team.

In 1966, he was noticed at the Casino in Deauville by the Italian director Vittorio de Sica, who was impressed by his good looks. He asked Lucan to do a screen test for a part opposite Shirley Maclaine. Someone in the film company said, 'Lord Lucan was great when he wasn't doing the test, but when the camera started rolling he became rather self-conscious and didn't seem to be able to smile. He laughed about not getting the part – just the kind of laugh and expression de Sica was looking for. The trouble was that before the camera he just froze up.'

All the while he had been gambling. One day he had a spectacular win of £20,000 at chemin de fer. He quit the bank and in about 1960 took up gambling as a profession.

Two years later Lucan's friend Bill Shand Kydd met and married a young girl called Christina Duncan – a blonde, slightly flashy, product of English country boarding schools for girls and the apartments in Chelsea and South Kensington – crowded, often sordid, hatcheries from which debs and ex-debs set out to look for husbands. Christina shared the flat in Melbury Road, Kensington, with her elder sister Veronica.

Their background was middle class and provincial, and for Veronica unhappy and disturbed. Their father was an Army major, who fought in the First World War and died in a car crash in 1939, when Veronica was two years old and her mother only twenty-one. Veronica showed signs of worry early on. Her younger sister grew up taller and more attractive and Veronica remembers her mother saying, 'Christina wears clothes so well and people like her so much.' Veronica was comforted for her early traumas with presents: new teddy bears, and occasional, troubled visits to the doctor. In the family, smallness was considered a sign of bad breeding – something with which Veronica became obsessed. She had to try harder. Her mother returned to Bournemouth after the war, then went to South Africa to marry her second husband, an ex-RAF navigator and prisoner of war, James Margrie. Veronica remembers that when she was growing up in South Africa the girls in her school used to ask her to dance during school break. She worked so hard at it that she ended up with her legs in splints. At the age of eight she began to receive psychiatric treatment.

Their stepfather came back to England to manage the Wheatsheaf Hotel, North Waltham, near Basingstoke, a mock-Tudor inn on the main road from London to Winchester. Someone in the Clermont Club described this as a 'pub on the way back from Ascot'. Both girls went to St Swithin's girls' school, near Winchester. Veronica hated it, left at 17 and enrolled at an art college in Bournemouth. One year later she was in London, picking up the underpaid jobs provided for girls of her class who were desperate to 'do something'. She found a job as a house model with a coats and suits fashion firm, near Cavendish Square. Later she started evening classes, became a temporary secretary, worked for the backers of a West End flop called *Little Mary Sunshine*. Finally she went into business herself with three friends, printing scripts. In the flat in Melbury Road, Christina was the star and therefore occupied the double bed. When Christina married Bill Shand Kydd, Veronica wore a red bridesmaid's dress to her wedding at the Church of the Holy Trinity, Brompton Road.

Then came the fatal meeting. For one weekend organized by Shand Kydd at his house at Leighton Buzzard, Christina invited Veronica and Veronica met John Bingham, as he then was. 'We had all gone off to a drinks party after a golf match,' said Veronica. 'You know the sort of thing – the men are out all day on the course and the women are hauled along for some light relief later in the day.' This was a hint of Veronica Lucan's astringency, for which she was later to become so unpopular.

That was spring 1963. In August that year Lucan asked her for another weekend with the Shand Kydds, and in London the next week Veronica remembered how Lucan had rung all his men friends one evening and in a voice thick with embarrassment and confusion had told them that he would not be joining them. Instead he seduced Veronica Duncan.

But Lucan didn't tell his parents of the engagement plans until they were sealed. There was a meeting in the House of Lords between the in-laws – Veronica Duncan's parents turned up in a battered old car. Veronica's mother thought Lucan's mother 'excitable'.

Night after night after that they went out for dinner together. Lucan talked about his powerboat endlessly. Veronica listened attentively. 'I was looking for a God,' she said, 'and he was a dream figure.'

Indeed Veronica must have wondered whether she was sleepwalking down the aisle at Holy Trinity, Brompton, where her sister had been married earlier in the year. 'The bride wore a gown of white silk with a train cut in one with the apricot tinted skirt. Her long tulle veil was held in place by a diamond tiara and she carried a bouquet of gardenias, lilies of the valley and freesias.' The four children who attended her wore emerald green satin coronets. The reception was at the Carlton Tower hotel.

Barely two months later, Lucan's father died and he succeeded to the title and £250,000. Veronica was now a Countess and on a par with her sister.

Lucan had given her lectures on gambling, books to read on the subject. He reassured her by saying that he would stick to the games of skill – poker, bridge and backgammon, and avoid the games of chance, baccarat, chemin de fer, roulette.

'He was rather a wild and reckless gambler in those days,' said Aspinall, 'and he suffered quite a lot of pain from his losses. But then he went through a metamorphosis in the years that followed. He realized that he couldn't afford to go on being a mug. His mentor in this was Stephen Raphael, a hardened old habitué of the bridge and poker rooms. He told him that if he wanted to go on gambling he would have to learn to survive. And in five or six years he became a shrewd gambler.' Raphael, now 62, is also a broker who managed whatever stocks Lucan had.

But Lucan was already an earl in decline, buoyed up by an

introverted, almost exclusively male world of smart professional gamblers. Many of Lucan's Eton friends, unable to integrate themselves into the world, had sought refuge in what one of them referred to as 'the boys' clubs'. The cause of being 'a man's man', which is how Lucan's friends always describe him, is a cause institutionalized in some of London's finest buildings, where he could always insulate himself: the St James's Club, White's Club, the Portland Club. 'He preferred the company of men.'

This need for exclusivity was of course defensive. In the Clermont especially there is a womb-like unreality. A few years ago Aspinall placed dwarfs, real live ones, in the alcoves – a fact noted by one reporter and splashed the next day over a popular daily newspaper. The atmosphere at the Clermont, as at the less cosmopolitan clubs like the Turf Club and White's, breeds alarming, truculent, right-wing talk of dictators and union bashing.

Dominic Elwes, son of the royal portrait painter Simon Elwes, and a witty and well-preserved playboy of the fifties, who became a close friend of Lucan, described it all as a 'hypercivilized, patrician kind of life'. Its ethos was concerned with 'power and success and to a certain degree survival. Anybody who has fallen by the wayside is dismissed. And there's the knowledge of course that in the end you are always prepared to go to work or marry a rich woman.'

The Clermont set shared a common belief in this ethos. Jimmy Goldsmith, old Etonian cousin of the French Rothschilds, made a fortune in food, and with some of his £52 million, bought an estate in Suffolk, a house 'jammed with marvellous French furniture', and took up the life of an English gentleman, hunting with the Quorn and Pytchley, and sending his own sons to Eton.

There was Charles Benson, who was in Lucan's house at Eton and who is 'Scout' – the racing correspondent of the *Daily Express*; Daniel Meinertzhagen, son of a merchant banker, old Etonian, heavy-weight boxing champion of the school and a gambler since he left.

There was the Earl of Warwick, Lucan's cousin of his own age, with whom the couple spent many weekends; Michael

Stoop, a top-class backgammon player, who volunteered immediately when in 1974 the first army of vigilantes was organized by Colonel Bill Stirling, former commander of Britain's Special Air Services; Ian Maxwell Scott, gambler and racing man who was once secretary of the Clermont Club and who played golf for high stakes with Lucan at weekends; Nicholas Soames, young and prematurely middle-aged son of Sir Christopher Soames, Britain's Minister to the EEC; Mark Birley, who ran Annabel's, London's most expensive night club, in the basement of the Clermont and whose wife, Annabel, had become Goldsmith's mistress and mother of his children. And there was Aspinall, Stephen Raphael, and Bill Shand Kydd.

All were united in a primitive view of English (and international) politics. Dominic Elwes's girlfriend at the time came from a surprisingly radical background and had earned the nickname the 'champagne pinkie'. Goldsmith liked to sit up talking to her, convincing himself of his faith in capitalism. She thought that Lucan's friends had never heard anyone putting forward anything approaching socialism within the same four walls. 'It was an unpleasant atmosphere, especially for women, who were treated with great suspicion. They all genuinely believed that the upper classes were racially superior. Goldsmith, for example, believed that we were living in a truly revolutionary situation; he believed in the right of anyone to make a fortune without any restrictions. While the threat was on, they were constructing walls of concrete around them but they thought that eventually they would be the masters again. Their arrogance was enormous.'

Lucan himself seemed almost a throwback, with his strange Crimean face, and views which appeared to be degenerating, under pressure, from paternalistic feudalism to the extreme right wing – views which are echoed by many of his friends. In the hearty ribbing that went on in the Clermont, Lucan would be teased for being a 'fossil', or because Irish peerages were dubious. One standard joke was that when the tenants on the Lucan estates in Ireland couldn't pay their rents during a hard winter, the roofs had been removed from their houses. Lucan, say his friends, had a great sense of humour.

But his politics were inclined to be rigid. His friend Charles

Benson says: 'He was very right wing and never compromised in front of people. He never watered it down in front of liberals. He would talk about hanging and flogging foreigners and niggers – equally to shock and to get a reaction.'

Although he never directly involved himself in politics, and only went to the House of Lords on State occasions, he was, according to Aspinall, 'very worried about the country'. As another acquaintance put it: 'His basic attitude was that wogs begin at Calais. He hated "abroad".'

In fact Lucan's own social world was narrow – it had no real links with power, or with the political or cultural life of London.

For elegance, the Clermont is perhaps the most impressive setting in Europe in which to win or lose the fortunes the high stakes provide for. It was designed by Thomas Kent, eighteenth-century genius, famous among other things for the Treasury building in Whitehall. The Clermont is the last Thomas Kent private house in London, with a ceiling painted by Kent himself; the great salon is hung with red silk drapes woven in Bruges. The decor is grand English country house style, standardized by interior decorator John Fowler.

Lucan became what is known in the Clermont as 'the good furniture'. His good looks and his title were used to attract big money, and Aspinall would double his hand. But after March 1972, when Aspinall sold the Clermont to Hugh Hefner and the Playboy empire, Lucan no longer had this protection.

Like many of his friends he resented the fact that any member of the Playboy Club could now come to the Clermont and dilute the exclusivity. One of them, describing the invasion said, 'They're hideous, they don't gamble, they're just noisy and they're skint. They just take up space and are unpleasant for people to sit with.'

Lucan, said Dominic Elwes, was not pleased that Hefner didn't lower the flags on the Playboy Club at night, and thus didn't know how to behave. Nor would he talk to people who did not have 'proper shoelaces'. He was dismayed at younger members of the upper class. He couldn't understand why they had to speak in 'red brick university accents'. 'He didn't really like women, or sex. He regarded it as almost disgusting,' said

Elwes. 'I think he saw women as an inferior race. He was often embarrassed in their company. If anything, I would say that he would perform only the occasional *boff de politesse.*' 'Boffing' was the euphemism for sex in Lucan circles.

He was usually generous, loyal, fastidiously polite to his men friends. But under the stiff exterior, and the heavy, emotionless face, which one person who played backgammon with him described as showing 'not so much control as blankness', Lucan's warrior blood would occasionally burst forth.

Charles Benson said: 'Very occasionally one did see a flash of temper, and then it was quite unpleasant. He would get very tensed up and shake, the classic bellicose effect. He would get angry with golf caddies who wouldn't listen and so on.'

From the vantage point of the St James's Club or the Clermont, where Lucan would start up with a vodka martini around midday, the outlook was bleak. Complacency gripped the land. Stern measures were required. (He had for years been disturbed by the possibility of a Russian-style class revolution and had bought jewellery because it was 'portable'. He had half-baked plans for leaving the country when the revolution came.)

Lucan's routine was almost unvaried. After the midday drinks he would lunch at the Clermont – usually with the same, mostly male, friends. 'In the decent days,' as one member describes pre-Hefner Clermont, there was a regular backgammon game after lunch. Lucan always ordered the same meal: smoked salmon and lamb cutlets in the winter; smoked salmon and lamb cutlets *en gelée* in the summer. Sometimes he would come home to bath and change around six, then back to the Clermont for the card games after dinner. Later on, he might go down to Annabel's for a drink and then, depending on the state of his insomnia, he would go home at two or three in the morning. There were some fixtures. On Mondays and Thursdays he would play bridge in the evening at the Portland Club and on Fridays he would invariably dine at the Mirabelle.

Veronica Lucan fitted uneasily into this routine. For a time she was occupied with the problems of the Belgravia young marrieds. Lord Lucan had received a marriage settlement from his parents of £25,000 with which he bought the house in

Lower Belgrave Street, and Veronica Lucan had done it up in thick satin drapes. 'I wanted to make a miniature castle in Belgravia,' she said later. She had herself photographed by Lenare with her newborn children. She stuck the usual photographs in the leather-bound albums: dinner at El Moroccos, weekends with the Fürstenbergs, Venice, Rome, the Cresta Run, yachting in Sardinia, pistol practice in Berkshire – even one with Lucan's face, flushed and roaring at his stag party before his wedding with a nervous-looking hostess by his side. He also took risqué pictures of Veronica, looking like a hooker in a short skirt and black stockings. At first Veronica Lucan imagined giving dinner parties, having a circle of friends. This, because of Lucan's routine, soon seemed a pointless ambition and the dining table became a storage area. She realized that the only way she could be with her husband and take part in his social life was to go herself to the Clermont. She would get dressed and arrive there around 9 o'clock to meet her husband for dinner. There would always be a large table, and she would sit, usually in silence, while the men held forth. Her husband ignored her, as he ignored most women.

The male world of the Clermont, however, was not geared to wives. ('Most of the men there were either unhappily married or not married at all.') Lady Lucan had the added disadvantage of having a mind that was far more perceptive and intelligent than that of her husband, and a tongue which could cut to the heart when her exasperation got the better of her. Michael Stoop, Lucan's backgammon partner, said: 'She was clever, astute and subtle – but aggressive and unbalanced. It made her an extremely dangerous type of woman.'

One of Lucan's few female friends, a great weekender who knew the rules about women, said that 'just walking through the front door of the Clermont Club for a girl is enough to give you a nervous breakdown. You've had dinner, and everything's fine. Then you know that you're just not going to talk or be talked to for the rest of the evening.'

As the evenings, and the years, wore on, Lady Lucan's manner became increasingly tense, her mood became brittle and she sat there night after night, occasionally dabbling in blackjack. Yes, that existence put pressure on her, said Lucan's friends, but her mistake was to have come at all, to have invaded her husband's world.

'He expected her to stay at home and reproduce,' said Elwes's girlfriend, 'but felt it was only fair to invite her out to dinner occasionally. He was very embarrassed when she was pregnant. He really hated it. He thought that she shouldn't be seen. She was very jittery when people spoke to her.'

'She would sit down on the banquette,' said John Aspinall, 'night after night and hardly speak to anyone. And she had a rotten life in that sense. But she had no business to come there.'

Michael Stoop also concedes that the 'situation was very difficult for her with John forming up at the Clermont night after night and having dinner with bores like myself'. Stephen Raphael, too, thought it would have been wise for her to stay at home. 'I think she made two mistakes,' he said, 'first she used to come gambling and see that he didn't get off with other girls, and secondly she didn't create a life of her own.'

The often cited climax to Lady Lucan's career as a Clermont wife – at least in terms of spectacle – came when she threw a wine glass at another woman in an argument about sex discrimination. A woman who was watching the television said: 'It's amazing how we women continue to love men despite what they do to us.' That struck a chord in Veronica Lucan, who said that 'some little tart was making a terrible noise near the backgammon table. I said "Shh . . ." and she lifted her wine glass, so I flung mine. We were in a common gaming house after all; whether it's tarted up or not makes no difference.'

Lady Osborne, John Aspinall's mother, once chided Veronica Lucan for such remarks. She told her that it was 'very bad taste' to refer to the Clermont as a 'common gaming house'. She predicted that never again in her life was Veronica likely to witness such 'grand, sumptuous and gay parties'.

Lucan's friends now say that Veronica turned her verbal guns on him incessantly, made deeply wounding remarks, taunted him and contradicted him. 'Lucan began to be eaten away,' said a close friend, 'by a long, bleeding attrition. But he was very long-suffering. She did him extra damage, you see, because

Lucan was an interesting young man and if he had had a half way presentable wife, he would have been asked out more.'

According to Charles Benson, Veronica Lucan simply became more lonely and 'more twisted' as time went on. 'Lucky was always having to apologize for acts of near lunacy on Veronica's part. She had the cunning of a lunatic. She would say wild inaccurate things with appalling venom.'

'Right from the beginning she was shrewish,' said Aspinall, 'and impossible. Lucan was a family man. He wasn't like Lord Rosebery, who said, "If a woman leaves you, there's always another on the next bus." She came down a couple of times to Howletts [Aspinall's zoo], and on every occasion would make the kind of remark that would reduce him in your eyes. There's nothing more embarrassing. Ah, you can't imagine. You know women . . . if they know you well enough they can always pick on the most wounding things to say. That's their business. She would taunt him, "You're not a gambler, you're a house player", and this would hurt him . . . a man trying to keep his end up with other people. It got to the stage where she would throw things at him, a glass of wine or a *crème de menthe*. But – you just didn't have them in the end, it was too embarrassing a thing to happen to a host. Because the atmosphere at a dinner party or a weekend is a very delicate thing and it can be easily ruined. So you have her once; if you're heroic you have her twice and then you say Lucan, yes, Veronica, no.'

The English country weekends were the worst time for Veronica Lucan. One of her hosts, Dicky Temple Muir, owner of a smart London restaurant, recalls her behaviour with a certain relish: 'A usual weekend. A bit of tennis, a rubber of bridge. A walk. She stayed in her room the whole weekend, wouldn't move. It wasn't that she didn't know how to behave. She just didn't behave in any way.'

But Veronica remembers these weekends, as other events, slightly differently. She remembers 'wretched weekends where you are a captive of the local horrors, who make you as miserable as possible'. She remembers dreading the mealtimes, her husband not waiting for her and going down first, she going down in trepidation, and groups of people standing around with drinks. She remembers one of them saying, 'It's not saying much tonight.'

After a while, she found herself, she said, 'under the sentence of death', gradually being ostracized and alienated from any form of social life, a feeling corroborated by Aspinall who said: 'The board went down on her, with everybody, stage by stage, and Lucan's long attachment to her began to curdle into hatred.'

There were always people to criticize her behaviour – and always those to praise that of Lucan, who was seen as the model husband, the perfect gentleman, whose patience in the face of his wife had bled him dry.

But what was happening at home in Lower Belgrave Street, and what was happening to Veronica?

Like a character in a fairy-tale tragedy, Veronica Lucan seemed to have forgotten her middle-class background. Perhaps her husband had fired her snobbery, or perhaps it was her only chance. She began to see her title as something of supreme importance, viewed with jealousy from all sides. At one weekend dinner she left the table when her sister was given pride of place to herself. She became obsessed by precedence – as sensitive to it as the declining aristocrats of Proust. She learned *Debrett* (known as the 'stud book') almost by heart, and once said she did it because no Honourable could then put her down. Her talk was interlaced with old snob words: vulgar, common. 'Common, vulgar, nouveau riche, stockbroker – a ghastly social climber, and a Jew.' Girls were usually 'scrubbers', or 'tarts' and she despised their behaviour. 'Women are loathsome. They can't rise above what's between their legs. That's their misfortune too.'

She became convinced that her sister hated her even more when she produced an heir, George Bingham. She considered herself a 'threat' to most of the people she met. She and Lucan wanted their children to reconstitute the family. 'After the tragedies of the Light Brigade and a socialist mother,' she said, 'it was his life's work.' She hoped for a 'killing' for her daughters.

And the pressure was telling on her. She felt she was branded as a social embarrassment but once remarked that it was her husband and his friends who were the real social embarrassments. 'That's why they had to stay at the Clermont all the time.'

But what his friends ignored was that, with the impending breakup of their marriage, Lucan's behaviour was taking a dangerous turn. Veronica Lucan began to suffer from depression. Lucan told his friends that she was going mad. In 1967, after the birth of George, Lady Lucan was told by her husband one day that they were 'going for a drive' in the country. They ended up at the Priory, a private psychiatric nursing home in South London. Lucan had contacted the doctors beforehand.

Veronica Lucan refused to be admitted and Lucan drove her home. She was prescribed injections of Moditen, a powerful drug with the unpleasant side effect of Parkinson's Disease, given for anxiety and depression. She spent the next three years doing the rounds of psychiatrists, and taking antidepressant drugs – an ordeal that, characteristically, she survived. But in 1971 Lucan drove her to another psychiatric hospital, Greenway, in Hampstead. This time she knew where she was going, but when she saw the green paint on the walls and the 'filthy' furniture, she ran out into the road, jumped on a bus; changed to a taxi and walked around Regent's Park for several hours before returning home.

By this time she had persuaded Lucan to come home to Lower Belgrave Street for dinner. Before he left again, around 10 P.M. for the Clermont, he would make her swallow four barbiturate sleeping pills. The effect of this, in her run-down state, was to induce hallucinations and fears as she overcame the sleeping effect of the drug.

Lucan then became obsessed, himself, with the bringing up of his children, a fact corroborated by his mother. He would tell his friends how Veronica was mistreating them, and that she was unfit to look after them.

One day in January 1973, Lucan walked out, convinced that he would be able to get custody of his children. 'He pinned all his hopes on a deterioration of her condition,' said a close friend, 'and he was also watching for any signs of unhappiness in his children which he could use.'

At the end of 1972, Lucan bought a small tape recorder that fitted into his breast pocket and began to record conversations with his wife. He also recorded the nannies, whom he asked to his flat in Elizabeth Street and fed on whisky. He recorded his children, and even on one occasion their school choir singing a Christmas carol.

Lucan would play these recordings back to his friends. His manner, on the tapes, is cool and rational. But then he would slowly provoke Veronica, winding up the argument, picking on old wounds, until she would lose her temper and insult him violently. There was an argument about a memorial service, in particular, to which Veronica had gone without reminding her husband. 'I can only think it's the action of an irrational person,' he says. 'Please note my extreme displeasure. I don't want to talk about it anymore, you behaved disgracefully. Finish. Nobody is interested in you.' Veronica replies at one stage, almost in triumph: 'I have borne Binghams out of my body,' and 'Why should I feed you with my intelligence, which I've been doing for years?'

Lucan now seemed to set out to drive his wife into madness or suicide. But there he made a serious underestimation of her resilience. She had survived as a Clermont gambler's wife for nine years – which was already a record. She barricaded herself into the house in Lower Belgrave Street, friendless and isolated, but determined not to lose her children.

She began to receive threatening telephone calls through an exdirectory telephone line that was linked to the safe in Lower Belgrave Street; only Lucan knew the number. He planted private detectives around the house and they followed Lady Lucan down the street on the rare occasions when she went out.

At night Veronica sometimes saw him drive slowly past the house, always wearing dark glasses. Then in May 1973, armed with a High Court order, Lucan and two private sleuths cornered the children and the nanny in Green Park, bundled them into a taxi and took them to Lucan's flat in Elizabeth Street. Lady Lucan spent another week in a psychiatric hospital.

It wasn't until the custody proceedings opened in May that Lady Lucan realized not only that her husband had been taping her for some months, but just what the rest of her family thought of her. Among the mass of affidavits that Lucan's lawyers had marshalled to show what a bad mother his wife had been, was one from her sister Christina and one from Lucan's mother. Lucan, say his friends, thought the case was cut and dried.

It was held *in camera* and thus never reported, but Lucan talked about it afterwards. The judge was apparently not impressed by his arrogance, nor by the fact that he had lied about his treatment of Veronica. One of the nannies had testified that Lucan had on occasions beaten Veronica up, pushed her down the stairs, and on one occasion tried to strangle her. He had also caned her, although more in sexual passion than anger.

Aspinall said: 'He did beat her up once or twice. Not surprising with a wife who's behaving badly. Eventually your temper frays and you give her a few blows or something. And when he was asked if he'd ever beaten her he said "no". I think some intellectual honesty would have stood him in good stead there. He said something like "I beat her up twice, you would have beaten her up thirty times".'

Lady Lucan, on the other hand, was a convincing witness – then as later. In court she appeared calm, clear and lucid. To Lucan's dismay, she won the case and the children were returned to her, and Lucan was left with a bill of £40,000 – money which by that time he just did not possess. 'Judges are mostly middle class,' said Dominic Elwes, 'and don't understand about not working.'

Lucan was living by this time in a furnished flat in Elizabeth Street, surrounded by a collection of Hitler's recorded speeches, many books on psychiatric illness and countless detective novels. His wardrobe contained rows of identical pin-striped suits. He also had a grand piano, had taught himself to play Bach and, latterly, Scott Joplin rags. 'This was one of the things he disguised from the world,' said Dominic Elwes, 'because people would have thought it soppy.'

Having lost the case, Lucan's personality began to change dramatically. He sat in his flat brooding for hours; his friends noticed unexplained disappearances and teased him about 'having a hooker in Paddington'. He behaved irrationally, say his friends, as if he was trying to inflict punishment on himself. 'He was fairly autocratic in those moods,' said Charles Benson. 'He didn't brook arguments or slowness.' Sometimes his self-control would snap. He would shout, 'Give me some money' when he started losing, and sign the cheques with a simple straight line in place of a signature.

'There is nothing worse for a gambler,' said Aspinall, 'than an unstable situation on his home ground. All this wrecked his capacity to survive as a gambler. He lost his nerve and his ability.' Benson remembers his rudeness one night when he sat blowing cigar smoke into the face of his backgammon opponent and making provocative remarks. 'A sign of lowering standards.'

He had become a chain-smoker, drank a great deal of vodka, talked on and on about his children – how Veronica was mistreating them, how the nannies were always leaving, how she spent his money. He developed an exaggerated interest in the latest bugging devices.

Dominic Elwes said: 'The last links with reality had gone by the board. He has lost his children, his estates, his money. There was a change. We began to see the dark side of the moon. The custody case had removed his faith in human nature and the law.'

Lucan had been hit, like many others, by the stockmarket crash of 1974. He had run up debts and overdrafts of £85,000 before he disappeared. He had put the family silver up for sale at Christie's auction rooms (it made £17,000) and in the last month before his disappearance he had borrowed £3,000 at the staggering interest rate of 48%.

And at Lower Belgrave Street the nannies came and, for one reason or another, went. Lady Lucan had become completely isolated. The children never went to parties. She never went out. The only calls she received were obscene and anonymous. Hazel Drobbins stayed four days in the house. Mrs Murphy, who was always incapacitated by alcohol by 9 P.M. and has since died, stayed two months. Two Spanish girls, Tina and Teresa, stayed from August until November 1973. Veronica Lucan remembers them saying: 'You have everything and we have nothing.'

Then came a girl from Veronica Lucan's own background – Christobel Martin – who became a confidante. 'When I first went there,' she said, 'Lady Lucan looked terrible. She seemed a completely beaten person. She was terribly thin, her hair was straggly, she was very nervous.' And in fact Lady Lucan looked like someone in the advanced stages of anorexia. Her veins were sticking out, her eyes looked haunted and she was frightened. Money was short. Lucan had cancelled her account at Harrods. 'Her only personal expense was cigarettes,' said Christobel Martin. 'When I got there the milk bill had been stopped at £48.'

Christobel Martin left – she had been a temporary. Then came Pierrette Goletto, then Nadia Broome, a teacher, and then, for the last few weeks of her life, Sandra Rivett.

Veronica Lucan had always had trouble with the nannies – that was one of the accusations made by Lucan and his friends against her: 'She couldn't keep staff.' In most cases it was not her fault, and often she would have to suffer the tension of Lucan waylaying them and questioning them about the children. The two nannies I spoke to were, in retrospect, very fond of Veronica Lucan, and sympathized with her. Sandra Rivett, however, was special.

Her mother and her father, Mr Albert Hensby, a 60-year-old factory worker, live in Coulsden, Surrey, where Sandra was born. Her husband had left her, and she had been taking odd domestic jobs around London. When she met Veronica she had just left a job looking after an old couple in Paddington. She and Veronica got on well and the children grew fond of her during the six weeks she stayed at Lower Belgrave Street. The moment of commitment, on both sides, came when Sandra went back to Coulsden to get her black cat. Since they were the same height Veronica offered her some of her dresses to try on, but Sandra had a rounder figure and couldn't wear them. The two had one bond in common – their husbands had both left them. They often talked about it.

Sandra liked good times, drinking, boyfriends – but she never brought them to the house. She would often go to the Plumber's Arms in Lower Belgrave Street and chat with the other customers. One day she picked up a married man with three children – a milkman – and had a brief affair. 'The milkman couldn't believe his luck had changed,' said one of Sandra's friends, 'and he couldn't believe it had changed again when she dropped him like a stone.'

Sandra's day off was Thursday and she would usually stay out with boyfriends until the early hours. But on Thursday, 7 November 1974, she had a cold and decided to stay in.

That evening, an hour or so before she was killed, she rang her mother to discuss her Christmas plans. Mrs Eunice Hensby told the *Daily Express*: 'She sounded so happy about everything. She told me she was really enjoying looking after Lady Lucan's children. She felt she was being treated like one of the family.'

Lucan's movements in those last two days were not noticeably different from his usual routine. Not, at least, for someone who was intending to commit a perfect murder.

On Wednesday at noon he visited his old friend and his piano teacher, Caroline Hill in Old Church Street, Kensington. In the afternoon he went to Heywood Hill's bookshop in Curzon Street where he bought a book about the Greek shipping millionaires. That evening he went to a supper party, played bridge with John Aspinall, Charles Benson, and Aspinall's wife, Sally. He went on to the Clermont Club to play backgammon and met Andrina Colquhoun, a young ex-debutante with whom he had become distantly friendly in recent weeks.

He left late. He was drinking heavily.

The next morning, Thursday, Lucan rose early – which was unusual. At 9.50 he telephoned his lawyers. At 10.30 he was telephoned by Andy Colquhoun, who asked him about his dinner plans. She found them 'rather a muddle'. She looked for him at lunchtime in the usual haunts and when she couldn't find him, she packed her pair of 20-bore shotguns into her car and drove to the country.

Then there is a gap until 4 P.M. when Lucan called in at his chemists asking them to identify a pill belonging to his wife. The chemist told him it was a Limbitrol, a strong tranquillizer.

Later that afternoon Lucan visited an Old Etonian friend, Michael Hicks Beach, a literary agent, to discuss an article on golf which Lucan said he was writing for an Oxford magazine. Hicks Beach said Lucan was behaving normally, that he was relaxed, but Michael Stoop who also saw him that afternoon said Lucan was 'definitely uptight'.

Lucan drove Hicks Beach home to his flat in Fulham in Michael Stoop's Corsair, leaving his own Mercedes outside his flat. A few drinks in Fulham, then Lucan returned to his own flat and changed out of his pin-striped suit and into a pullover and a pair of cavalry twill trousers – not the kind of clothes that Lucan would like to be seen in at the Clermont. Nevertheless Lucan now seems to be trying to establish an alibi, however full of loopholes it later appeared.

He got into his Mercedes about 8.15 and drove past the Clermont Club, wound down the window and asked Billy the doorman whether any of his friends had arrived. (Lucan had booked a table for four at the Clermont earlier in the evening – a party of four of his friends were going to see *Cole* at the Mermaid theatre. He would meet them afterwards, he said, making, of course, a table for five.)

The Inquest, seven months after the murder, was to go into some detail about the events of that night. But the bare bones of the information are quite enough to fill the gap: Lucan then went back to Elizabeth Street, switched back to the Corsair and drove over to Lower Belgrave Street.

Looking through the basement kitchen window and seeing that the place was dark, he let himself in with his own latchkey, walked through the hall and went down the short flight of carpeted stairs into the basement kitchen.

He had already checked that Thursday was the nanny's day out. From his frequent trips past the house on other occasions, when he looked to 'see whether the children's lights were off', he knew that Veronica still kept to her habit of going downstairs around 9 o'clock to make a cup of tea.

Lucan was carrying a US Mail bag and a piece of lead piping, carefully wrapped in medical sticking plaster. He took the light bulb in the basement from its socket, positioned himself in the dark alongside the end of the staircase and waited.

Just before 9 o'clock he heard the expected noise of footsteps coming down the main staircase towards the entrance to the basement.

As the short female form rounded the entrance to the small

staircase and began the last flight downstairs. Lucan had no reason to doubt that it was his wife. He raised the cudgel and brought ferocious blows raining down, so hard that blood and pieces of skull went flying up towards the ceiling. On the first blow the figure fell forward with the tea tray, scattering cups. As she lay on the ground he hit her again and again, although his victim probably died from the very first stroke.

There were large amounts of blood on the floor. In the dim light from the street Lucan performed the awkward manoeuvre of putting the body into the US Mail bag.

When did Lucan realize that he had made a catastrophic mistake? Did he recognize Sandra Rivett from her weight, or from what remained of her face as he stacked her in, or was it when he heard Veronica, his wife, shouting down the stairs, 'Sandra, Sandra'?

For a second time, and presumably now in some state of panic and confusion, Lucan again waited and this time walked up two or three steps before hitting Veronica with the cudgel. She suggested later that 'good breeding' was the only reason why her skull had withstood that first blow – which, from the photographs, looks as bad as the marks on Sandra's own head. She screamed. Lucan told her to 'shut up'. He managed to get two or three more blows to her forehead, but Veronica by this time was fighting for her life, twisting herself down on to the stairs between Lucan's legs. She grabbed his balls. The adrenalin was already running out of Lucan and his violence subsided.

Then, as only an Etonian could, he *apologized*. Veronica Lucan, through her tears and fear, began talking, saying that she would help her husband out of the mess. They went upstairs to the bedroom. Lucan went into the adjoining bathroom. When she heard the taps running Lady Lucan jumped up and fled down the stairs and through the door.

A few seconds laters, Mr Derrick Whitehouse, the head barman of the Plumber's Arms further down Lower Belgrave Street, and his clientele witnessed an extraordinary scene. The door burst open and a figure covered in blood stood in the doorway. For several seconds, nobody moved – they sat on the bar stools and stared. 'She was bleeding badly,' said Whitehouse, 'and the blood was pouring down her face. She had deep cuts around her head. She was shouting and screaming and saying, "I've just got away from being murdered. He's murdered my nanny, he's in the house." She went on screaming about her children.' Lady Lucan then collapsed on the floor.

The police from Gerald Road station arrived at the house within a few minutes. Lucan's mother, the Dowager Countess Lucan, arrived soon afterwards. They found, at the bottom of the stairs leading to the basement, the teacups that Sandra Rivett had dropped when her attacker struck. They found the light bulb, removed, lying on a chair. And they found the body of Sandra Rivett in a US Mail bag, hideously beaten. They also found the murder weapon. A welded iron banister had been prised away by Lady Lucan as she struggled with her attacker. There was blood everywhere.

Lucan, by now, was driving, apparently at great speed, to Uckfield in Sussex, 44 miles away, in Michael Stoop's Corsair. At some point on the journey he made two telephone calls to his mother in St John's Wood. Mysteriously the calls came neither from a call box – in which case his mother would have heard the familiar pips – nor through the operator.

'My son said, "There's been a terrible catastrophe at No 46. Veronica is hurt and I want you to collect the children." He said to ring Bill Shand Kydd and went on to say Nannie had been hurt. I said, "Badly?" and he said, "Yes, I think so." He mumbled about "blood and mess".'

The only evidence of Lucan's movements after he left London comes from Susan Maxwell Scott, wife of Lucan's golf partner Ian Maxwell Scott (who gave her story to the *News of the World* after the event). Lucan, she said, looked dishevelled, his hair was rumpled. She gave him a large Scotch and water and listened to his version of the events. Lucan told her: 'I've been through the most nightmarish, most awful experience.' He then said that he had seen an 'intruder' struggling with his wife as he drove past Lower Belgrave Street, went in using his own key, the killer ran off, Lucan 'slipped in a pool of blood', Veronica then, he said, accused him of having hired a man to try and kill her. When Veronica ran out of the house he panicked.

Before he left he wrote two letters, which give a confusing

picture of his state of mind, but could also be seen as a careful attempt to support the 'intruder' theory.

The first, to Michael Stoop, said that he had had a 'traumatic night of unbelievable coincidences'. 'I won't bore you, except when you come across my children, please tell them you knew me and all I care about is them. The fact that a crooked solicitor and a rotten psychiatrist destroyed me between them will be of no importance to the children. I gave Bill Shand Kydd an account of what really happened but judging by my last efforts in court, no one, let alone a 67-year-old judge would believe – and I no longer care except that my children should be protected. Yours ever, John.'

The second, to Bill Shand Kydd, read: 'Dear Bill, The most ghastly circumstances arose tonight which I have briefly described to my mother when I interrupted the fight at Lower Belgrave Street and the man left.

'V. accused me of having hired him. I took her upstairs and sent Frances up to bed and tried to clean her up. She lay doggo for a bit. I went into the bathroom and she left the house.

'The circumstantial evidence against me is strong in that V. will say it was all my doing and I will lie doggo for a while but I am only concerned about the children. If you can manage it I would like them to live with you. V. has demonstrated her hatred for me in the past and would do anything to see me accused. For George and Frances to go through life knowing their father had been in the dock accused of attempted murder would be too much for them. When they are old enough to understand explain to them the dream of paranoia and look after them.'

Then at midnight he telephoned his mother again. She told Lucan that she had the children. He said, 'That's all right.' She asked what he was planning to do 'but got nowhere'. Did he want to speak to the police? 'No,' he said. 'I'll ring in the morning and also talk to you.' Lucan's mother said: 'He sounded more on all fours, more solid than when he phoned earlier. On that occasion he sounded in a highly shocked condition.'

Mrs Maxwell Scott said that Lucan left the house around 1.30, intending, she thought, to drive to London. He told her:

'I must get back. I must find out what that bitch has done to me.'

In fact Lucan's car was found the next morning at Newhaven, the South coast port 14 miles from Uckfield. It had been parked near the harbour between 5 A.M. and 8 A.M. How it got there is not known – did Lucan drive it, or an accomplice of Lucan trying to plant a false trail? Whatever trail there was went cold at this point and Lucan vanished into thin air.

Lady Lucan had been taken to hospital with wounds that, superficially, looked as bad as those which had killed Sandra Rivett. On Friday, while she was lying in hospital, John Aspinall held a lunch for some of Lucan's friends to discuss how to deal with the situation. Goldsmith was not among them. Their telephones had been jammed since the early morning – instructions were given for everyone to make themselves scarce, not to answer their telephones until the friends had been able to establish what kind of protection Lucan might need. It was the beginning of a deep mutual dislike between the police, the press and the Lucan inner circle.

'People were worried,' said John Aspinall, 'about what to do if he turned up. He might have turned up at Howletts, he might have telephoned from Brazil, so every contingency was looked at.'

Nobody seemed to have the least sympathy for Lady Lucan, although at some point during the day Dominic Elwes was sent to the hospital to find out what was her version of the events. He went with Christina, Veronica's sister, and Hugh Bingham, Lucan's younger brother. They got to Veronica's bedside with some difficulty. When Veronica told Elwes what had happened – that Lucan had tried to kill her – Elwes burst into tears. He was the only one of Lucan's friends who believed, early on, that Lucan had in fact done the deed.

The detectives assigned to the case, Detective Chief Superintendent Roy Ranson, and Detective Inspector David Gerring, began piecing together the bare events of the previous night. Lucan had visited the house in Lower Belgrave Street, had left in a hurry. He had telephoned a friend, Mrs Floorman in neighbouring Chester Square, before leaving London. Mrs Floorman says she does not remember much of the call. She does remember that the doorbell rang for a very long time, but she was 'too frightened' to answer. She went back to sleep. Then she answered the telephone and she, also, is certain that it didn't come from a call box.

'I'm quite sure it was him,' she said, 'although he didn't give his name. He just said, "Madeleine, Madeleine, I know you, I know you . . ." perhaps in a slightly different expression. Then a lot of words that didn't make sense.' Some days later, she 'found' bloodstains on her doorstep which proved remarkably difficult to obliterate; she rang Dominic Elwes in consternation later the next week and persuaded him to scrub the stains from the Portland stone.

The police had broken in to Lucan's Elizabeth Street flat an hour or so after discovering the body, but found no traces that Lucan had been there since the murder. A suit was lying on the bed, an empty glass and a book beside it. They took away Lucan's copious address books and began to work their way through them.

On Saturday 9 November, the newspapers began the year's longest-running story: 'Police Seek Earl after Nanny is Murdered; Lucan Car Found at Newhaven; Dawn Search by Frogmen for Lucan's Body', and only three days after Lucan's disappearance, 'Murder Warrant for Lord Lucan'. The charges were murder (of Sandra Rivett) and attempted murder of Veronica Lucan. For seven months the English libel laws prevented anyone suggesting that Lucan had done the deed.

David Gerring spent 11 days at Newhaven, following the discovery of the Corsair. He discovered how easy it was to get out of the country unnoticed on a 60-hour passport. (The document is in three sections. The French authorities tear off one of these, and should send it back to the issuing authority, where it is matched up. But this they rarely do. Nothing has been done to tighten up this procedure.)

In the gale force 8 wind of that November night only the *Valençay*, the cross channel ferry, and one other boat which went around to St Catherine's Dock left Newhaven. If Lucan had jumped off, the police speculated, several things might have happened. If the body had been caught up in a trawl net, as bodies frequently are, the trawlermen might have spiked it with a boat hook and sent it to the bottom, rather than risk confiscation of their catch and hours in court.

When police searched a five-mile radius of Newhaven, which included the Downs, with their impenetrable brambles, they came across human bones, and a corpse hanging in a copse. It was not Lord Lucan's.

A few weeks later, on the river Ouse which runs out between Seaford and Newhaven, a skill, rib cage, leg and thigh bones were discovered – which at first were thought to be Lucan's. They turned out to be the remains of a judge who had died in 1965. His car had been found only a few hundred yards away, and the search at that time had revealed nothing. But even if remains of Lucan are found, identification, which is often done through teeth impressions, may be impossible. For some unexplained reason, his medical files are missing from the Guards records office.

It was Lucan's three address books which gave the police their greatest problem. Not only did they have to work through what looks like the guest-list for a gigantic charity ball, Lucan had filled them up with names of almost everyone he had ever met. Some people had no idea why they should have been recorded. A young monocled soldier of fortune gave the police enough trouble for them to look into his background. Within a few days he was being taken back on a train to Marseilles by a military policeman from the Foreign Legion, from which he had deserted.

The 'nob squad' came in for criticism themselves. 'They became very chippy,' said one of Lucan's friends, 'they were looking for things that weren't there.' Stories of their social discomfort became social currency. They were reported as saying, 'We are specialists in upper class crime'; to have raided the St James's Club in full force after a bogus tip off. They were treated with a certain arrogance, portrayed as 'Mr Plods', who 'panted' about like retrievers in raincoats and hobnailed boots, and then had to be dragged out of Annabel's at 3 A.M. 'We came up against the attitude,' said Ranson, 'of some of these people trying to take one over us, to take us on and beat us.'

And indeed Lucan's friends treated the police with contempt.

The newspapers caught on to this early on. The *Guardian* said that the police 'have to delve into the peculiar society which made up Lord Lucan's world – a snobbish aristocratic clique devoted to high finance and gambling in a closed circle in which an ordinary policeman is, to put it mildly, not exactly at home'. The police could not depend on the usual underworld informants and local knowledge. In Gerald Road police station they began to talk about the 'Eton mafia'. As they travelled around the countryside searching stately homes, like Holkham Hall, belonging to Lord Leicester, and Warwick Castle, belonging to Lucan's cousin, the Earl of Warwick, their tempers began to fray. They could not understand such apparent approval among Lucan's friends for the act of murder. They told of how one of them had said that Sandra Rivett's death was such a pity 'because nannies are so hard to come by nowadays'.

The hardened crime reporters from the *Daily Express* began to complain that they could get nothing from the Lucan crowd. 'To try to talk to this tightly knit circle of friends is like finding a traitor in Colditz. They shrink from interview . . . for fear of breaking that masonic style bond which links that certain breed of men whose "stud book" lines mostly lead back to the same stables – privileged prep schools, Eton, Oxford, the Household Brigade. The honour code binds their silence.'

John Aspinall was annoyed with the police when they asked him whether he was proud to be the friend of a man who had tried to bash his wife to death. 'I said if she'd been my wife I'd have bashed her to death five years before and so would you. I said don't come that line with me because who knows into what red hell one's saintly soul will stray under the pressure of a long dripping attrition of a woman who's always out to reduce you, to whom you are stuck and from whom you've had children.'

Aspinall himself was widely rumoured to have harboured Lucan, or to have helped him. Many believed that he had, at Lucan's request, fed him to his tigers at his country zoo, so that no trace would have been left and the family honour would have been saved. 'Aspinall's tigers eat the bones as well,' was the conventional wisdom at the time.

'If a close friend of yours came in covered with blood,' said

Aspinall, 'having done some frightful deed the last thing that would have occurred to you is to turn him in. It goes against every last instinct of human loyalties, and to hell with the law or the common norms of civic behaviour or something. If he had begged asylum he would have had it. I would have helped him.' Did you help him? 'Oh no. But if he had turned up at Howletts I would have taken him aside and had a long talk and looked at the problem. It may have involved him giving himself up or getting him funds to go to Costa Rica. He could certainly have had a lot of money. I had many people calling me and saying if Lucan wants money he can have it.

'I think he is probably alive, because he must have made some provision of some description if things went wrong. He had a lot of friends in America. And – crucial in a situation of pressure like this – he is the sort of person one would tend to trust.'

Most of Lucan's friends, however, believed that he was innocent of murder. In *The Observer*, Peter Deeley made a telling point: 'There appears to be a certain code of honour among Lucky Lucan's friends. The police do not find anyone who will speak ill of him, but many who will pass on unsupported gossip about Lady Lucan.'

That was perhaps the most fascinating aspect of the enormous rumour industry that grew up as the story gathered momentum. I remember that the Lucan affair was discussed everywhere you went all through Christmas and into the spring. Evidence was pieced together, with rumour built upon rumour, until it became almost a national obsession.

One thing was taken for granted: that Lord Lucan was a man of great charm, a dashing but modest family man, who had been tricked into some terrible situation by a wife who was not only vicious, but 'mad'.

Lucan indeed became a popular hero, a man to be sympathized with. The problem for Lady Lucan, who was by now totally alone, without a single member of her own family, including her own mother, or of Lucan's family to help her, was that her detractors had the monopoly of the gossip.

At one cocktail party, after I had been myself assigned to the story, the daughter of a former Tory Minister said that Lady

Lucan was 'the most disliked woman in London'. The girl had never met her, and added: 'You know how it is – when you hear that someone is so disliked, you think she must be awful.'

But more than that were the rumours. First the 'cat story' which related how Lady Lucan had received from her husband a black cat as a present for the children. She had torn the cat apart and pushed the pieces through the letterbox of Lucan's flat. They all suggested a morbid popular imagination. There was the story of Lady Lucan excreting on the dinner plates at Lower Belgrave Street; of her making her children mould sculptures of genitals out of plasticine; of her lesbian affair with Sandra Rivett. All the rumours seemed to strain to find Lucan innocent of the crime.

The rumours were fired by the fact that the information available was sketchy. Until the Coroner's Inquest into Sandra Rivett's death, which was delayed in the hope that Lucan would appear and be tried for murder – which would have dispensed with a lengthy inquest altogether – laws of contempt prevented journalists from writing whatever hard evidence they had gleaned in the endless days of drinking and talking with the police and the witnesses.

The real tragedy – the fact that Sandra Rivett, the factory worker's daughter from Coulsden, had been murdered because of someone else's paranoid hatred for his wife, and in this case her employer – was largely forgotten in the reporting of a society scandal. 'Of course, out of politeness, one says it's very hard on the nanny,' said Aspinall, 'although I don't, of course, feel a personal sense of loss.' Shand Kydd hired private detectives, determined that Sandra Rivett had been killed by a jealous boyfriend.

She was buried at Croydon cemetery on 18 December. Apart from those of her family, the only floral wreath was placed there by the police.

I began to get close to the story in February. There was one angle that had been ignored and which fired my interest – the question of whether Lady Lucan had, in fact, been driven from mild depression to the edge of a breakdown directly as a result of Lucan's character and behaviour. I had time, unlike the daily reporters, and I moved for some weeks through the cocktails and expensive lunches.

I also met Dominic Elwes, who wanted to put across a favourable view of Lucan, and who had become a close friend in the previous two years. Elwes was a remarkable and very distinctive person to discover in that rather mindless world of the Clermont.

His life had been a failure – with some strange interludes. He was sent by his father to Downside, the Catholic public school, went into the army at sixteen, and was dismissed before he even reached the rank of officer. He became a playboy, and something of an upperclass con man in the fifties, ran away to Cuba with an heiress whom he had illegally married. All Elwes's energies were devoted to talk – he was a brilliantly funny raconteur, quick witted, highly intelligent. He had become something of an entertainer to the Clermont world.

One day Elwes made a strange request. He asked me to destroy his cuttings in the library of the *Sunday Times*. I asked him why, and he replied that he wanted to stand as a Tory candidate in the next election and felt there were episodes from the past that would work against him.

When I refused, point blank, he threatened to withdraw his co-operation with the article. I went to the files and found some interesting items. Elwes had gone to Hungary to fight against the Russian invasion of 1956. More interesting was an episode when an RAF officer had been court-martialled for giving Elwes secrets during the Yemen civil war in 1965. Elwes's role in the war was vague, but he was connected through friends with Colonel Bill Stirling, who was helping the Royalist forces with arms and men, despite Britain's 'neutral' attitude to the struggle. (It was Colonel Stirling who emerged again in 1974 calling on all patriotic Britons to join his private army – an army that would have crossed picket lines and helped to 'run the country' in the event of a national strike.) After that Elwes never mentioned the subject again.

Then one day I knocked on the door of 46 Lower Belgrave Street. Lady Lucan opened the door on a short chain, peered cautiously out, unhooked the chain and let me in. We talked in the hall. One of my reasons for writing the story, I said, was to discover her version of the events. There were rumours about cats . . .

Lady Lucan was dressed in a little black velvet two-piece suit. Without a word, she pointed down the hall where two black cats were strolling towards us. One was the cat that should have been dismembered and put through Lucan's letterbox. The other belonged to Sandra Rivett – who had been buried some weeks before.

The house was freezing cold, the furniture in a state of dilapidation. Lady Lucan was hard up – unable to afford to keep a drink for visitors. She talked fast and lucidly, and was very polite. At our second meeting, she re-enacted the scene of that traumatic night – the fight on the stairs, the US Mail bag in the basement – as if her mind had shut out the horrors.

She described the worst moments of her isolation when under the influence of the strong drugs prescribed for her she had begun to hallucinate in her insomnia, and had begun to hear voices telling her that she should kill herself. She said that if she had allowed herself to have a breakdown she would have lost everything. She described the weeks of pacing about the house, trying to contain her energy, going over and over again the details of her life, the breakdown of her marriage and the events of the night when Sandra Rivett was killed. She also raged against Lucan's friends. She had a line of rampant snobbery I could hardly believe still existed as she cut and hacked her way through her own detractors.

Later, I had to check some passages with her for reasons of libel. She objected to being described as 'pretty'. 'Pretty?' she said, '*Pretty?* I am ravingly beautiful. You mustn't use that word. I want people to think that he did have a good-looking wife, even if she was a bitch.'

The article appeared the day before the Coroner's Inquest in June. By the time we assembled in court for the five-day hearing, there was a marked shift of feeling towards Lady Lucan by the reporters present, as a result of the facts in the article, which injected a fresh impetus into the gossip columns. She was now the lonely, hard-done-by martyr and mother.

The courtroom bristled with the hosilities of Lady Lucan's relatives towards her. Christina Shand Kydd, deeply tanned and dressed to the eyes in black velvet and a silk roll-neck blouse, sat directly in front of her sister, her bouffant hair blocking her view of the proceedings and a huge ruby clasp which held her pearls together staring back into Veronica's face. Next to her was her husband, Bill Shand Kydd, dressed in Gucci and St Laurent. And next to him, the Dowager Countess. Right in the back of the court were Sandra Rivett's relatives, scrubbed and polished in their Sunday best.

The purpose of the Inquest was to determine the cause of death to Sandra Rivett. But because of the unique situation – in which the cause, i.e. possibly Lord Lucan, was not there to give evidence – the Inquest took on the form of a criminal trial. An Inquest can name the murderer, if murder was committed, and the Dowager Countess had hired a top attorney, Michael Eastham QC, to protect her son's name. His brief was to prove that Veronica Lucan was lying when she said that Lucan was her attacker. The question was – would the Coroner allow such evidence purely for an Inquest?

In the end the Dowager and Shand Kydd were not allowed to produce evidence of Veronica's madness. But the proceedings left no doubt about Lucan's responsibility and they added some gory details. Lucan could not have seen an intruder fight with Sandra Rivett (or his wife) in that particular part of the basement through the Venetian blinds as he drove by. There were no signs of an intruder breaking into the house. Lucan never gave a description of the man he said had attacked his wife except to say that he was 'large'. The blood, which was splashed all over the walls and ceiling with the upswing of the violent blows from the murder weapon, was a mixture of groups A and B – which fitted Sandra Rivett and Lady Lucan.

And then a winning piece of evidence for the police. An exactly similar weapon – lead piping wrapped in bandaid – was found in the boot of Lucan's car at Newhaven. The car was also covered in blood groups A and B. If Lucan had pushed Sandra Rivett's body into the sack, he would have been covered in blood. Mrs Maxwell Scott noticed a 'dark stain' on his trousers – and the letters he wrote were also covered in blood.

Lady Lucan gave her own description of what had happened that night. She said that she and her ten-year-old daughter

Frances were in her bedroom watching television. Sandra Rivett had gone downstairs to make a cup of tea. When she failed to appear, Lady Lucan went downstairs to investigate. She called out 'Sandra, Sandra?' Then she heard a noise.

The Coroner: 'And what happened then?'

Lady Lucan: 'Somebody rushed out and hit me on the head.'

Coroner: 'Was there more than one blow?'

Lady Lucan: 'About four.'

Coroner: 'Did you hear anybody speak at that time?'

Lady Lucan: 'No, not then. But later I screamed and the person said "shut up".'

Coroner: 'Did you recognize the voice?'

Lady Lucan: 'Yes.'

Coroner: 'Who was it?'

Lady Lucan: 'My husband.'

She then told how Lucan had thrust two gloved fingers down her throat and that they had started to fight. Lucan tried to strangle her, but Lady Lucan got between his legs on the ground, grabbed hold of his 'private parts', and Lucan stopped. She asked him if she could have a drink of water. (He repeated the phrase, 'I must make a decision, I must decide what to do.')

'Together we looked at my injuries,' said Lady Lucan, 'I think I said, "I don't feel very well", and he laid a towel on the bed and I got on to the bed. My daughter was sent to her bedroom as soon as we went upstairs and the television was switched off.'

Lucan then said he would get a towel to clean up her face. As soon as she heard the taps running she ran out of the house.

But the most moving and poignant account came from Frances Bingham who had made a statement to the police. It began with the revelation that on a recent access weekend Lucan had asked his daughter which day of the week was the nanny's day off.

After tea, she said, she played in the nursery and then watched television with her mother on her bed. Sandra went downstairs to make the tea. 'After a while Mummy said she wondered why Sandra was so long. It was before the news came on at 9 P.M. I said I would go downstairs to see what was keeping her but Mummy said she would go down. I offered to go with her but she said no.

'Mummy left the room to go downstairs. She left the bedroom door open, but there was no light in the hall. Just after Mummy left the room I heard a scream. It sounded as though it came from a long way away. I thought perhaps the cat had scratched Mummy and she had screamed. I was not frightened. I went to the door and called, "Mummy", but there was no answer.

'But about 9.05 P.M. when the news was on the television, Daddy and Mummy appeared in the room. Mummy had blood over her face and was crying.'

Her mother told her to go to her bedroom, but Lucan did not say anything to her. 'I didn't say anything to either of them, I only caught a glimpse of her.'

'As far as I can remember Daddy was wearing a pair of dark trousers and an overcoat. I did not hear any conversation between Mummy and Daddy.'

She said she went to her bedroom and went to bed. After a while she heard her father calling for her mother. She got up and 'saw Daddy coming from the bedroom on the floor below. He went downstairs. That was the last I saw of him. He never came up to the top of the house, either to look for Mummy or to say goodnight to me.'

In fact when the police arrived, they found Frances standing by her bed, and the other two children, Camilla and George, lying in bed, both awake. The television had been switched up to maximum volume.

The Coroner's jury's verdict was murder by Lord Lucan.

There was one witness conspicuously absent from the Inquest. That was Greville Howard, Lucan's friend who had made an affidavit to the police saying that two weeks before the murder Lucan had told him that he would kill his wife and drop her body in the Solent. Howard was, in fact, in hospital while the proceedings were going on, certified as being medically unfit to appear.

The search for Lucan went on all through the summer. There were 'sightings' all over the world, and there was one white Mozambiquan who impersonated Lucan in order to get help from another Englishman to escape the country. Clairvoyants and ESP practitioners sent in bundles of letters. Lost for an initiative, there was an enormous press and police expedition to the Brittany Coast in June. Whether it was the press or the police that initiated the binge is not clear, but the intake of alcohol made it all look more like a wine tasting expedition which had gone madly out of control than a serious search for Lucan. It is still a mystery to those newsmen present how a single line of copy was filed. But filed it was. One headline even read, 'Lucan Traced to Cherbourg.' On closer examination, it seemed that a Monsieur and Madame Guilpain, proprietors of the Grand Hotel in Cherbourg, had simply seen the main chance and come up with the goods. They said they never checked Lucan's identification on the occasions he had visited the hotel, because he spoke such perfect French. Lucan's French, of course, was almost non-existent.

But then a more sinister tale directly connected with the Lucan affair was brewing inside the Lucan circle, which ended in a tragedy almost on a parallel with the death of Sandra Rivett.

The article I had written for the *Sunday Times Magazine* appeared on 8 June. Not only were the contents unpopular with the Lucan crowd, their sympathizers or the Lucan experts whose theories had been undermined – the pictures were worse.

I had obtained the pictures of the Lucan family albums from Lady Lucan herself. But the cover showed a photograph of Lucan, dressed in a blue open-necked shirt with a coral necklace, and Annabel Birley, wife of Mark Birley and mother of Jimmy Goldsmith's children, looking at him in a longing and affectionate way, her arm around his neck.

The inside showed several other photographs of a house-party in Acapulco in March 1973, made up of Lucan, Annabel Birley, Jimmy Goldsmith, Dominic Elwes, and their friends.

By extraordinary chance I happened to find myself sitting opposite Annabel Birley's sixteen-year-old son Robin Birley, at an Eton housemaster's lunch the day after publication of the story. I had been sent by *Die Zeit*, the German newspaper, to write a story about Eton. Robin Birley courageously attacked me in front of the housemaster and the boys for the photograph on the cover which showed his mother, and demanded to know who was responsible for it.

That week it was obvious just how angry Birley and Goldsmith were about the picture. Their world had been penetrated and pictures of their lunch parties splashed over one and half million copies of a British magazine.

They did not like it at all. Great efforts were made to find the origin of the pictures. To this day I never revealed the source, but I made it clear that, whoever the source was, it was not Dominic Elwes.

On 7 June, the beginning of the week of the Royal Ascot Races, Elwes received a letter from young Robin Birley, blaming him for selling the photographs to the *Sunday Times*. Elwes sat up all night writing a reply, denying any responsibility.

Then Mark Birley wrote to Elwes, excommunicating him from the clubs Birley owned – Annabel's, and Mark's Club in Charles Street. To make it more humiliating, the waiters had been instructed not to serve him. The *Daily Express* wrote of my article: 'While several of Lucan's friends assisted the author with background material, Elwes is considered by some others to have been a little too forthcoming.' Birley admitted writing the letter and said it was, indeed, because of the article. (Elwes in fact helped no more than anyone else and less, perhaps, than John Aspinall.)

On Friday 20 June, the columnist Nigel Dempster met Elwes at Heathrow airport on their way to Nice. Elwes had been sent to Lord Compton's house at Cap Ferrat by his friend Daniel Meinertzhagen because he thought he was cracking up under the pressure of the blame.

Dempster found Elwes in tears. He told Dempster that all his friends had turned on him – that Goldsmith was blaming him for selling the pictures to the *Sunday Times*. Dempster, with a certain panache, immediately telephoned Goldsmith, described Elwes's state via a secretary (Goldsmith would not take the call directly), and assured him that Elwes had nothing to do with the pictures. Goldsmith sounded as if he didn't want to hear the denial.

At that point things were going badly wrong for Elwes in other directions. He wrote to his former girlfriend, in a handwriting that scrawled all over the page: 'Please ring. Not at all well. Feeling rotten. Need cheering up but don't want to go on.' His mother had been taken into psychiatric care by nuns, his father was dying, he had lost what little money he had left due to a bad investment by a close relation. Trying to joke about it Elwes used the upper-class cliché, 'Is life worth living on these terms?'

Dempster told him that, at least, nothing could get worse. In fact he was wrong. On 1 July, Elwes went to the property development he had been working on as a designer for some years at Cuarton, behind Algeciras. He fell down a cliff, broke his painting hand and his foot. Finally, he told Dempster that he thought that his former wife, Tessa Elwes, had a serious illness.

When he came back to England in late August, Elwes was obviously suffering from severe depression. In early September, he was found dead in his small flat off the Kings Road by his closest friend, Melissa Wyndham, a 26-year-old interior decorator.

Elwes, who was sprawled across the bed, half dressed, had taken a large overdose of barbiturates and alcohol. He had written two notes. In one of them he blamed Goldsmith and Birley for his misery. 'I curse Mark and Jimmy from the grave,' it read. 'I hope they are happy now.' There were many religious passages, some lines distributing his possessions to his girlfriends, and instructions for his memorial service. He asked his friend Kenneth Tynan to deliver an 'apologia'.

The service was held on 25 November at the Church of Our Lady of the Immaculate Conception in Farm Street, Mayfair.

'His laughter, which still rings in my ears, was a triumphant yelp of victory – a cackle of conquest – over drabness and pretension. People of quite remarkable ordinariness are permanently lodged in my mind because of the skill with which they were sketched by this superb verbal cartoonist,' said Tynan.

'As a raconteur and mimic, he had the most ebullient and imaginative flair I have ever encountered. Nobody has ever made me rejoice more. Even Peter Ustinov, a superlative talker, is reputed to have said that Dominic was the only person to whom he would defer in conversation. He loved the world of wealth and ceremony far more than it deserved, and his politics were those of a romantic monarchist. For him, England's king over the water was the Duke of Windsor. Certain rich people elected him their court jester, and he happily embraced the role, but they never really accepted him, because in the final analysis he did not have quite enough money. It may be that he set too much store by the favourable opinions of people many of whom were manifestly his inferiors. Towards the end of his life he said to me, with a grin of self-deprecation: "I thought I was a hermit, and I found I was a pariah."'

Aspinall spoke after Tynan. He mentioned the word genetics four times, quoted Beowulf in an Anglo-Saxon accent ('He unlocked the word hoard'), and lectured the attendant family on how emotionally ill-suited Elwes was to modern life. He then read out a poem which he had composed. Its first lines:

> Why did you leave us Dominic?
> Why did you die?

After the service a distant cousin of Elwes walked up and delivered Aspinall a solid right hook to the jaw. Aspinall slumped on to a parked Mercedes and said: 'I'm used to dealing with animals.' The punch, said the *Daily Mail*, 'summed up the bitterness, acrimony and resentment that has festered beneath the surface of the privileged and once tightly knit group of Lord Lucan's friends.'

Tynan remarked that it was sad that his friend had been laid to rest, quoting Evelyn Waugh, 'to the sound of the English country families baying for broken glass'. In fact the incident deserved the same epithet used by a Brigadier in White's Club when the news of the Lucan murder broke some months before: 'A bad day for Eton,' he said.

Nigel Dempster, the *Mail* columnist, was uncharacteristically incensed by the behaviour of Goldsmith and Birley after this affair – and suddenly saw the Clermont crowd as something more than simply fodder for his column. I was so surprised by his torrent of words that I wrote it down: 'They have become an embattled race . . . the curtain, they know, is half-way down on them but they don't know when the final drop is coming so they've occupied the high ground. They think the scum are baying for their blood so they form clubs to keep the scum out, secure in the knowledge that they can behave boisterously and badly. When one of their class, like Dominic Elwes, seems to have been talking to the enemy – which is you and me – he is last seen heading down the hill into the enemy camp like a prairie dog, holding a white flag in his teeth.

'Whenever I get fed up with this job, I just think of those people and I'm at it again, waiting for someone to slump over a table in an exclusive Mayfair club.'

May 1976

Curry at the Laburnums

SHENA MACKAY

Rain set in. The hills were hidden and the village enclosed in dull grey curtains of mist. The river threatened the supports of the bridge. Children gauged the water level, hoping, as sometimes happened, that they would be cut off from school. The playground was roofed over by umbrellas, floral patterned transparent pagodas, under which waiting mothers complained. Little inadequate sandbags appeared outside their houses. Fields lay under a glaze of water. Some cows were temporarily marooned and a rotten tree trunk, caught under the bridge, bobbed uncannily like the head of a drowned cow. The river continued to rise, grass and nettles disappeared and alders stood in water which poured over the sides of the bridge and reduced the road to a narrow sluice.

Commuters returning to houses draped with wet washing were bored and alienated by tales of muddy dramas, trees swept downstream, rescued water rats, coaches forcing their way through the water and taking children miles round the back roads to school. They were more interested to hear that water had got into the cellars of the pub. They became a different species from the gumbooted inhabitants of the heart of the flood, irritated by wives shut up all day with small children and felt that the trials of water in the brakes, an abandoned car rota, and a go-slow on the trains were far greater than those of the home front.

The platform was jammed. What many found hardest to bear was the unfailing cheerfulness of Lal, the ticket collector, with whom Ivor, from vague liberal principles, often made a point of speaking, exchanging comment on the weather, and last Christmas he had thrust, almost aggressively, a pound note into his hand. Since the go-slow, he somehow hadn't liked to be seen chatting at the ticket collector's box and had restricted himself to a curt nod.

Lal laughed and joked and even made mock announcements over his microphone. Many were quite indecipherable, and the packed, soaked travellers eagerly turning to gaze at the signal which still showed red, and hearing his high-pitched cackle crackling over their heads, stared angrily up the receding tracks and understood only that they had been duped. In his efforts to entertain them, Lal had brought along his own transistor radio from home and played it loud enough to cheer up those at the farthest ends of the platforms. Many of them seemed not to appreciate Radio One.

'I wonder if you know that it's illegal to play transitor radios in public places?' a lady asked, shaking a rain-drop from her noise.

'I must keep the customers happy,' he replied. She reported him to the Station Manager who told him to turn it off.

'Bolshie so-and-so, playing the radio while his fellow Reds hold us to ransom.' A voice was heard in the aftermath.

'Blacks, more like,' replied another.

Camaraderie flowered among the wet heads and shoulders as stranger muttered to stranger imprecations on Blacks and Reds. Ivor and Roger were edging along the platform to try to get some sense out of Lal. He seized his microphone and shouted:

'All passengers Wictoria and Vaterloo, you might as well go home' and cackled. Then, as the two men reached his box, he received a telephone announcement, the signal went green and he called: 'All Stations Wictoria. Stopping train Wictoria!'

Twenty minutes later, the grateful commuters saw the train's round caterpillar face crawling towards them and those who could, fought their way aboard and stood steamily, agonizingly pinioned together, fainters held upright, pregnant women loathed for their bulk, dead limbs slowly filling with pins and needles, trapped ever tighter by a seemingly impossible influx at subsequent stations.

So it went on. Drivers reported late and were sent home. Rule books ruled. Trains ran spasmodically. At least the rain began to peter out and there were occasional flashes of watery sunshine.

Ivor and Roger were on the platform, at the edge of a group of older men, doyens of commuters, whose trousers were of necessity hoisted high over round bellies by braces and fell in soft cuffs on to polished shoes, whose muscles were adapted only to the hoovering of lawns with electric mowers, or hitting golf balls; electors who kept Chubleigh a safe Tory seat. At election times, its windows broke out in a blue rash of posters depicting Sir John Upton, who seemed to be conjured up only then, opposed only by an occasional doomed orange placard.

'. . . Harold Wilson,' Ivor caught.

'Heh heh heh,' laughed the old boys; products of small schools set back under the dripping beeches of Surrey. A pekinese-faced lady, with steel blue fur brushed up from a pink powdered forehead, bared her little teeth and laughed.

'Just let them try to treat cattle like this,' said one, 'and they'd soon have all the do-gooders up in arms.'

Their two weeks of inconvenience led these men, holding briefcases packed with the data of unnecessary companies, to compare themselves with Jews transported across Poland in freezing cattle trucks. One licked his livery lips, spotted like sloughed snake skins, and said: 'Did you hear about the Epsom incident? Some chaps got hold of one of those blighters and locked him in the, er, Ladies.'

'Heh heh heh,' laughed the old boys.

'Ha ha,' laughed Ivor.

'Next train to Vaterloo approaching Platform One in about twenty minutes,' broadcast Lal.

No train materialized. Some people went home. The coffee machine was jammed; a squirt of dirty water rattled into the plastic cup. Ivor and Roger trailed after the group to a little shack in the forecourt which sold such fare as sausage sandwiches, sulphurous rock cakes and tea. They blocked the doorway and jostled the taxi-drivers seated on benches round the walls, shooting spray over them as they closed their umbrellas, and brayed at the woman in broken slippers frying bacon at the stove. The kettle was shrieking; all was steam noise and succulent wisps of smoke.

'What's yours, Tony?'

'Name your poison.'

'Your shout, I believe, you old rascal.'

'Heh heh heh.'

The woman removed the whistle from the kettle and unfortunately the words '. . . Bloody unhygienic, ought to be prosecuted' hung in the air.

A huge man in shirtsleeves hoisted himself up from the bench.

'Right,' he said. 'Everybody out. We don't want your sort here. You're all banned.'

'Now look here . . .'

'Out.'

The taxi drivers rose, a menacing semi-circle confronting former customers.

'Well really, I must say . . .'

'Out.'

'Now look here, my dear chap, it says "ALL WELCOME" outside. Do you realize you're contravening the Trades Descriptions Act?'

'We demand to be served,' said Ivor from the back.

'Berks.'

The drivers stepped forward. The commuters retreated.

'If that's their attitude . . .'

Step by step the commuters were forced backwards into the forecourt, out of the delicious smell of bacon and hot tea into the cold drizzle.

'Good mind to call the police.'

'Well I for one shall be contacting the Inspector of Health and I suggest you all do the same.'

A stomach brayed expressing everyone's disappointment.

'My wife was sold a mouldy pie the other day,' volunteered Roger and was ignored.

Ivor felt specially outraged, like a little boy who arrives late for school dinner and finds the hatches closed and his comrades wiping gravy and custard from their lips. Marian had neglected to make muesli and he had left with only a small bitter cup of coffee. He and Roger went back through the booking hall and found themselves at Lal's box. Ivor was lightheaded and on the point of telling Roger he was giving up and going home. His mouth opened and hung open. Surely not? It couldn't be – a hot pungent drift of curry caught his nose. He stood swooning as it washed over his empty stomach. Roger caught his arm.

'The last bloody straw.'

He looked. The youngest porter, a lowly boy in a too-big jacket, who swept the platforms, was crossing the line bearing foil dishes of take-away curry.

'As you say, the last straw.'

Lal started across the platform through the passengers, smiling and rubbing a knife and fork in his hands, to receive the food. As he reached the edge of the platform and bent forward, Ivor and Roger exchanged a glance, each took an imperceptible step forward and thrust a foot under Lal's ankles. He swayed, the dishes in his hands, and crashed over, hitting his head on the rail, curry erupted and engulfed him. He sat up and half turned, scalding juice running down his hair, tomatoes, ladyfingers, yellow rice slipping down his face, and fell back, a knife sticking out of his striped waistcoat. Ivor and Roger were among the first to jump down. The tearful boy was sent to phone for an ambulance.

'Heh heh heh.'

The old boys couldn't see the knife, and laughed away their humiliations in the café.

Lal now lay on the pile of empty mail sacks on the platform. It occurred to nobody that it wasn't an accident. The ambulance klaxon overtook the sound of the approaching train.

The incident made the evening paper; a small paragraph on the front page under the banner headline proclaiming a return to work by the railmen after the personal intervention of the Prime Minister. It seemed that Lal was comfortable in hospital with burns and a punctured lung.

Ivor rolled uneasily all night in bed, behind the window which still bore an orange shred from the last election; the quisling of the station snack bar; all his principles slithering with scalding curry down Lal's surprised face. If he could become completely evil he could forget all this, or laugh at it, continue with the girl in the office, or a succession of women, refuse to attend

Family Service, neglect the garden, drink himself to death, then everybody would be sorry. Would he have to use another station?

He practised a sneer on his changed face as he shaved, but the eyes in the mirror had a puffy frightened look.

'Bye dear, have a good day,' he said as he left.

An incomprehensible curse seemed to batter against the front door as he banged it. He sensed something in the atmosphere as soon as he and Roger arrived at Chubleigh station.

'Deny everything,' he muttered as they squared their shoulders, the wooden floor of the booking hall resounding hollowly like the hearts in their chests. The young porter, promoted, inspected their seasons. A knot of people was down the platform, by the far seat, obviously holding some sort of conference. Roger's elbow caught Ivor painfully on the muscle of his arm. They stopped and glanced frantically back at the booking hall, but people blocked the entrance.

'Wait for the 9.12?' said Roger stepping back a pace. A patch of bristle under his nose denoted a shaky hand. Ivor shook his head. The cluster broke. A woman pointed at Ivor and Roger.

'A necktie party,' said Roger.

'I am completely evil,' said Ivor to himself.

His umbrella was slippery in his hand. Two students were coming down the platform towards them, his long blue jeans bent and straightened, eating up the asphalt, her skirt trailed tiny chips of grit; they heard the flap of her bare feet. The two avengers garbed in their tatty integrity moved down the platform towards them. Ivor stared at the yellow tin newspaper stand and became absorbed in a blotch of rust, dog-shaped. He scratched at it with a forefinger, to elongate its stumpy tail and a flake of rust pierced the soft skin under his nail. He stared at it. 'Your nails are so neat,' Heather had said, 'just like haricot beans.'

He felt detached pity for those polished beans, as if they were to be violated in some inquisition or boiled for soup. Meanwhile Roger was finding it necessary to search his briefcase, and not unexpectedly found only *The Guardian* within, and squinted at its sideways folded print.

'About the accident yesterday – '

'Look here,' Roger started to say, but Ivor caught his sleeve.

'We're getting up a collection for Lal's family from the regulars.'

A balloon burst in Ivor's chest, suffusing his veins and face with warm liquid. His leather wallet leaped to his hand and he was stuffing a fiver into the jagged slit of the improvised collection tin, round which was pasted a piece of white paper with the simple message FOR LAL, which the girl held out.

'Turrific,' she uttered.

The male student scowled in silent accusation of ostentation. Roger managed fifty pence, which landed dully on Ivor's note.

'Right,' said the student, taking the tin and giving it a shake, and they moved on to the next passengers.

Roger and Ivor sat at opposite ends of the compartment, as if each thought the other had behaved rather badly.

The following morning the students were waiting. The boy hovered over them, his jeans seemed to sway with self-effacement.

'Personally I think the little old lady who gave 20p out of her pension should take it, but Maggie,' who had her hair in stubby pigtails today, 'seems to think you genuinely love the guy, so here you are. From us all.'

He thrust the heavy tin at Ivor, who stared up at him hopelessly.

'Give him the address, Maggie.'

She gave him a piece of paper. As if divesting themselves of a necessary but distasteful contact with the spoils of capitalism, they loped off.

'Pompous sentimental young twit,' said Roger.

Ivor, who had the tin, said nothing.

'You'd better go tonight,' suggested Roger. 'Get it over with.'

'Yes, we will,' said Ivor rolling the weighty embarrassing tin into his briefcase.

They met in a bar at Waterloo and fortified themselves for their task; from his seat under the red and yellow lights, above the platform, Ivor watched all the lucky commuters going home; all the fortunates who didn't have to take a tin of money to the wife and children of a man they had pushed on to the railway line for no reason.

'The more one thinks about it, the more impossible the whole thing becomes,' said Roger.

Ivor grunted. Roger went to telephone Martha.

'That's settled then,' he said as he came back.

'Same again?'

It struck Ivor that Roger was looking forward to the evening with cheerful or morbid curiosity. He almost told him to go home, but the thought of facing Lal's wife alone was worse.

'No thanks,' he said standing up. 'The woman will be busy putting the kids to bed, maybe after visiting the hospital, we don't want to turn up stinking of booze.'

Roger sighed and followed him out. It transpired, however, that they had twenty minutes to wait for a train, and they returned to the bar. Marian had hung up on him when he telephoned; too late he remembered that it was madrigal night.

Croydon was golden when they left its station. They hired one of the taxis blazing in the forecourt and gave the driver Lal's address. The street turned out to be a long hill of terraced houses, which the taxi climbed slowly looking at the numbers.

'Bet it's that one.' Roger leaned forward and pointed at a blue-painted house with its brickwork picked out in pink, and windows and door, with hanging baskets of plastic flowers, pale green.

'They go in for that sort of thing. Really lowers the tone.'

It was at none of the picked-out houses that the taxi finally drew up. Lal's house was a discreet cream, with only a wreath of stucco leaves above the door painted dark green and a laburnum tree trailing leaves and pods over the gate, with the name 'The Laburnums'.

Ivor was fumbling with the lock of his briefcase as Roger knocked. A plump dark boy in school trousers opened the door.

'Does Mr Kharma live here?'

'My dad isn't here.'

A voice called something foreign from within. The boy answered in the same language, keeping his lustrous eyes on the two strangers, standing on a hectic yellow-orange carpet which swirled up the staircase behind him like a colony of snakes. The hall glittered with dark eyes from behind doors and the spaces of the banisters.

'Are you from the newspaper?' asked the boy.

'No, we – '

A woman came from somewhere at the back of the house and stood behind the boy. Ivor thrust the tin at her over his head.

'On behalf of the regulars at Chubleigh Station, we'd like you to accept this small token. We were all very sorry about your husband's accident. He was very popular.'

He spoke slowly and loudly, feeling a flush seep up his neck from his collar. She stared at him almost with hostility. A smell of cooking came from the kitchen. The boy seemed to translate.

'Her eyes are like pansies, those dark velvety pansies,' thought Ivor.

'My mother says please come inside.'

'Well that's awfully kind of you, but we really mustn't impose,' began Ivor.

'Please.'

The woman and children moved back, the boy held the door wide.

'Well, just for a minute.'

Ivor and Roger stepped in. They were led into the front room and told to sit on a black leatherette sofa backed with red, encrusted with gold thread, embossed by a bright picture of a Bengal tiger. Bamboo pictures hung on the walls and coloured brass ornaments stood on the mantelpiece and windowsill. Roger shifted his feet on the blue carpet.

'Have you seen your dad? How is he getting on? That was a rotten thing to happen.'

'He can talk now. His burns pain him. Did you see the accident?' answered the boy.

'Yes we were right there. We did what we could.'

The woman interposed a question to her son.

'Is one of you Mr Ivor and Mr Roger?' asked the boy.

'No,' said Ivor at once, but Roger was saying heartily, 'That's us. Great pals of your dad, we are.'

This was translated with some vehemence.

'All is lost,' thought Ivor. He wanted to run.

Three little girls came and sat opposite them, two on chairs and one on the arm, swinging an impossibly thin brown leg and foot in a rubber flip-flop. Lal's wife said something to the boy and went out of the room. Ivor tried to remember if there was a telephone in the hall. He placed the tin, FOR LAL, on a little carved table covered with a silk cloth, beside a Monopoly game.

'My mother says please wait. She is getting you some food. She is very grateful to you.'

The men exchanged a helpless glance. Ivor wondered if the plump boy was teased at school, and if his own children could cope so well with a second language. He was not really like a child, rather a small self-contained man in his white shirt, with sleeves turned back to show a heavy gold watch on his wrist. He seemed not to have inherited his father's jocularity; rather his mother's gloom. But of course they had something to be gloomy about, Ivor reminded himself.

The mother called from the kitchen and one of the girls left the room.

'Lovely kids,' muttered Roger. 'Beautiful eyes.'

'I don't like the way they're staring at us. I think they know. Let's get out.'

'Can't. Look worse.'

He raised his voice to the little girls. 'Do you speak English?'

'Yes.'

'Jolly good.'

The tallest girl returned with two thin conical glasses on a brass tray. Her hair was tied back in a long plait like her mother's and she had tiny gold stars in her ears.

'Would you like a drink?'

'I say, thank you very much.'

The two assassins each lifted a glass and put their lips to the thick sweet liquor.

'Cheers.'

'Cheers,' said the girl, unsmiling. She held the tray behind her back; there was nowhere to put the glasses, so they drained them. She held out the tray and went out again. The young girls were whispering and stopped when they caught Ivor's eye. He wished someone would turn on the television or the transistor with which Lal had cheered up his customers.

'Please tell your mother she mustn't go to any trouble on our account,' he told the boy.

'She wants to repay your kindness.'

'Mustn't offend Eastern hospitality,' mumbled Roger, 'besides, I could do with some nosh. Wonder what it'll be? Smells good.'

The girl returned with the filigree glasses refilled. This time Ivor took a sip and set his glass on the floor.

'Good stuff,' said Roger, a little thickly.

'Don't know how it mixes with Scotch though.'

'It is called Muth,' said the boy, and the mother called again from the kitchen. The little girls opened a drawer in the sideboard and took cones of incense and stood them in little brass hands and lit them. Ivor thought he heard the front door click. He reached down for his glass, the fragile stem swayed in his hand and slopped the liquor on to the floor. A child ran for a cloth and the oldest girl took his glass and brought it back brimming.

'Very clean,' remarked Roger, jerking his head at the floor.

'Is your house dirty then?' retorted the boy.

'Touché,' he laughed.

'Would you like to come through,' said the boy politely. 'I'll show you the bathroom first, if you'd like to wash.'

The strange drink and heavy incense swirled round in Ivor's head, he had to put his hand to the wall as he followed the children. Fresh soap and towels seemed to have been put out in the bathroom; he glanced back as he left to make sure he had left it tidy.

'Did you put the towels back?' he whispered to Roger.

'What?' He pushed past him into the kitchen. There, Ivor felt suddenly gross among these small people as he hovered at the table and sat down clumsily on the indicated chair.

'Aren't you having any?'

'We have eaten earlier, before the hospital,' explained their little host.

Bowls of steaming rice and dishes of food smelling of every delicious spice of the orient were placed before them. The family grouped round the kitchen to watch the Englishmen eat. Incense was burning here too, the air was thick with it, sweet and acrid scents mingling.

'Please eat,' said the girl. Lal's wife drew out a chair and sat down at the opposite end of the table from Ivor. He heaped his plate until it was swimming with beautiful coloured vegetables and marbled with red and yellow juices. A full glass stood by his plate.

'It's great, it's delicious. I don't know what it is but it's great!' Roger said.

There was no need to translate this; his spoon was already digging again into a dish.

'Have some more ladyfingers, Ive.'

He scooped a heap of the little pods on to Ivor's plate and took another drink.

'Everything's all right,' thought Ivor, as he bit into the strange delicious ladyfingers, he straightened his shoulders which were stiff with tension, and relaxed in his chair.

'I am totally evil,' he thought, and sniggered a little at himself.

Roger put down his spoon and fork.

'D'you know,' he said, spitting rice. 'D'you know, if every immigrant family in this country was to ask one English family into their homes, just one each, for a meal like this, it would put an end to racial prejudice at one stroke. Eh, Mrs Lal? What do you say to that? I call you Mrs Lal,' he explained, 'because you people put your surnames first.'

Ivor was terrified again. If Roger was drunk would they ever escape those velvet eyes and glittering earrings, fusing, shifting, miniature watchful Lal faces, dark and golden?

'We Anglo Saxons are a funny lot.' Roger was leaning over the table. 'We're very reserved, but if you people would just take the initiative, not be so stand-offish, you know? We're very nice when you get to know us, aren't we, Ivor?'

'For God's sake, Roger!' Surely Indians were teetotal?

'Now some people think, and I know they're wrong, that your lot are a bit stuck-up, you know, toffee-nosed, unwilling to adopt our customs, living in the past. You spread the word, Mrs Lal, you give us an inch and we'll take a yard.'

He stopped suddenly and resumed shovelling. No one spoke. Ivor kept his eyes on his plate; if he stopped eating his head might crash forward into the curry; like Lal's. He blew his nose.

Roger was waving a fork at the boy; his mouth opening and shutting, trying to get the right words out. He lurched up and put his arms round two of the girls, pulling them together so that they almost kissed. The boy stepped forward to protect his sisters. Roger released them.

'These kids. Our kids. It's up to them. They're the generation that counts. You and me, Ivor, we've had our chance. They're the last chance this rotten old world's got.'

He began to cry and sat down, spooning food now into his wet mouth, now down his tie. Ivor's whole head broke into bubbles of sweat; he blotted it with his handkerchief, and saw runnels under Roger's nose. He loosened his tie. He made an effort to salvage the evening and their honour.

'How did your husband seem, Mrs Lal? In himself, I mean.' He said very slowly and courteously.

'He is as well as can be expected,' said the boy.

'Good. Good.' Ivor nodded solemnly. His eyes were caught by Mrs Kharma's; the pansies seemed drenched with dew; he had to shake his head to shift the image of himself unwrapping the gauzy sari, like the cellophane round a flower, to reveal the dark orchid within. He thought one of the little brass incense burners clenched and unclenched and almost felt the metal fingers on his throat. He kicked Roger and stood up.

'Mrs Lal, my friend and I would like to thank you for a most excellent meal. We mustn't take up any more of your precious time.'

He hauled Roger to his feet.

'It has been a privilege to meet Dad's friends. Please convey our thanks to all the kind people who contributed. But there is more to come.'

One of the girls was taking from the fridge aluminium shells of ice cream pitted with green chips of pistachio. Roger made a clumsy move towards the table. Now or never. Ivor got him into the hall.

'Mrs Lal, I want you to know,' he heard himself saying, 'I

want you to know you can count on me, as a friend of your husband. He's a good man, and I'm proud to be his friend – '

'So long, Gunga Din.' Roger was ruffling the boy's hair as the front door nearly clipped his fingers.

'Gloomy lot, never smiled once,' he said. 'Did you notice? No sense of humour.'

He tangled with the laburnum.

'More like some weird ritual than a meal.'

'At least one of us kept his dignity,' replied Ivor.

Ivor woke, clawing his chest as if wrenching out a knife; his pyjamas were sodden. He had a terrible pain; he was about to be sick. He bumped through in the dark, gagging himself with his hand, biting his palm, whooshing and whooping into the bowl, a burning poisonous volcano. At last he lay back on the floor, pressing his forehead on the cold tiles, then doubled up and vomited again where he lay.

'Are you all right?' came Marian's annoyed voice from the bedroom.

Spasm after spasm racked him; it was pouring from his mouth, down his nose, and when there was nothing left his stomach still heaved towards his raw throat. His insides felt sore and pink and mangled.

'Ivor?' She had forced herself out of bed.

'Go away,' he groaned. 'Just go away,' trying to pull the door shut with his foot. She took one look, and fled to be sick in the sink.

'O God, O God, I'm dying, let me die, I can't bear it. Let me die,' a voice was groaning over and over. He lay sweating and shivering for a long time. Then he pulled a towel over himself like a blanket and half dozed in the appalling smell. An iron band was screwed round his head.

Some time later he pulled himself, frozen, to his feet and set about cleaning up the fouled bathroom with newspaper and disinfectant and Ajax, washing its walls and floors and the interstices of the hot water pipes, specked and freckled with his guilt. Every time he bent, the burning vice tightened on his skull and his teeth clattered uncontrollably. He put his pyjamas in the dirty linen basket for Marian to wash. He stood in a towel at the open window, watching the strange sky lighten over the heavy oaks. The telephone drilled.

Martha Henry's frantic voice battered against his caved-in chest. He couldn't bear to put the receiver to his ear.

'He won't die,' he said, and put the phone down.

Sitting on the bath's edge, watching it fill, steam flowering up the turquoise sides, in the sour aftermath and draught from the open window, he thought: 'You've got to hand it to them. Not a word of the pain we caused them. Not a flicker of emotion. Just a silent revenge. You've got to respect them for that.'

June 1976

Bar Italia
(to L.S.)

—— HUGO WILLIAMS ——

This is how we met,
Sheltering from work in this crowded coffee bar.
This is where we sit,
Propped at some narrow shelf,
Each day more crowded than the last
With undesirables.

I wish we could meet again
In two years' time,
Somewhere expensive where they remembered us
From the early days, before the crash.
Instead of here, instead of now,
Facing our reflections in the Bar Italia.

You would be frowning of course,
After all this time,
But then you would hold out your hand and say,
'Well, where are your three pages?'

I haven't written them. One day I will.
Anywhere but here it might seem possible.

August 1976

•

It's Disgusting
at Your Age

—————— MARTIN AMIS ——————

Two young men, very early twenties, wearing jeans and plain shirts, sit at a table in a tidy though ill-equipped kitchen. They are educated, middle-class: JAMES, taller, prettier, weedier-looking; FREDDIE, stockier, more robust, but with the same puppyish air. JAMES sits erect with his hands palm-upwards on the table; FREDDIE lounges with his arms folded. Their talk is slightly stylized, having that defeated, ironic twang peculiar to their class and age-group.

JAMES I can't cope any more. She's started sending me obscene poems now. I can't cope with this.

FREDDIE What sort of obscene poems?

JAMES (*running the back of his hand haggardly across his forehead*) Stuff about my 'diamond crown'. And stuff about her 'amber jewel'.

FREDDIE What sort of stuff about them?

JAMES Just stuff like that about them.

FREDDIE How disgusting. Well what are you going to do about it, James?

JAMES That's just it. What *can* I do about it? I can't say – Look here, don't send me any more obscene poems, okay? . . . I just can't cope any more. And the horrible things she makes me do in bed – they're . . . She's insatiable, Freddie. Insatiable.

FREDDIE (*starts to look hunted himself, at which JAMES seems to perk up a little*) Felicity's exactly the same. We should never have got mixed up with them. They're far too posh. Posh girls, they're after one thing and one thing only.

JAMES Your body.

FREDDIE Sex sex sex.

JAMES   It's all they ever think about.

FREDDIE   They're totally obsessed with it.

JAMES   Totally.

FREDDIE   Why couldn't we have taken up with two nice working–class girls?

JAMES   I know.

Silence.

JAMES   Tell you what – we were insane to give in on the first night like that. They don't respect you if you come across straightaway.

FREDDIE   Exactly. They just use you.

JAMES   Yeah, if only we had held out for a couple of weeks. Then they would have valued more what they were getting.

FREDDIE   Trouble is, you do that nowadays and they just don't want to know. If you don't come across, they're off. There's plenty of others who will.

JAMES   And they're so persistent. Won't take no for an answer.

FREDDIE   They just nag until you do.

JAMES   I mean, we have feelings, same as anyone else. We're not just lumps of flesh.

FREDDIE   No use telling *them* that, *oh* no . . . Well it's got to stop. Tonight.

JAMES   Mm. What's the time?

FREDDIE   Mm. Better get changed I suppose.

Their faces go slack with foreboding. Then animate.

FREDDIE   Bags the first bath.

JAMES   Look, I've got to wash my hair.

FREDDIE   Tough. I've got to wash mine.

JAMES   You washed it yesterday.

FREDDIE   No I didn't. Day before.

JAMES   Yes you did. Anyway, you shouldn't wash it that often otherwise it'll go all . . .

They leave the kitchen, arguing contentedly.

Cut to a feminine bedroom. The tall and angular MIRANDA, in panties and bra, is trying to unscrew a jar of face-cream, her features contorted angrily. She grunts, and throws the jar with a clatter on to the dressing-table. FELICITY, broader and even more formidable-looking, strides in, violently shaking at some dress.

FELICITY   What's up?

MIRANDA   Bloody jar. Can't get the top off. (*Looks grimly into mirror.*) Guess I'll just have to go rugged tonight.

They start getting dressed, briskly, negligently.

FELICITY   How are we going to work it?

MIRANDA   I suppose we'll have to go through the motions first. It's only civilized. How about a film? Then at least we won't have to small talk.

FELICITY   That's a point. I'm going to gag if I have to listen to Fred whining on about the art gallery.

MIRANDA   Or James droning on about the death of the novel. You'd think he was married to the bloody thing.

FELICITY   (*deliberately worsening her deb accent*) I don't know – the things a girl has to put up with these days.

MIRANDA   (*also in shopgirl*) The sacrifices we have to make.

FELICITY   Well, it's got to end. I can't take another night like the last.

MIRANDA   Look, let's be half-an-hour late, then take them to that long Charles Bronson murder film at the Classic. Then it'll be too late for dinner and we can whisk them off straightaway.

FELICITY   Your turn to go there. I'll get Freddie back here.

MIRANDA   Say you want to show him those pictures for the gallery.

FELICITY   But what if bloody James decides he wants to see them too?

MIRANDA   I'll say I've got to get the book I left at their place.

FELICITY   Right. And if they start moaning about not splitting up just bundle him off.

MIRANDA   Got to be firm with them. Tonight, anyway.

FELICITY   (*looks at her watch*) We've got ages. Let's have one on the way. Got a brush?

MIRANDA   (*pokes dubiously among the rubble on the dressing-table*) It's . . . perhaps it's in the –

FELICITY   To hell with it anyway.

Cut to JAMES, standing slightly arched backwards in front of a bedroom mirror, combing or brushing his hair with as much concentration and complexity as the actor's locks allow. FREDDIE's voice from neighbouring room.

FREDDIE   James! Have you got my belt again?

JAMES   (*looks startled*) Yes.

FREDDIE   (*enters, elaborately clothed*) Well get it off.

JAMES   Come on, Freddie. Please. I lent you the waistcoat.

FREDDIE   Get it off.

JAMES   (*despondently does so*) Well let me wear the blue scarf.

FREDDIE   No.

JAMES   Come on.

FREDDIE   All right. If I can have the hat.

JAMES   I wanted that.

FREDDIE   No scarf then.

JAMES   (*agonized decision*) Oh *okay*. But I wear the belt next time.

FREDDIE   Oh all right. Christ, James, you're like a bloody girl sometimes. Like a bloody *girl*. (*Straightens the lapels of his velvet jacket.*) Well how do I look?

JAMES   Bit of shaving cream on your chin.

FREDDIE wipes it off. JAMES folds his arms, leans back, and stares at FREDDIE for at least five seconds.

JAMES   Mm, well, I was never sure about that shirt, as you know. I mean, those *cuffs* . . . And the jacket's all gone to hell under the arms of course. But all right on the whole. (*Posture relaxes.*) Apart from those revolting boots. And me?

FREDDIE   . . . Well, the colour–scheme isn't one I would have chosen, but you can get used to anything in time, I suppose. The shape is good. (*Leans forward and arranges a curl of James's hair.*) The effect, the general *effect* is good, even though the details are all out of whack. Mmm – wish I had your complexion.

JAMES   Ah shut up. Bitch bitch bitch. At least I haven't got dishcloth hair. I mean, look at it, Freddie. You can't do a thing with it, can you? You can't, can you?

FREDDIE   Ah shut up. I just don't happen to need to arrange my hair to cover my face, like some sort of veil. Do something about it, James, please. Just cope with it. You ought to try this new cream they've come up with. Apparently it –

JAMES   Ah shut up. And look, what are we going to *do*?

FREDDIE   Relax. I've got it all worked out. We've been pushed around for long enough.

JAMES   Treated like dirt.

FREDDIE   Like scum. Well it's going to be different tonight. Is there any Campari left? We'd better get Dutched.

JAMES   It goes straight to your paunch, you know.

FREDDIE   Ah shut up.

Cut to a public house, FELICITY and MIRANDA are leaning virilely against the bar, half-full pint glasses of beer in front of them, chain smoking. Their voices are raised in the normal oblivious upper-class style.

FELICITY   I always used to wonder whether it was worth all the sweat. Getting dressed up. The dinner. The small talk.

MIRANDA   Going through all the motions.

FELICITY   I like to take it easy on my evenings out.

MIRANDA   It's all too much like hard work.

FELICITY   Still, it's good exercise. Keeps us in shape.

MIRANDA   What's Freddie really like then?

FELICITY   *(expression grows slightly wistful)* Well, Freddie's . . . He's got a funny figure really. He's a bit short in the shank – that's why he wears those yob's boots. But he's got a good back and nice shoulders. And his –

MIRANDA   But what's he really *like*?

FELICITY   *(realizes she has misunderstood)* Oh. Well, he was a bit nervous and shy at first, of course. Romantics always are. Lots of stupid inhibitions. Completely green, really. For instance he wouldn't even . . .

Fade dreamily to two discotheque alcoves, the boys in one, the girls in the other, a glass screen between them. The discotheque to be done as uncornily as possible. We don't need to see anything but the alcoves, so we can get away with lights flashing off-camera and background music. Centre on boys:

FREDDIE   I don't know why the hell we still come here. I don't know the hell why we still do.

— 239 —

JAMES   It's *so* tacky. Look at that dirty fool in the orange bell-bottoms.

FREDDIE   Bell-bottoms. I mean, really, I ask you.

JAMES   His hair's a total mess. A write-off. God, I loathe people who dance like that. As if he's covered in lice.

FREDDIE   He probably is. At least he's an improvement on that fashionable Chink. What is it with you Chinese these days? What makes you think you're so flash?

JAMES   Mm. Wonder where he got that jersey, though. Think it's cashmere?

FREDDIE   . . . No. Cashmere gives off a kind of –

JAMES   *(freezes with a glass at his lips)* Oh God. That girl's giving me the eye.

FREDDIE   *(equally alarmed)* Which one?

JAMES   *(out of the corner of his mouth)* Next door. The blonde.

FREDDIE   *(out of the corner of his mouth)* Well just pretend not to notice.

Move over to MIRANDA and FELICITY.

MIRANDA   What about them?

FELICITY   *(looks interested but unimpressed)* Mm. Which one do you fancy?

MIRANDA   I'm not fussy.

FELICITY   You can't afford to be in this dump. *(Looks around wearily.)* There were a couple of half-way decent Greek-type efforts over by the door just now but I think they've already been pulled.

MIRANDA   Yes, they were all right. Looks like these two then.

FELICITY   Looks like it.

MIRANDA   It's your turn, isn't it?

FELICITY   Yours, I think.

MIRANDA   Okay.

FELICITY   No, I'll do it.

Back to JAMES and FREDDIE.

JAMES   Yawn. They're coming over. I think they're coming over.

FREDDIE   Yawn. Are they?

— 240 —

JAMES   God. They *are*.

FELICITY   What's all this then? What are two nice boys like you doing in a place like this?

JAMES and FREDDIE stare haughtily into space, as if nothing has happened.

FELICITY   And I suppose you want to dance now.

FREDDIE   *(looking doubtfully at JAMES)* Do we?

FELICITY   Good, because we'd much rather drink. Come on, they're on us.

JAMES   Oh all right.

THEY get in, FELICITY next to FREDDIE, MIRANDA winks at FELICITY and smiles glaringly at JAMES, who looks diffidently at the table. Meanwhile, FREDDIE is trying vainly to attract the attention of a waitress, saying 'Uh . . . Uh', and snapping his fingers weakly. FELICITY sighs.

FELICITY   Hey.

WAITRESS instantly appears.

FELICITY   *(to boys)* What's it to be?

JAMES   Um . . . Campari and soda, please.

FREDDIE   Don't have that, James, please. It only makes you giggly.

JAMES   Ha ha. I want a Campari and soda.

FREDDIE   Well don't make a spectacle of yourself. I'll have a, a Dubonnet. With lemon but no ice. No ice. Just lemon.

JAMES   Look who's talking.

FELICITY   And two whiskies.

MIRANDA   *(handing round cigarettes – FELICITY accepts, boys refuse)* Big ones.

JAMES   We don't smoke.

MIRANDA   Haven't seen you down here before. I'm Miranda, by the way.

FELICITY   *(smiling)* I'm Felicity.

Silence.

FELICITY   Well what are your names, for Christ's sake?

FREDDIE   Oh. That's James. I'm called Freddie.

FELICITY   How do you do. I said we haven't seen you down here before.

FREDDIE   *(dryly – slight stress on 'not')* We do not come here often.

MIRANDA   Yes, I know what you mean.

Silence.

MIRANDA   Where do you usually go?

JAMES and FREDDIE turn to each other. They shrug, and sip at the remains of their drinks.

MIRANDA   *(to FELICITY)* This is fun, isn't it?

WAITRESS reappears.

WAITRESS   Bar's closed.

Girls' postures flop.

FREDDIE   *(looking at his watch)* Is it that late? James, oughtn't we better –

JAMES   *(to waitress)* Have you got any Fanta? *Lemon* Fanta?

FELICITY   Fanta! Fuck *Fanta*. *(gathering her things)* Our place. There's some wine. Let's go.

FREDDIE and JAMES look at each other with exaggerated bewilderment.

JAMES   But it's nearly . . . it's nearly . . .

MIRANDA   *(with tired contempt)* Come on. Let's go.

JAMES and FREDDIE look at each other expressionlessly. They shrug.

Return to the pub. The girls are flushed and ironical, enjoying themselves.

FELICITY   Talk about getting swept off your feet.

MIRANDA   I was helpless, your Honour. He was like – like some sort of animal.

FELICITY   Anyway he's pulled his socks up and he's really quite daring now. Or at least *he* thinks he's quite daring now. What about James? *(Hardly moving her lips, like a ventriloquist)* Seen the one by the fruit-machine?

MIRANDA   *(Follows FELICITY's glance. Her eyes bulge a little bit and she nods quickly three or four times)* Oh, James. *(Bored)* Same sort of thing. *(Wags her head at the dartboard.)* Want a game?

FELICITY   *(attracts the barman's attention and forks her fingers at the beer-glasses)* Two more.

Cut to JAMES, sitting erect and quite still at the kitchen table, smoothing the creases of the inside elbows of his jacket with slow, robotic hands. He watches with interest as FREDDIE pours out the drinks, places them on the table, and sits down beside him.

JAMES   Thanks. Freddie, you really *are* putting on weight. *(Gestures vaguely, unhappily.)* Your gut.

FREDDIE   *(stares at his stomach)* It's this shirt.

JAMES   Do something about it, Fred. Please do something about it. It's disgusting at your age.

FREDDIE   I have. I am. I've done an hour's callisthenics every morning for three months. And cut out carbohydrates. And cut out beer. And cut out all fried foods.

JAMES   And?

FREDDIE   And I've gained five-and-a-half pounds. Thanks a lot.

JAMES laughs wealthily.

FREDDIE   What is it with you anyway? *You* eat really startling amounts of food, you've got a really hideous appetite – and does it show? Not on you, *oh* no. I think it's bloody unfair.

JAMES   Cheer up about it, Fred.

FREDDIE   Well, I do. Bloody unfair.

JAMES   Has Felicity said anything about it yet?

FREDDIE   Well, oddly enough it doesn't really show when I'm stripped. *(Seems momentarily cheered by this, but then a shadow of foreboding crosses his face.)* Oh God. *(Shudders.)* Wonder what she's dreamed up for tonight.

JAMES   Give you three guesses.

FREDDIE   Wham-bam-thank-you-man. You can place money on that. Well tonight they've got a little surprise coming.

JAMES   Let's not even talk about it. It's going to be a nightmare, Freddie. A complete nightmare.

FREDDIE   I know. *(Sniffs the air a few times.)* This Cologne. Think it's a bit . . . I mean, you know.

JAMES   A bit what?

FREDDIE   You know.

JAMES   A bit. I prefer a tangier flavour on the whole. Not Eau de Sauvage, anything like that. Too many people wear it. What I like are the ones that . . .

Dreamy, faded return to girls' flat (night the four met, continuation of discotheque scene). MIRANDA and FELICITY stride into the room;

the boys follow gingerly. There is a double bed in one half of the room and a collection of cushions in the other.

FELICITY *(pointing at the bed)* Dump your coats there. *(Thinking better of it)* Or on the floor.

Unselfconsciously, and with practised movements, the girls pour out wine, put on soft music, subdue the lights.

JAMES *(whispers to FREDDIE)* Don't let them get us drunk.

FREDDIE Stick together.

They settle on the cushions.

MIRANDA *(to JAMES)* What do you do?

JAMES *(looks at FREDDIE and back again)* Sort of interior decorating.

Silence.

FELICITY *(to FREDDIE)* What do you do?

FREDDIE *(looks at JAMES and back again)* Sort of in an art gallery.

Silence.

MIRANDA Aren't you going to ask us what *we* do?

JAMES Oh. What do you do?

FELICITY Nothing. Idle rich, darling.

JAMES and FREDDIE's eyes confer wearily. So do MIRANDA and FELICITY's, but more secretively, with narrowed lids.

MIRANDA *(to JAMES)* An art gallery, eh? Better come over and see some prints I bought.

JAMES No – he's the one who works in an art gallery.

MIRANDA *(taking JAMES's hand)* Never mind. These are etchings. Come on.

MIRANDA leads JAMES out of camera. (They have gone to sit on the bed; their intimate mumbles can be heard.)

FREDDIE watches them go, cold, betrayed.

FREDDIE *(bitterly, under his breath)* Slag.

Meanwhile FELICITY is arranging herself at his side. FREDDIE's eyes bulge as she crooks an arm on his shoulder.

FELICITY So you're the one who works in the gallery?

FREDDIE Yes.

FELICITY *(moving in, throughout the conversation)* Whereabouts is it?

FREDDIE The Bond Street area. Mayfair.

The sounds of JAMES's scandalized giggling comes from the other end of the room.

JAMES *(playfully)* Don't. Stop it!

FELICITY What do you do there? In the art gallery.

FREDDIE I'm an assistant. The assistant.

FELICITY Oh. So you just sit there with clean fingernails being nice to Americans?

FELICITY puts her hand on his knee; FREDDIE removes it with finger and thumb, as if he were taking her pulse.

FREDDIE Some selling, too.

JAMES *(coos from the other end of the room)* Ooh! You mustn't!

FREDDIE looks brokenly at where the voice has come from. He gulps. FELICITY then leans forward in front of him. FREDDIE's clenched hands come up to his chin. She kisses him on the mouth. FREDDIE's hands drum feebly on her shoulders for a few seconds – token resistance – then fasten round her back in fluttery surrender.

Return to the pub. The girls finish their game of darts and saunter back to the bar. Once again FELICITY forks her fingers at the beer-glasses.

FELICITY *(quizzically)* Two more?

MIRANDA *(protrudes her lower lip and nods)* Why not? At least we'll be late.

FELICITY *(attracting the landlord's attention; he is young and presentable, and they make eyes at him in a jokingly aggressive way)* Yes, and it's just that the returns are so poor. And I don't just mean all the chatting-up and coaxing and flattery you have to go through first.

MIRANDA *(emphasis on 'proper')* We need some proper men.

FELICITY *(seriously)* Do we? I don't think I do. The awful thing is I quite like little butterflies like Freddie. *(Puzzled pause.)* I mean, I hate them really. But I quite like them.

MIRANDA Yes it's funny, isn't it. I do too.

FELICITY God knows why.

MIRANDA 'Ooh, James, what a super shirt!' *(Exhales.)* And he doesn't even say 'I'm glad you like it' or anything. He simply hugs himself with the ecstasy of it all.

FELICITY I get worse. Fred's got a thing about his paunch. It's the only subject that interests him any more. His paunch is all he's prepared to talk about now – even when we're in bed – prodding it, looking at it from different angles. He's got a real thing about it.

MIRANDA   The fat little fool just eats too much.

FELICITY   No. He's just so vain that he hasn't eaten anything at all for three months.

MIRANDA   He should corset.

They sigh.

MIRANDA   Well tonight we're going to be firm.

FELICITY   Don't let them simper their way out of it.

MIRANDA   Don't let them sidetrack us.

FELICITY   Hey – why don't we just go straight ahead. Forget the film. Do it as soon as we get in there. Just get it over with.

MIRANDA   *(Face lightens up, then darkens)* Ah, but they'd be so hurt. So huffy. 'That's all you came round here to do' – you can imagine it. Anyway, it'd be too embarrassing to do it with the four of us there. Wouldn't it?

FELICITY   Suppose so. Well let's just play it by ear . . . How late are we?

MIRANDA   *(not looking at her watch)* About half-an-hour.

FELICITY   Bit longer?

MIRANDA   Yeah.

JAMES and FREDDIE are sitting like tailors' dummies at the kitchen table.

JAMES   *(wistfully, dreamily)* Perhaps they're not coming . . .

FREDDIE   *(looking at his watch)* What a break.

JAMES   *(perplexed)* Don't you think they are coming?

FREDDIE   How should I know? Actually, I couldn't help noticing that Miranda looked pretty unenthusiastic last time. Perhaps she had a better idea for tonight.

JAMES   Oh yeah? Well Miranda says, actually, that from what Felicity tells *her*, that *she's* the one who's doing all right.

FREDDIE   That's not what Miranda tells me.

JAMES   *(slightly taken aback)* When did she speak to you about it?

FREDDIE   Oh, only when she cornered me in the bathroom one evening. And that reminds me – have a word with her about it, will you, James? She was all over me. It was *very* embarrassing.

JAMES   *(not taken in – or trying to seem so)* I bet. Don't start making a fool of yourself, Freddie, please.

FREDDIE   *(shrugs coolly)* Anyway, that's hardly the issue any more. We've got to think what's a shrewd way to work it tonight. *(JAMES still looks downcast, cowed, so FREDDIE says)* . . . That scarf with that shirt, James – it works.

JAMES   *(stares down and examines the two garments)* You think so?

FREDDIE   No doubt about it. I thought that they wouldn't quite . . . wouldn't quite *make* it. But you were right. They really work.

JAMES   It wouldn't have been better with the yellow tassle things?

FREDDIE   *(frowning)* I don't *think* so. The thing about that sort of look is – Well, take my blue velvet overalls. I mean, what a catastrophe *they* turned out to be. For a start they . . .

FELICITY and MIRANDA are walking animatedly down the street, looking at each other as they talk.

FELICITY   *(laughing)* The one who called himself 'Peanut'? 'Peanut'! I couldn't believe it!

MIRANDA   Nor could I. How was it you didn't just burst out crying with laughter. Rather you than me, girl.

FELICITY   *(affectionately, accusing)* At least he wasn't a hairdresser.

MIRANDA   Yes, that was Peanut's strong point. You could say that for Peanut: he wasn't a hairdresser.

They laugh and link arms.

MIRANDA   Was that the worst we've ever done?

FELICITY   I hope it was. But maybe those hitch-hikers. The Devon ones . . .

MIRANDA   What, The Tike and The Gingerboy?

FELICITY   The ones that blew their noses on their vests and combed their hair all night.

They laugh.

MIRANDA   *(in a fruity voice)* Heard the one about the – *(Halts.)* Oh, God.

They have reached their destination. FELICITY extends a hand gingerly towards the bell (one of many). They look at each other like two commandos about to make a perilous dash.

FELICITY Well here goes.

Cut to the kitchen. FREDDIE and JAMES, in their drowsy style, are having a shriek and a giggle. Their faces are animated. JAMES's hand flaps playfully on FREDDIE's forearm.

JAMES And then you got those really bad-buy shiny blue trousers from Biba!

FREDDIE *(smiling ruefully)* Yes. They were a mistake.

JAMES They were so shiny you could see your face in the seat. You looked quite revolting, Freddie – everyone said so.

FREDDIE Wasn't it about then that you were wearing your belt *outside* your jersey.

JAMES *(tickled, pawing a hand helplessly in the air towards FREDDIE)* Aah! Don't! Please!

FREDDIE And I said, 'James, are you quite sure that the belt thing is good?'

JAMES And what did I say – I said –

The bell rings. The boys freeze.

JAMES Oh, God.

FREDDIE *(looking at JAMES grimly)* Well here goes.

Cut to the boys' sitting-room. Things seem surprisingly normal: the boys help the girls off with their coats, kiss their cheeks, mutter pleasant hellos. The boys are unexpectedly solicitous, the girls unexpectedly diffident. Once they are settled, though, a silence falls, a silence so complete and clueless that it could almost be the night they first met.

FELICITY What are we going to do?

JAMES *(folding his arms)* Well for a start we're going out to dinner.

FREDDIE *(folding his arms)* For a start.

MIRANDA But it spins the evening out so much.

JAMES No. We insist. Freddie and I've decided.

FELICITY But we wanted to go to the murder film at the Classic.

FREDDIE Too bad. What's wrong with going out to dinner?

MIRANDA It takes hours.

FREDDIE   Only as long as a film.

MIRANDA   But in a film you don't have to . . .

FREDDIE   Don't have to what?

JAMES   *(bitchily)* You never even watch the film anyway. It's just back-row stuff as far as you're concerned.

FELICITY   So?

FREDDIE   *(bitterly)* You get enough of that later on. I mean, all James and I want to do is hot things up with a bit of conversation, that's all.

FELICITY   That's what's wrong with dinner. Conversation.

FREDDIE   *(sharply)* Now what do you mean?

FELICITY   *(sighing)* It's just that you're a bit boring, Fred.

A silence.

JAMES   *(hesitantly)* . . . Miranda, I'm not boring, am I?

MIRANDA   A bit, James.

FREDDIE and JAMES turn to each other in frank consternation, then back to the girls. During the following speeches the girls look at each other boredly.

JAMES   Well thanks very much.

FREDDIE   Yes, I suppose people like you would find anything not actually physical 'a bit boring'.

JAMES   I mean honestly, can't you ever think about anything else?

FREDDIE   We're not machines – we're human beings.

FELICITY   *(tonelessly to MIRANDA)* I've got it. Why don't they go out to dinner and we go to the film?

JAMES   . . . And what? . . . Meet up after?

FREDDIE   *(still bitter)* Yes, I suppose that's all we're good for. Not for talking. Not for going out together. Just for that. That's the only thing we're any good for, isn't it? Isn't it?

FELICITY   *(fairly nastily)* Not really.

FREDDIE   *(stunned)* I think you'd better leave.

MIRANDA   So do I.

JAMES and FREDDIE stare at each other as the girls pick up their coats. They leave.

Cut to FELICITY and MIRANDA walking along the street, springy-stepped.

FELICITY   *(brightly)* Well that was fairly painless, wasn't it?

MIRANDA   Didn't even have to go out with them.

FELICITY   Didn't even have to let them down easy.

MIRANDA   Didn't even have to get them on their own.

FELICITY   Didn't even have to waste an evening on it.

MIRANDA   I feel better already.

FELICITY   Me too.

MIRANDA   A quick one, the film, and a club–crawl?

FELICITY   You bet.

Cut back to the boys' kitchen. They sit at the table, blank and becalmed.

JAMES   Fancy them just saying that.

FREDDIE   We saw them in their true colours tonight. They're *all* the same.

JAMES   Still. We did what we set out to do. I mean, it was what we wanted to do, wasn't it?

FREDDIE   Oh yeah. Absolutely.

JAMES   I could do with an early night.

FREDDIE   Got all that ironing to do.

JAMES   Give me a chance to wash my hair.

FREDDIE   Try my conditioner if you like, James.

JAMES   Can I? That green stuff?

They get up to leave the room.

FREDDIE   Yes. Makes it far more manageable and gives it that bit of bounce.

JAMES   Doesn't it go all fluffy though?

FREDDIE   Not if you wait for a few minutes after the second rinse. Then add a little water and . . .

They disappear.

September 1976

The Soho Hospital
for Women

—— FLEUR ADCOCK ——

I

Strange room, from this angle:
white door open before me,
strange bed, mechanical hum, white lights.
There will be stranger rooms to come.

As I almost slept I saw the deep flower opening
and leaned over into it, gratefully.
It swimmingly closed in my face. I was not ready.
It was not death, it was acceptance.

Our thin patient cat died purring,
her small triangular head tilted back,
the nurse's fingers caressing her throat,
my hand on her shrunken spine; the quick needle.

That was the second death by cancer.
The first is not for me to speak of.
It was telephone-calls and brave letters
and a friend's hand bleeding under the coffin.

Doctor, I am not afraid of a word.
But neither do I wish to embrace that visitor,
to engulf it as Hine-Nui-te-Po
engulfed Maui; that would be the way of it.

And she was the winner there: her womb crushed him.
Goddesses can do these things.

But I have admitted the gloved hands and the speculum
and must part my ordinary legs to the surgeon's knife.

II

Nellie has only one breast
ample enough to make several.
Her quilted dressing-gown softens
to semi-doubtful this imbalance
and there's no starched vanity
in our floppy abundant ward-mother:
her streaked silvery hair's in braids,
her slippers loll, her weathered, classical
features hold a long, true smile.
When she dresses up in her black
with her glittering marcasite brooch on
to go for the weekly radium treatment
she's the bright star of the taxi-party –
whatever may be growing under her ribs.

Doris hardly smokes in the ward –
and hardly eats more than a dreamy spoonful –
but the corridors and bathrooms
reek of her Players number 10,
and the drug-trolley pauses
for long minutes by her bed.
Each week for the taxi-outing
she puts on her skirt again
and has to pin the slack waistband
more tightly over her scarlet sweater.
Her face, a white shadow through smoked glass,
lets Soho display itself unregarded.

Third in the car is Mrs Golding
who never smiles. And why should she?

III

The senior consultant on his rounds
murmurs in so subdued a voice

to the students marshalled behind
that they gather in, forming a cell,
a cluster, a rosette around him
as he stands at the foot of my bed
going through my notes with them,
half-audibly instructive, grave.

The slight ache as I strain forward
to listen still seems imagined.

Then he turns his practised smile on me:
'How are you this morning?' 'Fine,
very well, thank you.' I smile too.
And possibly all that murmurs within me
is the slow dissolving of stitches.

IV

I am out in the supermarket, choosing –
this very afternoon, this day –
picking up tomatoes, cheese, bread,

things I want and shall be using
to make myself a meal, while they
eat their stodgy suppers in bed –

Janet with her big freckled breasts,
her prim Scots voice, her one friend,
and never in hospital before,

who came in to have a few tests
and now can't see where they'll end;
and Coral in the bed by the door

who whimpered and gasped behind a screen
with nurses to and fro all night
and far too much of the day;

pallid, bewildered, nineteen.
And Mary, who will be all right
but gradually. And Alice, who may.

Whereas I stand almost intact,
giddy with freedom, not with pain.
I lift my light basket, observing

how little I needed in fact;
and move to the checkout, to the rain,
to the lights and the long street curving.

September 1976

Lorca

—— D. M. THOMAS ——

Lorca
walking
in a red-light
district at night
heard one of his own songs
being sung
by a whore

he was moved
as if the stars
and the lanterns
changed places

neither the song
to himself
belonged
nor the girl
to her humiliation
nothing
belonged to anyone

when she stopped singing
it went on

death must be a poor thing
a poor thing

September 1976

Two Poems

———— CRAIG RAINE ————

The Gardener

Up and down the lawn he walks with cycling hands
that tremble on the mower's stethoscope.

Creases blink behind his knees.
He stares at a prance of spray

and wrestles with Leviathan alone. Victorious,
he bangs the grass box empty like a clog . . .

The shears are a Y that wants to be an X –
he holds them like a water diviner,

and hangs them upside down, a wish-bone.
His hands row gently on the plunger

and detonate the earth. He smacks the clods
and dandles weeds on trembling prongs.

They lie, a heap of dusters softly shaken out.
At night he plays a pattering hose, fanned

like a drummer's brush. His aim is to grow
the Kremlin – the roses' tight pink cupolas

ring bells . . . For this he stands in weariness,
tired as a teapot, feeling the small of his back.

The Window Cleaner

The college quad is cobbled like a blackberry
and shining in the rain and dangerous . . .

The window cleaner cups a telescopic caber –
Blondin never trod so warily.

He wears a sad expression on his face,
half a dress, and heather-mixture trews –

all day he listens to the squeak of puppies,
litters he is paid to drown and strangle.

All day he sees himself in the glass darkly
and waves goodbye, goodbye, goodbye.

All day he wrings his hands, crying buckets.
He'd rather shave shop windows clean

than climb this bendy Jacob's ladder
and risk the washboard fall of seraphim . . .

April 1977

Living on Capital

—— JONATHAN RABAN ——

I suppose that everyone is really the father of their own family. We make them up, these private sanctuaries, prisons and sunny utopias. Visiting other people's families, I've always found it hard to square what I've seen with the legend as it was told to me in the car on the way. The characters are always much bigger or smaller, nicer or nastier, than they ought to be. It's like seeing a play performed by a weekly rep working from the wrong text. One's own legend is doubly distrustable. One has all the ruthless impartiality of a critic writing up a show in which he has both been casting director and one of the stars. Legend it must be, not accountancy or gritty realism; and like all Genesis myths, its garden, its rib and its fruit of the tree are symbols. When it comes to his own family, no one can afford to be a fundamentalist.

Once upon a time, before the idea of 'family' ever took hold, there was just my mother and I. We lived in a sweet cocoon, and it was much like having an idyllic extra-marital affair. My father was away 'in the war': he was a photograph on the mantelpiece; he was the morning post; he was part of the one o'clock news on the wireless. He was not so much my father as the complaisant husband of the woman I lived with – and I dreaded his return. Meanwhile, we made hay while the sun shone. I had contracted a wasting disease called Coeliac, and I was fed, like a privileged lover, on specially imported bananas and boiled brains. We learned to read together, so that I could spell out paragraphs from *The Times* before my third birthday. We stoved in the bottoms of eggshells, so that witches wouldn't be able to use them as boats. We saved up our petrol rations, and drove to my grandmother's house in Sheringham. My mother's Ford Eight, AUP 595, had been bought in 1939 with money she'd earned writing love stories for women's magazines, and it was the perfect vehicle for conducting a romance. Bowling along Norfolk lanes at a hair-raising thirty, with the windows down and the smell of pollen, leather and motor oil in my nose, I felt that this was the life. I meant to keep on as I had started; riding in the front seat with kisses and confessions, and the Ribena bottle conveniently near the top of the hamper.

I was a bag of bones. But I had already acquired the manner of a practised gigolo. My illness gave me the right to constant attention. With my forehead in my mother's hands, I was sick until my throat bled. When I wasn't being sick, I was being loquacious. Since my mother had only me to talk to, I'd picked up an impressive vocabulary which I was perpetually airing and adding to. Too weak to play with other children – whom I regarded from a distance as rough, untutored creatures – I looked to grown-ups for the concern and admiration that was clearly my due. I feared the mockery of the few children who were allowed ('No rough games, mind!') to enter my bone-china world. My one friend was the doctor's son, who'd been crippled with polio and went about in a steel frame that was almost as big as himself. When I was three, my mother told me that children like him and me would go on scholar ships to nice schools, but the village children would all go to knocky-down schools like the one up the road. I saw myself and my mother sailing out in my scholar ship, its sail filling with the offshore wind on the beach at Sheringham, its prow headed into a romantic sunset, away from the line of jeering, unkempt children on the shore.

I hadn't reckoned with my father. I had once made my mother cry, when I had enquired whether he was likely to be killed by Germans; and I was often puzzled by the depth of her engrossment when a new batch of letters arrived from North Africa, then Italy, then Palestine. Curiously, I have no memory at all of my father coming back on leave. He must have blended into the other occasional visitors – many of them in uniform – to our house. Was he the man who took us both out to lunch one Sunday at a Fakenham hotel, where I remember the stringy rhubarb and a fit of sickness in the lavatory? I'm not sure.

At any rate, he was a complete stranger when he turned up late one morning, carrying a khaki kit bag across Hempton Green – the moment at which family life began for me. My first impression of him was of an unprepossessing roughness. The photo on the mantelpiece showed a junior officer so boyish he looked too young to shave. My father's jowl was the colour and texture of emery paper. His demob suit, too, seemed to have been woven out of corn-stubble. When my mother and he embraced, right there in the open on the green, I was mortified. I studied the faded white lettering on his bag: Major J. P. C. P. Raban R.A. By what right did this tall soldier in his ill-fitting civilian suit horn in on our household? The question took me several years to even begin to answer.

My father must have been a bit shaken too. His spindly, solemn son can hardly have been the beamish three-year-old he might have looked forward to. He was obviously unused to children anyway, and had no practice at dealing with precocious little invalids who cried when he spoke to them. He brought with him the affectedly hearty manners of the mess, and tried to make friends with me rather as he might have jollied along a particularly green subaltern. On the afternoon of his arrival, he carried me by my feet and suspended me over the water-butt in the back garden. As I hung, screaming, over this black soup of mosquito larvae, my mother rushed out of the house to my defence.

'Only a game,' said my father. 'We were just having a game.' But I knew otherwise. This terrifying Visigoth, fresh from the slaughter, had tried to murder me before we'd even reached teatime. I ran bleating to my mother, begging her to send this awful man back to the war where he so clearly belonged. My father's fears were also confirmed: unless something pretty firm in the way of paternal influence was applied here and now, I was going to turn out a first-rate milksop, an insufferable little wet.

My father's feelings about 'wets' may have been streaked with anxieties of his own. Before the war, he had been a shy young man who had scraped through School Certificate at a minor public school. From there he had gone to a teachers' training college, and had done a probationary year of teaching (at which he had not been a success) before enlisting in the Territorial Army. In the army, he blossomed. He was rapidly promoted. He got married. He found himself suddenly a figure of some considerable poise and authority. When the war ended, he had hoped to transfer to the Regular Army but had been discouraged from doing so. By the time we met, he was 27, already at the end of a career he had been able to shine at. He had, along with his forced officer-style jocularity, a kind of preternatural gravity; he had learned to carry his own manliness with the air of an acolyte bearing an incense-boat. My father in his twenties was a profoundly responsible young man who had grown up late and then too quickly. He was stiff, avuncular and harsh by turns. I think that he felt my namby-pamby nature obscurely threatened his own manhood, and he set about toughening me up.

I was frightened of him. I was afraid of his irritable, headachey silences; afraid of his sudden gusts of good humour; afraid of his inscrutable, untouchable air; and afraid, most of all, of his summary beatings, which were administered court-martial fashion in his study. A toy left overnight in the path of the car got me a spanking; so did being unable to remember whether I had said 'thank you' to my hostess after a four-year-old's birthday party. He introduced me to a new cold world of duties and punishments – a vastly complicated, unforgiving place in which the best one could hope for was to pass without comment. Perhaps my father had cause to believe that the world really was like this, and was simply doing his best to rescue me from the fool's paradise unwittingly created for me by my mother. I felt then that he was just jealous of my intimacy with her, and was taking his revenge.

For weeks after the war he hung about the house and garden. He clacked out letters to potential employers on my mother's old portable Olivetti. He practised golf swings. He rambled round and round the birdbath in his demob suit. He made gunnery calculations on his slide-rule. I played gooseberry – a sullen child lurking in passageways, resentfully spying on my parents. I felt cuckolded, and showed it. When my father eventually found a job, as the local area secretary of TocH, his work took him out of the house most evenings: when he drove off to Wisbech and Peterborough and King's Lynn, I would try to seduce my mother back to the old days of our affair. We listened to *Dick Barton* on the wireless over cocoa, and then I would launch into an avalanche of bright talk, hoping to buy back her attention and distract her from the clock. I felt her joy at having my father home, and I think I did sense her distress at my conspicuous failure to share it. I also felt a twinge or two of shame at our snugness. From my father, I was beginning to learn that my behaviour was distinctly unmanly, and these cocoon–evenings were clouded with guilt. When my father said, as he did several times a week, 'You are going to have to learn to stand up for yourself, old boy', I shrank from the idea but knew it to be unarguably right.

But my father and I grew grim with the responsibilities that had been placed on our shoulders. I think we both felt helpless. He had inherited a role in life which he could only conceive of in the most old–fashioned terms: he had to become a Victorian husband and father, a pillar of the family, the heir to the fading Raban fortunes. I had inherited *him*. And we both chafed under the weight of these legacies, both of us too weak to carry them off with any style. He bullied me, and he in turn was bullied by the family dead. If I feared him, he had Furies of his own – the ancestors and elderly relations who had set him standards by which he could do nothing except fail.

My father was not an eldest son, nor was his father. It must have been just his seriousness, his air of being the sort of young man who could take responsibility, his obvious dutifulness towards his own father, that marked him out. Whatever it was, it seemed that every dotty uncle and crusty great aunt had named him as an executor of their wills. Whenever anyone in the family died, my father got busy with auctioneers and lawyers; and our house began to fill with heirlooms. Vans arrived with furniture and pictures and papers in tin boxes. Things went 'into store', then had to be brought out because it cost too much to keep them in the repository. We were swamped by my father's ancestors.

They looked down on us disapprovingly from every wall. In vast, bad, oxidized oil portraits, in pencil-and-wash sketches, in delicate miniatures, in silhouettes, they glared dyspeptically from their frames. There was the Recorder of Bombay. There was General Sir Edward. There was Cousin Emma at her writing desk. There were countless Indian Army colonels and mean-mouthed clerics. There were General Sir Edward's military honours mounted on velvet in a glass case. On top of the wireless stood the family coat of arms (a raven, a boar's head, some battlements and a motto that I don't remember). They were joyless, oppressive trophies. They represented a hundred-and-something years of dim middle-class slogging through the ranks of the army and the church. The faces of these ancestors were like their furniture – stolid, graceless but well-made in that provincial English fashion which equates worth with bulk. There was no fun in them, and only the barest modicum of intelligence. They looked like people who had found the going hard, but had come through by sticking to the principles that had been drummed into them at boarding school.

We revered them, these implacable household goods. We tiptoed around their hideous furniture ('*Don't* play on the games table; it's an *an*tique – '); we ate our fish fingers with their crested forks; we obediently tidied our own lives into the few humble corners that were left behind by the importunate family dead. My father bought books on genealogy (*How to Trace Your Family Tree* by L. G. Pine), and buried himself in index cards and the 1928 edition of *Burke's Landed Gentry*. Summer holidays turned into sustained bouts of ancestor-worship of a kind that might have been more appropriate to a pious Chinese than to an English middle-class family on its uppers. In a Bradford Jowett van (my mother's Ford had been sold, and I now rode second class, in the back) we trailed through Somerset, hunting for churchyards where remote cousins were supposed to have been buried. My father scraped the lichens off tombstones with a kitchen knife, while I looked for slow-worms under fallen slates. On wet days, he took himself off to the record offices in Taunton and Exeter, where he ploughed through parish registers, checking births, marriages and deaths in eighteenth-century villages. 'We come,' he said, 'from yeoman stock. Good yeoman stock.'

Then there were the living to visit. Most seemed to be elderly women living with a 'companion', and they stretched, like a row of hill forts, across southern England from Sussex to Devon. Each holiday, my father appeared to discover a new great aunt. Their houses were thatched, and smelled of must and dog. The ladies themselves were mannish, always up to something in the garden with a hoe and trug. The few men were immobilized, wrapped up in rugs, and talked in fluting falsetto voices. My grandfather, Harry Priaulx Raban (grown-ups called him 'H.P.'), had retired from his parish in Worcester-shire to a Hampshire cottage where, on his good days, he used to celebrate an Anglo-Catholic mass of his own devising in a little room that he'd turned into an alfresco shrine. I sometimes acted as his server on these occasions, piping the responses to his piped versicles. A plain crucifix hung above the improvised altar, surrounded by framed photographs of Edwardian boys at Clifton College. At Prime and Compline and Communion, my grandfather paid homage to his own past in a way that had come to seem to me perfectly natural – for anyone in our family.

My father was barely thirty, yet we lived almost exclusively in the company of the old and the dead. Sometimes his old regimental friends would call, and there was a steady stream of youngish clergymen and colleagues from TocH; these contem-poraries brought a boisterous, irresponsible air into the house, a hint of fun which seemed alien to it. Its proper visitors were aunts and elderly cousins – people who nodded at the portraits on the walls and left their sticks in the rack by the front door. In private with my mother, my father had a lightness I have not done justice to. He liked *Punch,* and told stories, and spent a lot of time in the garage tinkering with the car: there was a boyishness about him which was always being forcibly squashed. The lugubrious solemnity was practised as a duty. He behaved as if it was incumbent on him to appear older, stuffier, more deferential than he really was. The silly world of gaiety and feeling was my mother's province, and I think my father felt a stab of guilt every time he entered it. It was *not manly*, not quite worthy of a serious Raban. So he overcompensated, with a surfeit of aunts and ancestors, and made his amends by constructing a vast family tree which he kept rolled up in a cardboard tube. Each year, new lines appeared; forgotten cousins many times removed were resurrected; our yeoman stock inched steadily back through the Georges and into the reigns of Queen Anne and Charles II.

I was five, then six, when my younger brothers were born. These additions to the tree struck me as needless. With ancestors like ours, who needed children? But I had been cuckolded before, and had learned to live with infidelity. Our household was already bulging with family, and my brothers simply added to the clutter. Though my own status was eroded. My mother constantly mixed up our names, and the two leaking babies and I got rechristened, for convenience's sake, as 'the boys', a title that made me cringe with humiliation. I hated their swaddled plumpness, their milky smell, and felt that their babyhood somehow defeated what little progress I had made in the direction of manliness. Lined up with them on the back seat of the Bradford van, surrounded by their cardigans, their leggings, their bootees, their plastic chamber pots and teated bottles, I used to daydream myself into a state of haughty solitude. I acquired a habitual manner of grossly injured dignity.

If I have a single image of family life, it is of a meal table. There is a high chair in the picture, dirty bibs, spilt apple puree, food chaotically laid out in saucepans, a squeal, a smack, my father's suffering brow creased with migraine, my mother's harassed face ('Oh, *Blow!*'), and the line 'William's made a smell' spoken by my younger brother through his adenoids. And over all this, the ancestors glower from their frames and the crested silver mocks from the tabletop. It isn't just the noise, the mess, the intrusive intimacies; it is that hopeless collision between the idea of Family as expounded by my father and the facts of family as we lived them out. We had ideas that were far beyond our means.

At this time my father must have been earning about £600 a year. Like most other lower-middle-class households, we were over-crowded, we had to make do on a shoestring budget and we had neither the money, the time nor the space for the dignities and civilities that my father craved. 'We are,' he reminded us, 'a family of *gentlemen*.' Was my teacher at school, I asked, a gentleman? No. A nice man, certainly, but not quite a gentleman. Was Mr Banham up the road a gentleman? No: Mr Banham was in trade. People in trade were not gentlemen, it was explained; it had nothing to do with money; it was a matter of caste, taste and breeding – and we were gentlemen. This distinction caused me a great deal of anxiety. The few friends I made never turned out to be gentlemen. Some were 'almost'; most were 'not quite'. Their fathers were often much better-paid than mine, their accents (to my ears) just as clear. My mother was always keen to stretch the point and allow all sorts and conditions of men into our privileged class; but my father was a stickler for accuracy and knew a parvenu when he saw one. Consequently I was ashamed of my friends, though my mother always welcomed them, at least into the garden if not into the house. They didn't have ancestors and family trees like ours, and I half-despised and half-envied them their undistinguished ordinariness. Once or twice I was unwise enough to let on that I was marked by a secret distinction invisible to the eye – and the consequences tended to support my parents' conviction that the state system of education was barbarous and fit only for young hooligans. I was, predictably (especially since I started to get asthma the moment I stopped having Coeliac), a thoroughly unpopular child. At primary school, I started to keep a score of the number of days I had lasted without crying in the playground. It stayed at zero, and I gave it up. But I always believed that I was bullied because I was 'special'. That too happened to you because you were a gentleman.

There was another family on our horizon. Uncle Peter – my mother's brother – lived on the suburban outskirts of Birmingham, and we saw him twice or three times a year. I was his godson, and after I was seven or eight I was occasionally allowed to stay at his house. For me, he was pure legend. Balding, affable, blasé, he would drop in out of the blue in a Jaguar car, smelling of soap and aftershave. Like my mother, Uncle Peter had been brought up by my grandmother in Switzerland, in the last days of servants; but somehow he had managed to escape being a gentleman. He'd taken a degree in engineering at Birmingham University, and during the war had served in the RNVR. If Macmillan had wanted a symbol of postwar meritocratic affluence in the age of You've-Never-Had-It-So-Good he might well have chosen Uncle Peter, with his car, his sailing boat, his first-in-the-road TV set and his centrally-heated suburban villa. Uncle Peter had real class – with a flat *a* – but he was entirely innocent of the suffocating class snobbery which ruled our roost.

Staying at Uncle Peter's was like being admitted to Eden. There was no smell of guilt in the air, no piety to a lost past. Where we had ancestors, he had Peter Scott bird-paintings and framed photos of ocean racing yachts on his walls. Where we had shelves of family books (sermons, Baker's *Sport in Bengal, The Royal Kalendar,* first editions of Jane Austen, a Victorian *Encyclopaedia Britannica*), Uncle Peter had copies of the *National Geographic* magazine, *Reader's Digest* condensed books and greenback Penguins. I had often been enchanted by the bright theatre of an illuminated department store window at dusk – the impossibly soft rugs, the virgin upholstery of the three-piece suite, the bottles and glasses set ready on gleaming coffee tables, the glow of steel standing lamps . . . a room designed for immaculate people without memories or consciences. The inside of Uncle Peter's house was like one of those windows come to life. It was my Brideshead. I was dazzled by its easy, expensive philistinism; dazzled, too, by my girl cousins with their bicycles and tennis rackets and the casual, bantering way in which they talked to their parents.

On Sunday morning, no one went to church. I half expected a thunderbolt to strike us down for our audacity, but in Uncle Peter's family church was for weddings, funerals, baptisms and Christmas. Instead, we sat out on the breakfast patio, sunbathing. Uncle Peter stretched himself out on a scarlet barcalounger, put on dark glasses, and settled into his *Sunday Express.* I was nearly delirious. I hadn't realized that it was possible to break so many taboos at once, and Uncle Peter was breaking them all without so much as a flicker of acknowledgement that he was doing anything out of the ordinary. I also felt ashamed. I was so much grubbier, more awkward, more screwed-up than these strange people with their Californian ease and negligent freedom; like any trespasser in Eden, I was always expecting to be given the boot.

Given his belief in stock and blood-lines, it would have been hard for my father to be too openly critical of Uncle Peter. My mother's family (doctors and Shetland crofters) was, of course, not quite up to Raban standards, but Uncle Peter was still definitely a gentleman. So my father limited himself to a few warning shots delivered from a safe distance. 'Don't suppose he gets more than 15 to the gallon out of *that car*.' 'Can't think what he must be paying for moorings for *that boat*.'

'He's always going abroad to conferences,' said my mother.

'One conference, dear. One conference that we actually *know* of.'

To me, he was spoken of as '*your* Uncle Peter', which gave me a certain pride of possession, as I happily took responsibility for the 3.8 Jag, the decanter of Scotch and *that boat*. At Christmas and on my birthday he sent postal orders, and I was briefly *nouveau riche*, happily about to squander the money on status symbols on my own account, like fixed-spool fishing reels and lacquered cork floats. 'You'd better put *that* in your post-office savings. Hadn't you, old boy?' So Uncle Peter was laid up where neither moth nor rust corrupted. I loathed my savings-book. When, years later, I first heard the phrase 'The Protestant Ethic', I knew exactly what it meant: it was my father's lectures on the subject of my post-office savings account.

'It's all very well, old boy, your wanting to throw your money down the drain on inessentials now. But when it comes to the time, what are you going to do about the Big Things, eh? Now, the money you've got in the post office; that *grows*. Sixpence on the pound mounts up, you know. Suppose . . . suppose, in, say, three or four years you want a bicycle. Where do you imagine that bicycle is going to come from? I'm afraid, old boy, that bicycles do not grow on trees.'

But in Selly Oak I had ridden in the Jag, and skipped church on Sunday, and a splinter of doubt had lodged in my mind. There were, I now knew, places in the world where bicycles did grow on trees.

When it was announced ('Daddy has had a calling') that my father was going to seek ordination, I lay on the floor and howled with laughter. I can't remember why – it certainly wasn't in any spirit of satire. I think it may have been straightforward nervous hysteria in the face of the fact that my father was on such intimate terms with God. The question had been put to Him, and He had made His position clear. It all sounded a bit like having an interview with one's bank manager. But I was awed and proud. We were high Anglicans – so high that we could almost rub noses with the Romans. The priest, in his purple and gold vestments, was a figure of glorious authority. He was attended by boys swinging incense. He chanted services in plainsong. High in the pulpit, his surplice billowing round him, he exercised a mystique of a kind that, say, a politician could not hope to match. Had my father said that he was going to stand for parliament, I would have been impressed; when he said he was going to be a priest, I was awestruck. I grew intensely vain on the strength of his vocation. I was not only a gentleman; I was about to be the son of a priest. When bullied in the playground, I now thought of myself as a holy martyr, and my brows touched heaven. 'Daddy's vocation' had singled him out from the ruck of common men, just as I expected soon to be singled out myself. I waited for my calling, and pitied my persecutors. At night I had vivid fantasies in which God and I were entwined in a passionate embrace. By day, I spent my time staring out of the classroom window in a fog of distraction. I was not a clever child. My distinction was a secret between myself, my ancestors and God.

My father was thirty-three – a year younger than I am now – when he became a theological student. For the first time in my life, I realized that he was not actually as old as he had always seemed. We took a rented house on the outskirts of Bognor, and my father bicycled the six miles between there and his college in Chichester, staying in the house only at weekends. He wore a college scarf and went about in cycle clips; he played for the college cricket team and swotted up his notes. Now that he was more often away from the family than inside it, he lost his irritable hauteur, and I began to lose my fear of him. On Saturday afternoons, my mother brought my brothers and me to support his team from the boundary, where we were the centre of a group of pious, hearty young men with the arms of their white sweaters tied round their necks. At college, I think my father must have recaptured some of the ease that he'd felt in his wartime regiment. Most of the other students were younger than him, and he was like an easygoing adjutant among subalterns. I sensed – again for the first time – that he was proud of his family, and we were proud of him.

For those two years we were 'living on capital' – an ominous phrase which meant, in effect, that my parents were blueing their post-office savings; and this hectic, once-in-a-lifetime gesture seemed to liberate and frighten them in equal parts. They went on a spree of economies, putting one gallon of petrol at a time in the car and buying everything in quantities so small that my mother appeared to be going shopping round the clock. They also hatched what was as far as I was concerned their greatest folly. They decided to scrape their last pennies together and send me to public school.

For once, I was happy at school. At Rose Green Primary I had made some friends (no gentlemen, but with my father now a student we were turning into daring bohemians). With private coaching, I muddled, a little improbably, through the eleven-plus, and had a place waiting for me at the grammar school in Chichester. But my parents were expecting to move house at least twice within the next three years, and at ten I had already attended four different schools (a dame, a prep and two primaries). That was the rational side. The irrational side was all to do with ancestors, gentility and manliness.

'Take this business of your asthma, old boy. It's all psychosomatic, you know. Psychosomatic. Know what psychosomatic means? In the head. It's all in the head. It means you bring it on yourself. Public school will clear that one up in no time.'

The brochure arrived. My father had been at King's in the 1930s, and we pored over the blotchy photos of rugger pitches and the cathedral green. My father showed a new, alarming levity; we were boys together as he pitched into a slightly mad peroration about the joys of doing 'The Classics' and taught me the basic rules of rugger on the drawing room carpet.

'Pass the ball behind you – like this. Always pass the ball behind, never in front.'

His own fondest memory of King's had to do with being put into a laundry basket and having his arm broken. Somehow as my father told it it came out as pure pleasure. Every Sunday we checked over the public school rugby results where they were listed in small print at the back of the *Sunday Times*. When King's won, there was a celebratory air around the breakfast table; when they lost we were downcast too. My mother had some Cash's name-tapes made up: J. M. H. P. RABAN SCHOOL HOUSE. In the evenings, she sewed them on to piles of socks, pants, shirts and towels, checking each item against the matron's printed list.

When we made our annual trek from aunt to aunt, I basked in the phrase, repeated like a litany, 'Ah – Jonathan's off to public school, you know.' God, I was special. Suddenly elevated out of 'the boys', I towered with distinction. I could barely speak to my old friends at Rose Green – common little boys who played soccer and went on Sundays, if they went at all, to nonconformist churches.

At my confirmation service, the Bishop of Chichester preached on a text from Paul's Epistle to the Ephesians:

> I therefore, the prisoner of the Lord, beseech you
> that ye walk worthy of the vocation wherewith ye are called.

No one that year was walking more worthily than me. Already I was nursing my own calling and talking regularly to God. I walked in imaginary vestments, a halo of distinction faintly glowing round my person.

As my father pointed out, sending me to public school was going to mean sacrifices – enormous sacrifices. My mother was not going to be able to buy clothes; my brothers would have to live in hand-me-downs; with the price of tobacco as it was, my father was going to have to think seriously about giving up his pipe. This did frighten me. Despite the fact that I was living in an ever-inflating bubble of persecuted egotism, it did break in on me that the probable result of all this sacrifice was going to be that I was going to let everybody down. At nights, I strained to see myself sprinting away from the scrum towards the touch-line to score the winning try for School House; but the picture would never quite come right. When my father talked about the famous 'house spirit', I was troubled by a stubborn image of myself skulking grubbily, shame-faced, on the fringe of things. I had always been the last to be picked for any side. Would public school really change that? I tried fervently to believe so but some germ of realism made me doubt it. Certainly I felt singled out for peculiar honours, but my vocation was for something priestly and solitary; it wasn't for team games. I was scared by the other children whom I now affected to despise – and the prospect of living in a whole houseful of my contemporaries was frightening. I was beginning to suspect that I had my limits, and my faith in miracles was shaky. But with General Sir Edward and his cronies on one side, and the hand-me-downs and shiny skirts on the other, I went off to King's, teased by the notion that it was I who was the sacrifice.

One memory of being miserable at boarding school is much like another – and none are quite believable. I went when I was eleven; I left when I was sixteen; and I spent an unhealthy proportion of that five years wishing that I was dead. The usual story. For the holidays, I came home to beat my puzzled younger brothers black and blue. I was their monitor; they were my fags. So I was able to share with my family some of the benefits of going to public school.

Our family life seemed full of anomalies and bad fits. There was the problem of my father's age – one moment he was boyish, the next testily patriarchal. There was the mismatch between our actual circumstances and our secret splendour. There was the constant conflict between the superior Victorian family to which we were supposed to belong and the squally muddle of our everyday life. We were short on education, short on money, short on manners; and the shorter we got, the taller grew our inward esteem. In the Anglican Church, and in the succession of clergy-houses that we moved to, we found a kind of objective correlative for our private, family paradoxes. In the 1950s, the Church of England had not changed all that much since George Herbert was a parish priest. It hadn't yet been hit by 'existential theology' or the decadent tomfoolery of the Charismatic Movement. It still stood firm on Parson's Freehold and the idea that the priest was third in line to the squire and the doctor. Even on urban housing estates, where churches were plonked down in the middle to be vandalized before they'd had a chance to be consecrated, the vicar was expected to behave as he would in an agricultural village. The Church was smiled on by the housing authorities presumably because it felt that it might introduce a cheery, villagey note of 'community' into these godforsaken places. Put a beaming cleric in dog-collar and cassock in Churchill Crescent or Keynes Road, and you are halfway to creating another Tiddle-puddle Magna. In one sense, the clergyman was expressly hired to be an anomaly. Like our family, the Church had a grand past but was down on its luck. Like our family, it was succoured by a sense of its own inner virtue and stature in the face of utter indifference from ninety per cent of the rest of the world. Like my own, its public face was one of superior injured dignity.

My father was given the curacy of a council estate just outside Winchester, and we turned into a parsonage family. To begin with, the ancestors were moved into a council house, disdainfully slumming it in the cramped lounge-diner. They had probably known worse. Long suffering, ox-like men, their schools, like mine, had prepared them for temporary quarters and outposts of Empire. The Weeke Estate was much like an Indian hill station, with hard rations, lousy architecture and nothing to speak of in the way of society. It was no accident that the one author whose works we possessed in their entirety, in the uniform Swastika edition, was Kipling.

The parsonage was an island. People came to it when they wanted *rites de passage* – to be baptized, married and buried. Or they were in distress: tramps with tall stories on the look-out for a soft touch; pregnant girls, dragged there by grave, ashamed parents; middle-aged women who cried easily; and lots of shadowy people, talking in low confessional voices beyond the closed doors of my father's study. When they came to the house, their manners were formal; often they had put on best suits for the occasion. What is it that people want from a priest?

Understanding, surely, but not ease or intimacy. Most of all, I suspect, they feel that only a priest can clothe a bitter private hurt or mess with the gravity and dignity that they would like it to deserve.

My father seemed cold and inhibited towards me as if he found our biological connection an embarrassment. But to his parishioners he was able to show a sympathy, even a warmth, that perhaps depended on the formal distance which lay between him and them. In mufti, he was often still and blundering. In the uniform of his cassock and his office, he was gentle and considerate. The very things that might have marked him as a misfit outside the priesthood enabled him to be a good priest. I've known a number of people who have told me how much they have admired him, been grateful to him, and thought of him as a consummately good man.

At that time, though, for me he was pure Jekyll and Hyde. I thought of him as a hypocritical actor. Offstage, he seemed to be perpetually irritable, perpetually swallowing aspirins, never to be disturbed. His study – a chaos of papers under a blue pall of St Bruno Rough Cut tobacco smoke – was a place I was summoned to, for a long series of awkward, sometimes tearful, occasionally violent interviews. Once I tried to knock him down, and in my memory he collapses in an amazed heap among the parish magazines, narrowly avoiding cracking his skull on the duplicating machine. But that is probably an Oedipal fantasy. What really happened, I'm afraid, is that the amazement was on my face, and that the collapse too was mine – into weeping apologies. Usually, though, these confrontations followed a pattern as cold and stereotyped as a chess gambit. I stood; my father sat, shuffling papers, filling his pipe. While he stared beyond me out of the window, he would talk with tired logic about my misdemeanours (terrible school reports, insolence, laziness in the house, rumours of girls). The final line was always the same.

'I'm afraid that the trouble with you . . . old boy . . . is that you appear to have no thought for anyone except yourself.'

Long, long pause. Sound of pipe dottle bubbling in a stem. A faint groan from my father. A muttered monosyllable from me.

'What did you say?'

'Sorry.'

'Sorry – *what?*'

'Sorry – *Daddy.*'

Another pause, while my father gazes sadly out over a landscape of sandpiles, stray dogs and upturned tricycles.

'I do wish you'd make *some* sort of an effort.'

I did see his point. The sacrifices that were being made on my behalf were all too visible. My father's clothes had been worn to a bluebottle sheen. His shoes gaped. And I was at public school. Worse, I knew that I was wrong, perhaps even evil, when I accused him of hypocrisy. Here he was, wearing himself through on my behalf, and driving himself to nervous exhaustion in the parish; what right had I to ask even more of a man who was clearly two-thirds of the way to being a living saint? It was further evidence – as if I needed any more – of my own selfishness. With the help of a Penguin book on psychology I diagnosed myself as a psychopath.

The parsonage became a refuge for a number of people who, as social casualties go, were the walking wounded. Most had been left stranded – as we had – in the wrong age or the wrong class. School-mistresses, social workers, district nurses, they attached themselves to the fringe of the family, dropping in unannounced with small presents and staying on into the night talking with my father. The closest, most persistent ones were made honarary aunts, and they liked to busy themselves in the house, clucking over my brothers, 'helping' my mother, and making strained conversation with me, until my father, his cassock flapping round his heels, came home from his rounds.

'Hello, dear!' Having spotted the parked Morris Minors round the corner, he had the cheeriness of someone walking through the French windows in a drawing room comedy. He always discovered the lurking aunts with delighted surprise. 'Ah, Elspeth!' And Miss Stockbridge, or Miss Winnall, or Miss Crawley, glandularly mountainous in tweeds, would produce a tiny, astonished little Bo-Beep voice – 'Oh, he*ll*o, Peter!' – as if their meeting was a stroke of wild coincidence. From my room upstairs, I would hear my father's 'Hmmm . . . hmmn . . . yes

. . . yes . . . yes . . . *Oh*, dear. Ah, ha-ha,' while the high, put-upon frequency of the adoptive aunt was lost to all except my father and the neighbourhood dogs.

Much later, when they'd gone, I'd hear my mother's voice. 'Oh, poor old Elspeth – the *poor* soul!' And my father would answer, 'I'm afraid the trouble with *that* one . . .'

The social worker's dealings with his client do have some formal limits. But with a clergyman, nothing is out of bounds. People came to my father for reassurances of a kind no doctor or psychiatrist could offer. This meant that everyone who arrived at the parsonage – even those who came in the guise of my parents' friends – presented themselves as crocks and casualties. The ones who came and came again had things wrong with them that were far too vague to ever cure. They were spiritual things – weaknesses and discontents for which the doctrine of the Resurrection was the only answer. My father had put himself in the position of Miss Lonelyhearts, but he had more pride and less saving cynicism than the columnist in Nathanael West's novel; and his view of this world to which he'd opened our door was one of compassionate condescension.

'We in the parsonage . . .' 'In the parsonage family . . .' 'As a son of the parsonage . . .' My father's lectures nearly always started out with one or other of these riders. We were expected to be exemplary. Our standards of moral and social decorum – unlike those of the natives among whom we'd been posted – were supposed to be beyond either criticism or pity. Another favourite was 'More people know Tom Fool than Tom Fool knows'; and I went about the council estate aware that it was full of spies behind curtains. One slip from me, and my father's standing in his parish could come a cropper. On the estate as on the rugger field, I was always letting our side down. At twelve and thirteen, up to no particular good with boys of my own age from the youth club, I sometimes came face to face with my father on his rounds, and pretended not to see him. He misinterpreted these gestures, and thought I was trying to 'cut' him. I wasn't. I was simply ashamed to be caught fraternizing with the children of his problem families – boys who, as he pointed out, had not had my advantages, and whose obvious shortcomings deserved compassion, not uncritical collusion.

On the far fringes of the parish, where the houses stood back from the road behind trees and rhododendrons, the gentry lived. Like the ancestors, they were retired colonels and commanders, admirals and generals. Their children went to boarding schools. Their houses smelled of flowers, dry sherry and wax polish. They weren't problem families; and we visited them shyly when bidden, like poor cousins, trying as best we could to tiptoe through their loud gravel. It usually took fifteen minutes for me to find myself out on the back lawn with their daughter, where we would both stand awkwardly scuffing our heels and smiling fiendishly.

'Do you play tennis?'

'No.'

'Oh what a pity. When Henry's here, we play a lot of tennis. But Henry's at Dartmouth, you know.'

'Oh, dear.'

'Mummy said she thought you might play tennis.'

'I'm sorry.'

'Oh – not to worry!'

Desperation. With an hour to kill, we would inspect abandoned tree-houses like a pair of undertakers visiting a cemetery on their day off.

'I say, you didn't hear a bell, did you?'

'I don't think so.'

'I could have sworn . . . I suppose Mrs Hawkins must be late with tea. Awfully boring for you, I'm afraid.'

'Oh, no! No, no, no!'

'Are you in YF?'

'Er . . . I don't think so.'

'Ah, there's the bell. Good-oh.'

Then, quite suddenly in the middle of the 1950s, a lot of bells began to ring. The first one I remember hearing was Frankie Lymon singing 'I'm not a juvenile delinquent', which went to the top of the hit parade sometime in 1955, I think. Bill Haley and his Comets made their first British tour, and in Worcester, where I was at school, there was hardly a seat left intact after *Rock Around The Clock* was shown at the Gaumont. I read *Look Back In Anger*, Joyce's *Portrait of the Artist*, and Anouilh's

Antigone, and somehow managed to muddle them together into a single work of which I was the hero. There was the Chris Barber band and the Beaulieu Jazz Festival. There was CND, which for me meant the triumphant end of the CCF. All at once it was possible to think of oneself as a member of a generation and not as a member of a family; and the generation provided me with new standards that were even more liberated than Uncle Peter's. It seemed that overnight my minuses had all changed to pluses. The generation loathed my ancestors even more than I did; it despised team games; its heroes were sulky, sickly solitaries like Juliette Greco in her death-mask phase. At sixteen, I discovered that the inchoate mess of my relations with my father had been all the time, unknown to me, a key battle in the coming revolution. And I was on the winning side. It was like having my dream of scoring the winning try in the house match come true. We continued to have rows – about my wearing a CND badge at family meals, about bringing *that* rag into *this* house (the *New Statesman* into the vicarage), about girls ('Not really the kind of girl you'd wish to introduce to Mummy, is she?'), about the width of my trouser-bottoms (18″ was permissible, but 16″ was 'teddy boy'). But I too now wore an expression of distant superiority through these wrangles. An outsider looking in might have seen us as a pair of quarrelling mirror-images – two glazed faces speaking in the accents of the same old school.

I was much too absorbed in the enthralling process of my own adolescence to notice that bells had began to ring for my father too. Something happened. Perhaps it came about on his parish rounds, as he found himself drawn in to the tangle of other people's lives, unable, finally, to maintain his distance. Perhaps it had to do with the difficulties he found himself in when he skirmished with the local worthies who regarded the church as an extension of their own drawing rooms. Perhaps he just strayed one day from under the oppressive shadow of the family past and found the air clearer and the going easier. At any rate, he changed. The first thing to go was his Anglo-Catholicism, which he dropped in favour of a kind of basic, ecumenical Christianity. Sometime in the 1960s, he slipped out of his ancestral family Toryism and became a Labour voter. He exchanged his living in a Hampshire village for a vast parish of tower blocks in Southampton. His passion for ancestor-hunting turned into a scholarly interest in social history. On holiday one year, he grew a beard. It was as if a row of buttons on a tight waistcoat had suddenly given way.

I have written about him as if he was dead – the Oedipal fantasy again. But when we see each other now, I find it hard to detect more than shadows of the man I remember as my father. The ancestors are still hanging on the walls of his vicarage, but they have the air of inherited lumber now, and have lost their power to hex. We talk easily. We both think of ourselves as victims of our upbringing – and beneficiaries of it too. The solitariness of his priesthood and my writing is a shared legacy: we have each had to learn how to be alone in society in the practice of our odd, anomalous crafts. A little more than ten years ago, we both suddenly realized that we were chips off the same family block – and I think that the discovery surprised him as much as it did me. When I showed my father this piece in galley-proof, he said: 'What you've written here is really a confession on my behalf.'

It is certainly a confession on mine. Looking at the other man, it occurs to me that he may have been a wilful invention of my own. Did I conceive him on the green when I was three as a jealous, defensive fiction? And did I let this fiction die only when I was old enough to leave the family and do without a father to be afraid of?

Perhaps. I don't know. 'There's some *slight* exaggeration – I hope,' my father said, handing me back my galley sheets. I'm afraid so.

April 1977

The Savage Sideshow:
A Profile of Angela Carter

—— LORNA SAGE ——

Angela Carter's fictions prowl around on the fringes of the proper English novel like dream-monsters – nasty, erotic, brilliant creations that feed off cultural crisis. She has taken over the sub-genres (romance, spies, porn, crime, gothic, science fiction) and turned their grubby stereotypes into sophisticated mythology. Two writers she admires, John Hawkes and J. G. Ballard, are useful reference points for mapping out her imaginative territory, but she has written less trash than Ballard, and is a lot less fey and self-regarding than Hawkes has become. Like them, though, she writes aggressively against the grain of puritanism-cum-naturalism, producing adult fairy tales. She combines the compulsive qualities of children's stories with self-conscious and parodic wit. Increasingly she has become an analyst of mythologies, a sceptical fantasist who performs Frankensteinish experiments on her characters, and on her readers' sensibilities. She is fascinated above all by narcissism and by excess, and takes decadence rather shockingly for granted. Her last two novels have been about what happens when ordinary reality finally withers away, and people's uncontrolled wishes and fears have their chance.

Her first novels, however, misbehaved themselves in a way that was more titillating than offensive. *Shadow Dance* (1966) seemed a pure emanation of the sixties – a beauty-and-the-beast story, obsessed with appearances; the main locale was a junk shop full of Victorian lavatory chains and theatrical costumes, and the style likewise was cruelly knowing about the past. The plot was, literally, murder. *The Magic Toyshop* (1967) performed scandalous variations on a stock children's story motif, with a clean, dreamy orphan heroine plunged into deprivation and dirt, learning to pit her precocious wits against a wicked uncle who keeps lifesize puppets in the basement, and casts her as Leda in his climactic production of 'Leda and the Swan'. Critics spotted perhaps a successor to Iris Murdoch or Muriel Spark; at any rate *The Magic Toyshop* won the John Llewellyn Rhys Memorial Prize, and her next, *Several Perceptions* (1968), won the Somerset Maugham Award. Again, there were variations on a theme: Joseph, the hero, tries to end it all in Chapter I by igniting the gas like Beckett's Murphy, but is forced against what's left of his will to come back into the 'real' world, which consists of an excessively lifelike collection of characters: a derelict violinist, a richly ageing whore, an ex-actress, a psychosomatic cripple and an analyst who says things like, 'You're wedged in the gap between art and life' and 'Try to get plenty of fresh air'.

Anthony Burgess's tribute to *Shadow Dance* indicates pretty exactly the quality of all three novels:

> I've read this book with admiration, horror, and other relevant emotions, including gratitude that we seem to have here a very distinctive talent that's going to be a major one. Angela Carter has remarkable descriptive gifts, a powerful imagination and – what I admire and envy more than anything – a capacity for looking at the mess of contemporary experience without flinching.

More than that, she was entirely at home in the 'mess', the distinctive sixties atmosphere of doomed euphoria and *déjà vu*. From the beginning, places and people were subtly unreal and ominous. The writing was lucid, exact and unnatural:

> The muted and elegiac light seemed to be that filling a dead city. It was the light of the city of dream-come-true. Morris felt like his own shadow, moving silently past windows where television sets glowed whitely, bluely; where roses spread in a red, yellow and pink plastic fan in lustre vases; where plaster Alsatian dogs romped between plush curtains. They saw hardly another walker. A girl in shorts whirled by on a beautiful, young bicycle. A car slid by with cushions on its wheels. That was all.

This (from *Shadow Dance*) is an unusually quiet paragraph, probably because it heralds the horrid denouement; however, it reveals all the better the way life imitates art and takes on a synthetic bloom (lustre and plush) in her urban pastoral, even when there are few obvious signs of literary borrowing (the 'beautiful, young bicycle' belonged originally I think to *Lolita*). Shadowy Morris, like all the central characters in these books, has a choice between being merely unreal and spectacularly so, dressing up and acting an heroic part.

She had found a near-perfect formula, it seemed. Her next novel, *Heroes and Villains* (1969), boldly ditched it, and took off into gothic/sf allegory: the cataclysm suspended over the city streets has happened, and the shrunken world of the new Dark Ages is divided between Professors and Barbarians who raid the official culture from time to time. The student drop-outs, King's Road peacocks and junk-collectors of the earlier novels, have inherited the earth; the truths of history are pored over by scholarly relativists in high, quiet towers (where they often commit suicide), while out in the wilderness the Barbarians assemble a theatrical, flea-bitten patchwork out of the remnants of past, present and future. Probably the most striking consequence of accelerating the dissolution of traditional mores is that sex-roles come out reversed. Beautiful boys, called things like Jewel and Precious ('The Barbarians used whatever forenames they found lying about, as long as they glittered and shone and attracted them'), are described caressingly and coolly as sexual objects. The heroine, a hard-hearted deserter from the Professors named Marianne (a corrupted Alice in wonderland, as are most of Angela Carter's innocently-named girls), battles with Jewel, enjoys him and uses him up, before taking over the show.

Looking back, Angela Carter herself dates a turning-point in her career from *Heroes and Villains*: one of the reviewers, she said, observed while relishing the book, that she wouldn't be winning any more prizes. Both its method and its sexual fantasy were aggressive, and the self-possession of the writing now added to the offence. She suddenly *belonged* less. And in 1969 she uprooted herself, and went to Japan, but not before she had completed *Love*. In many ways it is her most faultless novel, since it combines the exotic detail of the allegories with the elegant, obsessive structure of an eternal triangle. The setting is back in the present, so is done with easy cunning: provincial glitter, pubs, clubs, working-class idlers and middle-class art-school dropouts – a casual, intense network of relationships, more holes than mesh. The central trio, Buzz, Lee and Annabel, sometimes one incestuous organism, at other times in violent conflict, act out the decay of experience into theatre. Annabel especially retreats (or advances) so far into fantasy that the two men become little more than surreal figures in her paintings and, when she gives up painting, in her day-dreams. She manufactures childhood memories of magical powers:

> Little Annabel slipped out of the grocer's while her mother discussed the price of butter and played in the gutter for a while until she decided to wander into the middle of the road. A car braked, skidded and crashed into a shop front. Annabel watched the slivers of glass flash in the sunshine until a crowd of distraught giants broke upon her head, her mother, the grocer in his white coat . . . all as agitated as could be imagined. 'You might have been killed!' said her mother. 'But I wasn't killed, I was playing,' said Annabel, no bigger than a blade of grass, who had caused all this huge commotion all by herself just because she could play games with death.

Passively, crazily, she makes things happen, until she becomes such a connoisseur of unreality that her climactic sexual betrayal of Lee with his brother Buzz can only be a scrabbling, savage travesty. Then, with perfect logic, she undoes the world by dying, 'a painted doll, bluish at the extremities'. The novel is particularly unnerving in its insidious description of Annabel's cosmos (and Lee's and Buzz's): their fictions cover the ordinary universe with an oily patina that sets, becomes opaque, and demands to be treated as real. The result is a kind of psychological dandyism. Characters wear their inner lives on the outside – Lee has his heart painfully tattooed on his chest.

Love was published in 1971, by a new publisher, Hart-Davis. (Angela Carter's nomadic habits with publishers seem to confirm her general air of displacement: first Heinemann, then Hart-Davis, then Quartet, and now Gollancz. When I rang Gollancz, I was told they knew more or less nothing about her, which of course is not unusual, but it meant that reviewers of her latest novel weren't equipped with the usual battery of reprinted raves, with predictable results.) On her return from Japan in 1972, she published *The Infernal Desire Machines of Doctor Hoffman*, her most ambitious novel to that date, and her most demanding – a magical anatomy of cultures and institutions in which mythical creatures rub shoulders with historically solid ones, and questions about animal, vegetable or mineral are hard to answer. Doctor Hoffman (a cross between Norman O. Brown and Frankenstein) fiendishly plots to liberate the unconscious, and, starting with things crawling out of mirrors, all possible creatures become actual. Centaurs have a social and religious organization as watertight as (say) river Indians described by a conscientious anthropologist. The encyclopedism works only because each milieu, whether it originates from Hollywood or *The Golden Bough* or an innocent Greek epic, is portrayed with tongue-in-cheek sociological expertise, and fascinated relish. Impossible objects have (at least) three solid dimensions – witness the archetypal prostitutes, caught like baroque sculptures in the process of turning into beasts, vegetables and machines:

> . . . if some were antlered like stags, others had the branches of trees sprouting out of their bland foreheads and showed us the clusters of roses growing in their armpits when they held out their hands to us. One leafy girl was grown all over with mistletoe but, where the bark was stripped away from her ribcage, you could see how the internal wheels articulating her went round.

These androids, somewhere between Bernini and the Bunny Club, aren't a bad emblem of the many worlds of *Hoffman*. There's more myth-breaking going on than myth-making, but the plot, which has reverted to the primitive form of the quest, keeps just ahead of the demolition, until the final cataclysm when the Doctor himself (who turns out to be a dull fanatic with the world's largest orgone box) is tracked down and destroyed.

With *Hoffman*, she became more self-conscious, having been excessively so to start with. The structure is looser, the exhibits wilder, and subjected to more analysis. The trees with breasts and carnivorous flowers that flourished in Annabel's paintings in *Love*, for instance, really grow in *Hoffman* in a mockery of

Eden. And in a brief afterword to her collection of tales, *Fireworks*, in 1974, she took the unusual step of to some degree explaining herself: the tales were a series of decorative abstractions ('I was living in a room too small to write a novel in'), and had the advantage of obvious fictionality:

> . . . the tale cannot betray its readers into a false knowledge of everyday experience . . . Its style will tend to be ornate, unnatural, and thus militate against the perennial human desire to believe the word as fact . . . I was living in Japan; I came back to England in 1972. I found myself a new country. It was like waking up, it was a rude awakening. We live in Gothic times. Now, to understand and to interpret is the main thing; but my method of interpretation is changing.

Part of that change is certainly the increasingly grotesque, and yet increasingly recognizable (borrowed, parodied) range of her symbolism, so that she seems bent on a general stocktaking, from the earliest innocent icons to their latest camp revivals. In the last three years or so she has been working on a book on De Sade, another sign perhaps that she's investigating the roots of her rootless dandies of the void. Her latest novel, *The Passion of New Eve*, carries on where *Hoffman* left off, and she sees it as the second instalment of a trilogy of 'speculative novels'. The setting is America, but an America disintegrating into a barbarous New World, and the plot is again a quest leading through 'a series of enormous solipsisms, a tribute to the existential freedom of the land of free enterprise'. Hollywood dominates the imagery, but Lilith, Tiresias, Oedipus are there too. The object of the quest is to track down sexual archetypes to their grisly lairs, to reclaim them from the ad-men and late-night thirties movies, and set them in motion. To rescue our shop-soiled and conflicting and vulgar myths for the imagination.

At the moment Angela Carter is completing a year as writer in residence at Sheffield University, and has been profanely re-writing classic fairy tales. She writes too for *New Society*. When she came recently to the University of East Anglia to read a story (Red Riding Hood, revised through gradual and immensely ingenious transformations, until she learns to take on the Wolf) she demonstrated her personal talent for shape shifting, being tall, spare and cropped as though for some tough expedition, whereas the only previous time I'd seen her, not long before, she'd had elf-locks and looked almost fragile. Her reading was triumphantly insidious: one effect was that several puzzled students demanded to know where she and her accent came from, since she read with a curiously un-English, innocent, flat lilt, that showed off her meticulous syntax to unfair advantage. All questions were answered decidedly; questions about the origins of symbols got a businesslike response: books read, films seen, footnotes noted. The inevitable unenchanted smart-ass got his nose metaphorically bloodied; as she says, she doesn't bring out in an audience much of the gallantry traditionally accorded lady writers. She clearly enjoys the fact, as she enjoys reading her work, and laments that prose writers are seldom asked to.

Interviewed, she was patient, also canny and disarming. She informed me that she was much more sane and sensible than I'd expected, which was true; like the students, I'd looked for more eccentricity and more aggressive assertions out of the blue yonder. We began with where she feels she belongs:

I always felt foreign in England, and I realized the reason I'd always felt foreign was that I was. My father's not into Scottishness at all, he married an English wife and had English children, and he never did things like go to St Andrew's Nights – because he was *Scottish* you understand. And also we come from a very un-Scottish part of Scotland, classic English colonial Scotland . . . My father points occasionally at a low range of hills in the distance, and says things like 'Look at the glory of the sunset over the Cairngorms,' but I don't think they *are* the Cairngorms. I started sending him histories of Scotland, and he dutifully glanced through them because he loves me; I said to him, 'Did you like them, father?' and he said, 'I couldn't read them, they were too bloody depressing,' which is his attitude to the history of his people. He never perceived himself as Scottish, as being different, but it *is* different, I think.

But you were born English?

Do you want the anecdotage? My little brother was evacuated from South London to Sussex at the beginning of the war, and my mother went with him, and since she was carrying me I had no option. They took the whole caravanserai, my mother and my Yorkshire granny. My mother went into labour as Dunkirk fell, and Eastbourne became the front line. My granny said, there's one place in England we shall all be safe, and that's my home town. Which is the village of Wath-upon-Dearne near Rotherham in South Yorkshire. Even the most rugged and insensitive of South Yorkshiremen shudders at the names of Wath-upon-Dearne and Mexborough. It was mining, totally – a one-horse street. My granny rented a cottage (I don't know how she got it, actually, because it was National Coal Board) next door to my great aunt Sophie and great uncle Sid, and that was where granny and me and my brother and occasionally my mother spent the duration.

You've made joky references to being a 'good socialist' – do you think your environment shaped you?

Well, my brother and I speculate endlessly on this point. We often say to one another, How is it possible such camp little flowers as ourselves emanated from Balham via Wath-upon-Dearne and the place my father comes from, north Aberdeenshire, stark, bleak and apparently lugubriously Calvinistic, witch-burning country? But, obviously, something in this peculiar rootless, upward, downward, sideways socially mobile family, living in twilight zones . . . I do actually believe that everybody is the product of their environment, and you get the seeds of how you transcend your environment from the environment itself. My mother's family were great examination-passers . . . and the last time I was in Scotland, I knew there was a book I'd read sometime that would explain the mystery of my family to me, and it was *The Rainbow*. Everything in it slotted into place, not literally – my mother left school at fifteen and worked in Selfridges, nothing in it correlates to any actual experience in my family – but the whole business of moving into the rootless, anomic, Bohemian bourgeoisie from

very secure roots explained a lot to me. It's one of the great
novels of social mobility . . .

*(Granny she recalls as a 'South Yorkshire matriarch' with an innate
conviction of the irreducible superiority of women, 'though she could
only just count – she couldn't give her quality to her daughters'.
Among her mother's most embarrassing memories were prize days –
'Grandfather came wearing his Kier Hardie hat, Gran with "Votes for
Women" on her lapel'. She herself passed the eleven plus, and went to
a direct grant school in South London, which her mother thought
suspect, because some people paid, which meant their kids were
probably stupid.)*

What did your family think of your writing?

I'm going to tell you an anecdote which always seems to me to
explain my family. When my brother, who trained as a
musician, was being interviewed for I think the Guildhall School
of Music, when he was about fifteen, the bloke in charge of
admissions asked my mother when he had started playing the
piano, and my mother said, 'Oh, when he could toddle, he
started playing tunes.' 'You mean with one finger?' 'Oh, no,
with both hands, and he'd hum the tunes . . .' And the man
said, 'Didn't you think that was rather unusual?' And mother
said, 'Oh, not in my family!' And very, very much later, when
I'd had some novels published, and my mother had been
prowling around I think Harrods book department, and she'd
noticed that my books were on the same display as Iris Murdoch's, she said to me, 'I suppose you think that makes you an
intellectual?'

A strong-minded woman?

She wasn't, that's the difficult thing . . . Basically we were an
eccentric family, and the fact that I had been scribbling away
and writing stories since almost as soon as I could write my
mother regarded as a perfectly normal activity for a child, just
as she regarded my brother playing the piano . . . My father

didn't notice, so it was never regarded as any kind of achievement.

Were you influenced by what you read, Gothic novels, for instance?

When I started writing, I was six, I'm afraid . . .

I didn't mean then, but later, did you have a sense of yourself as a particular kind of writer?

No, I didn't, I thought I was a social realist. In a very deep sense, I'm spectacularly illiterate. Well, yes, I'm an auto-didact . . . Actually, another anecdote about my mother illustrates the literate illiteracy of my home: when she caught me reading cheap novels, she used to say, 'Don't let me catch you reading novels, you remember what happened to Emma Bovary.' We were on first-hand terms with these people.

So your books don't relate very directly to a tradition?

There's been no cultural Scottishness around at all, but when I read Hogg, *Confessions of a Justified Sinner*, the landscape was immediately familiar to me, just like *Wuthering Heights*. I won't say my Yorkshire relations behave in exactly that fashion – they don't, and south Yorkshire's a long way from the moors – but the personality of Heathcliff was similar to people like my uncle Arthur; he married a Catholic girl, and the priest told her she was living in sin, so Arthur went round and roughed up the priest . . . These giant emotions were what life was made of. I remember in my childhood climaxes of violent parental strife, and then acres of boredom. The first writers that I read with excitement and conviction were Elizabethan and Jacobean dramatists, when I was about fifteen – *A Chaste Maid in Cheapside, Women Beware Women* and *A Trick to Catch the Old One*. Then we had this very good French teacher, and we did *Les Fleurs du Mal* and *Phèdre*, and the minute I read Racine, I knew that it moved me much more savagely than Shakespeare . . . plus the hint of Calvinism, the Jansenism. Anyway at this point I was completely lost to the English tradition. Anybody who's had a stiff injection of Rimbaud at eighteen isn't going to be able to cope terribly well with Philip Larkin, I'm afraid. There must be more to life than this, one says. It made the circumstances of my everyday life profoundly unsatisfactory. Later the surrealists had the same effect. One's washing around with all these things going on in one's head, and there are all these people unmoved by the notion. The savage sideshow.

(At or around eighteen she had anorexia, though it hadn't been fully invented; she got down to six stone something in a classic attempt to postpone womanhood, or whatever. She was working as a reporter at the time, and only recognized what she had when she reported a psychiatrist on someone else. In 1962 she went to Bristol to read English, and specialized in medieval literature.)

Were you part of a particular set at Bristol?

The Bristol renaissance? Of course not . . . I worked in an art gallery in the summer holidays; I think I saw Tom Stoppard across a crowded room once. But that was the provincial glamour circuit, and I wasn't on that at all. I was a wide-eyed provincial beatnik, and there were a lot of them around.

What did you do about your writing?

I wanted to publish it. My father was a journalist, and I mean, it's like the right true end of love. And also I was a reporter after I left school, and therefore there was no magic about seeing your name in print. I still do think that a book isn't finished until it's published. This was all very crude and incoherent in my mind because I wanted to be published anyway for reasons of psychological compulsion, to validate myself. I love about academics the way they say, 'I'm working on a book' – without any idea of the marketing, I find that very sweet . . . Sometimes when you say to people you're a writer, they say, 'Have you had anything published?' Which is a bit like saying to an actor, 'Have you ever been on the stage?' Because if it's not published, it doesn't exist.

How old were you when Shadow Dance *came out?*

I was twenty-six. I thought I was a has-been, actually, because when I was growing up it was the era of the child prodigy . . . Sagan, for instance. There were a whole crop of young writers, a lot were one-shotters. Then there was Shena Mackay, whom I do think is good. But the people I thought were *good* were Dostoevsky . . . and Colette – a corrupting influence. What's wrong with a lot of women is that they don't read enough Colette at an impressionable age. It's always been a problem for me to judge, because I'd think that, say, Joyce was good, and a whole lot of people were getting published and acclaimed who weren't as good as Joyce . . . or Flaubert . . .

'Gothic' writers are notorious for having good ideas and awful prose styles. Where did you acquire your polish?

That must have been from French. I'm quite distressed I'm too old, I'll never be able to write in French. It's the structure of sentences – French has got a much more subtle grammar than English, English grammar is very clumsy. In French you need fewer adjectives, you can do so much more with the subjunctive and the passive and what have you. If you do it in English it does sound odd.

Love *seems almost effortlessly written – the description of places and streets . . .*

That was my tribute to Balzac. There's a paragraph that begins 'In the street where the brothers lived with their aunt, during their childhood, it always seemed to be Sunday afternoon'. It's a real street, and usually I describe locations with that sort of detail when they are unreal, imaginary . . . It sounds very quaint, but one of the books I keep referring to is *The Princess and the Goblin* by George Macdonald . . .

The goblins with the soft feet?

Well any Freudian . . . And also there's a set of fairy tales, one about the giant who kept his heart in a paper bag. Well I do keep referring back, because he's got some iconographic imagery of a startling nature: the id-y goblins, and the very nice young working-class boy who actually only appears in a parody version – Lee in *Love*.

Nice? I found him frightening. Or at least it was a shock, when I first read Heroes and Villains, *I think to find savage, beautiful boys like Jewel – or Lee – described so fetchingly.*

But he was supposed to be nice . . . It's funny actually – I was discussing this with a gay friend. One of the things I was doing then unconsciously and am now doing consciously is describing men as objects of desire. I think a lot of the ambivalence of response I get is because I do this . . . But these flowers, you know, you can reach out your hand and touch them, and they'll *crumble* I tell you. It's lies, it's lies what your mother told you. They turn into grovelling masses, they go and they scrub out the lavatory . . . Well, my gay friend said Jewel wasn't his type, but nevertheless he could see what I was getting at, and he thought I'd succeeded, and he looked forward with pleasure to the time when I'd get around to describing his type.

One's not supposed to attend this way to male appearances? Men are supposed to be creatures of sensibility?

But men have been doing this to women in fiction and in poetry since the year dot.

There's a brand of feminist argument that says we should teach them not to do it?

Part of the 'remorseless dialectic' is to do it back to them – and also I think that sexual conflict is what-makes-the-world-go-round, is what produces the tensions that any society needs to continue forward, rather than just hanging around like the *'eeppies*, just lolling around in their own ooze.

Why French hippies?

French hippies are the most noxious in the world, they're all appearance and no essence, even worse than the Americans.

But your people's appearances are their essence?

Of course, it's a world of appearances. I call this materialism.

This character covered in skins and mirrors – you call this materialism?

Well, there's a bit that's very important in that novel, when they're walking across the beach, and Marianne says to him, 'You're a phallic and diabolic version of female beauties of former periods,' and of course that's what he is, though in fact he doesn't want to be – he's *id.* But you see, one of the things I love about Charlotte Brontë, about *Jane Eyre*, is that she won't *look* at Rochester until she's castrated him, he doesn't stand a chance. In fact she hasn't castrated him, she's given him a vasectomy – it's obvious that she retains the sexual use of him, therefore it's a peculiarly feminine and applaudable version. And also she's very nice to him, she can afford to be, this is where she can start behaving like a human being. Actually, in Freudian terms (not Freudian, Freud would be terribly upset) what she's done is to get him on an egalitarian and reciprocal basis, because in fact she hasn't castrated him at all, she's got rid of his troublesome *machismo.*

What do you mean by 'Freudian'? Surely he'd want to make you better?

I don't think he would. Like a lot of people, I love Freud as though he were an uncle. He'll go on and on about envy, then he'll sit down and write a letter to Lou Andreas-Salomé discussing all these concepts, and she'll have a think and write back, and go straight out and castrate Rilke – no problem. Obviously, like those racists who don't notice their best friends are black, he made a mental reservation for those women he knew and admired and respected, and who behaved in a very peculiar fashion. He must have noticed looking round his classes that they were full of these mad women. I think Juliet Mitchell's book on Freud is very good. You can't jump out of your time, he could only think of women as castrated men because he couldn't think any further. I mean I use 'Freudian' in the crass, popular sense, meaning unconscious imagery expressed in conscious actions and conscious imagery.

You, though, are a re-writer – you take myths and turn them inside out.

I have excellent precedents for this, from Shakespeare on . . . But I have done it consciously, because I do think we're at the end of a line, and to a certain extent I'm making a conscious critique of the culture I was born to. In a period like this of transition and conflicting ideologies, where there isn't a prevalent ideology, really all artists can do is to go round mopping up.

As in The Passion of New Eve, *and* Hoffman?

I can see *Hoffman* as an inventory of imaginary cities, and it's got quite a well worked out science-fictionish schema. But I embarked on this project of three speculative novels, and genre-wise there's a bit of everything in them. There are passages in *Hoffman* that still give me enormous pleasure – a French Legion fort out of *Beau Geste* and a rather Wagnerian castle at the end. It had a great vogue in the underground. The Moroccan acrobats who take themselves apart are called The Acrobats of Desire, and there's a rock group in Sheffield who call themselves that, which gave me great pleasure. They don't know me at all.

The structures of these books present some problems.

I suppose the picaresque is a mode I fall into, because you can get so much in, you can talk one minute about a castle, the next about a railway station, and move through space and time, with just the structure of the journey.

The images exert a static pull, though, like the revolving glass house in Eve?

Well, yes, it's a centrifuge, and America is a glass culture, but the revolving house, the whirling tower, is in Celtic mythology, it's a very antique image. That's one of the things about delving around in obscure corners.

Perhaps your most extraordinary images are the mechanical humans . . .

I don't systematically construe my own images as I go along. I mean I would like to be able to say that the clockwork prostitutes and the puppets are man under capitalism, but it's not consciously been so. They're not dehumanized by being that way, but that sort of parodic imitation of life, the closed system, the clockwork prostitutes going through the motions and being dependent on somebody else for their motive power . . . I think if I think about it I may spoil it, but the connections are obvious, they are women in a certain relation to men, when men are in a certain kind of relation to the economic system they live in.

We seem to come back to your expertise in appearances, outsides.

Everybody's appearance is their symbolic autobiography. I'm a part-time sociologist of fashion – I'm very interested in the iconography of clothes and gestures.

That must connect with going to Japan?

Well, I don't know what I got from Japan, or what it did to me. Yes, in that it's a country that is absolutely superficial, in the sense that they have no metaphors, the action is the man. I remember talking to a Japanese friend about hypocrisy as the British vice, and he said he thought hypocrisy was smashing, a tremendous moral regulator. Imagine: a man walks by a canal where a child is drowning, and in order to sustain the notion in the world that he is brave and good and kind, he leaps into the canal to save the child. He thought this was a beautiful paradox. He was incapable of understanding the nature of hypocrisy. Obviously, the Japanese love existentialism, Sartre's hit them like a bomb. They know it intuitively, that's what they knew life was about. It made me realize how much better, how much morally better, people are in a world without God.

Why?

Well, the man by the canal can't apologize to God about why he walked slightly on – 'I thought I would meet a man with a boat' or whatever – he can't make these specious rationalizations, he's got to explain to the parents of the child why he let it drown, which you can't do with any grace. All his actions are in the world of men, and are interpreted by the world of men, and therefore he cannot lie in an action. If you can't rationalize yourself out of behaving badly, you've got to behave well.

You feel one needs still to be anti-God?

Oh yes! It's like being a feminist, you have to keep the flag flying. Atheism is a very rigorous system of disbelief, and one should keep proclaiming it. One ought not to be furtive about it.

De Sade in this context is a hero?

I think a lot of the disrepute in which he's held springs from his irascible contempt for human folly. He can forgive man anything but his folly and his rationalizations. What I would really like to do if I had the intellectual energy would be a book about the morality of cruelty. Sade was the great influence on the romantics, they'd all read him.

As Mario Praz says in The Romantic Agony?

Yes, except that I don't think Praz *had* read him. Nietzsche is directly descended from Sade, without Sade's humanism. Sade's ideas about women, when he's not being mad and ironic and satirical, are very progressive for the time, and indeed are still quite progressive. He did think it was awful to hang women for procuring abortions, which they did at the time – inconceivably wicked, almost as wicked as getting pregnant . . . But he could understand that sometimes that happened to them in an involuntary fashion, and they needed an abortion . . .

(At this point, our tape ran out, and Angela Carter had to catch a train. There are, though, a few additional and relevant jottings: on women – 'lots of my sisters are still looking for Mr Right, or Miss Right, which is the same thing, or the great commune in the sky'; they have been 'the oppressed of the oppressed', and behave accordingly, witness their historical role as strike-breakers; there is a line that has always haunted her as a memento of men's dealings with women, from The Testament of Cresseid *by the Scottish Chaucerian Henryson, 'When Diomed had all his fill and more' is how she quotes it; actually, it goes 'Quhen Diomed had all his appetyte,/And mair, fulfillit of this fair ladie', which is no less cruel or ominous. Clearly for her it stands for one of the basic plots of experience, and explains why sexual conflict doesn't cease. As for more recent slogans, she uses them with heavy quotation marks and double irony, so that it's visible that for her they remain true, but absurd. E.g., 'The imagination must seize power'. Parody of this kind is a usual conversational mode with her: interpreting the troubled female household my daughter and I share, she read its signs with cruel accuracy as 'tea bags and Tampax and the TLS'; her own equivalent image, she said, was 'syringes and joss sticks and black men who beat me'.)*

Angela Carter's mental geography and her style should have made her a popular novelist, but the truth is that she is not. The very splintering of reality she writes about – the proliferation of subcultures – must be part of the cause. One reaction to the splintering is to take refuge in the old 'central' forms of the novel even though they are becoming vacuous, a kind of unconscious pastiche themselves. The genres she has borrowed or stolen from, gothic, science fiction, pornography, are of course traditionally the lonely, private and addictive kinds. And there is a degree of loneliness and displacement about the impression she gives. Personal biography rather slipped out of our conversation: the brief facts seem to be that she has been married and divorced; her journey to Japan was a sentimental journey; she has no children; her mother is dead and her father has retired to Scotland; besides London (and Tokyo) she has lived in Bristol, Bradford, Bath; she seems presently in the usual equivocal senses free, contemplating writer-in-residence jobs here or in America for next year.

However, when she remarked with some asperity, and heavy irony, 'I think I'm absolutely typical,' it struck me as true. Her particular circumstances and talents are precisely adapted – or rather, she has brilliantly adapted them – to mapping out the changeling worlds engendered by our decline and fall. Her alertness to signs and symbols, and her skill in re-creating them are of a piece with her nomadic sensibility. 'We live in Gothic times,' as she says, and she more than most is capable of riding the blast, picking up the pieces, and so on. Having apparently given up the self-contained and mild perversity of her earlier novels for something more adventurously subversive, she has run into some problems: in *The Passion of New Eve*, she admitted, some bits, notably the science fiction matriarchy in the desert, were perhaps not concretely enough imagined (it should, she said, have revealed a proper economic and social structure); and the ending, with new Eve pregnant but really still preoccupied with giving birth to herself, seemed to me to have the problems of prophecy: we don't really know what will emerge from rethinking sexual stereotypes. The positive enticements though, as always with her, easily lure one on past the gaps.

The desire and fear that fuel her plots (the magnetic attraction of fear is something she has all along relished and used) are not of the 'B' movie kind you can segregate in your consciousness. Where she does overlap with whatever 'B' movies stand for is in her urgency to retrieve and re-vamp in the highest style the most tatty and suggestive of our symbols. The opening of *New Eve* makes the point, 'Our external symbols must always express the life within us with absolute precision: how could they do otherwise, since that life has generated them? Therefore we must not blame our poor symbols if they take forms that seem trivial to us, or absurd . . .' Searching for a way to describe Angela Carter's relation to the old norms of the novel, I remembered a passage from Italo Calvino's *Invisible Cities*, where he describes the divided city of Sophronia. In one half are the roller coasters and shooting galleries, in the other the marble palaces and the factories. Every year one half of the city is dismantled, and goes off to a vacant lot somewhere else: they take down the marble pediments and leave the Ferris wheel and the carousels . . . It's altogether too whimsical an analogy, but it will have to do.

July 1977

Anniversaries

—— ANDREW MOTION ——

The Fourth

Anniversary weather: I drive
under a raw sunset, the road
cramped between drifts, hedges
polished into sharp crests.

I have it by heart now;
on this day in each year
no signposts point anywhere
but east into Essex,

and so to your ward,
where snow recovers tonight
the ground I first saw lost
four winters ago.

Whatever time might bring,
all my journeys take me
back to this dazzling dark:
I watch my shadow ahead

plane across open fields,
out of my reach for ever,
but setting towards your bed
to find itself waiting there.

The First

What I remember is not
your leaving, but your not
coming back – and snow
creaking in thick trees,

burying tracks preserved
in spiky grass below.
All afternoon I watched
from the kitchen window

a tap thaw in the yard,
oozing into its stiff sack,
then harden when evening
closed with ice again.

And I am still there,
seeing your horse return
alone to the open stable,
its reins dragging behind

a trail across the plough,
a blurred riddle of scars
we could not decipher then,
and cannot heal now.

The Second

I had imagined it all –
your ward, your shaved head,
your crisp scab struck there
like an ornament,

but not your stillness.
Day after day I saw

my father leaning forward
to enter it, whispering

'If you can hear me now,
squeeze my hand', till snow
melted in sunlight outside
then turned to winter again

and found him waiting still,
hearing the slow hiss
of oxygen into your mask,
and always turning to say

'Yes, I felt it then',
as if repeating the lie
had gradually made it true
for him, never for you.

The Third

Three years without sight,
speech, gesture, only
the shadow of clouds
shifting across your face

then blown a world away.
What sleep was that, which
light could never break?
What spellbound country

claimed you, forbidding you
even to wake for a kiss?
If it was death,
whose hands were those

warm in my own, and whose
astonishing word was it

that day when leaving
your sunlit room I heard

'Stay; stay', and watched
your eyes flick open once,
look, refuse to recognize
my own, and turn away?

The Fourth

The evening falls with snow
beginning again, halving
the trees into whiteness,
driving me with it towards

the end of another year.
What will it send for you
that this has abandoned?
You are your own survivor,

bringing me back the world
I knew, without the time
we lost; until I forget
whatever it cannot provide

I'll always arrive like this,
having no death to mourn,
but rather the life we share
nowhere beyond your room,

our love repeating itself
like snow I watch tonight,
which spins against my window
then vanishes into the dark.

August 1977

Summer Tides

—— ROBERT LOWELL ——

Tonight
I watch the incoming moon swim
under three agate veins of cloud,
casting crisps of false silver-plate
to the thirsty granite fringe of the shore.
Yesterday, the sun's gregarious sparklings;
tonight, the moon has no satellite.
All this spendthrift, in-the-house summer,
our yacht-jammed harbor
lay unattempted –
pictorial to me like your portrait.
I wonder who posed you so artfully
for it in the prow of his Italian skiff,
like a maiden figurehead without legs to fly.
Time lent its wings. Last year
our drunken quarrels had no explanation,
except everything, except everything.
Did the oak provoke the lightning,
when we heard its boughs and foliage fall? . . .
My wooden beach-ladder swings by one bolt,
and repeats its single creaking rhythm –
I cannot go down to the sea.
After so much logical interrogation,
I can do nothing that matters.
The east wind carries disturbances for leagues –
I think of my son and daughter,
and three stepdaughters
on far-out ledges

My father had been surrounded from birth by monumental edifices to trade and commerce. When he was born in 1889 there were sailing ships in Salthouse Dock. Those ships had carried cotton goods to Africa, refilled their holds with slaves, borne them in chains to the West Indies and returned to Liverpool in triumph loaded with sugar and rum. In the Gorée warehouses, behind the offices of the Mersey Docks and Harbour Board – a name intoned by my father as if he was calling O Jerusalem – beneath the rusticated arcade supported on columns of cast iron, slaves were tethered by the neck to bulky rings projecting from the walls.

Throughout my childhood, when I was small and we were still on speaking terms, he trailed me round the business sector of the town, detailing doorways he had stood in, windows he had gazed from, warehouses that had stored his cotton, his tobacco. They weren't of course his very own commodities but to his bones he was a man of commerce, a trader, and he loved his city. The docks, he told me, were formed out of a giant plateau of sandstone and granite. Why, even the lamp standards and the bollards were made of cast iron. Monuments to an age when things were built to last and nothing fell apart. Some years later in one of his paddies, reversing his car on the Albert Dock, he rammed one of these admired bollards with such force that he was bounced against the dashboard of his Triumph Herald and his false teeth, made of slighter stuff, shattered at the front.

From the Dingle to Gladstone Dock my father took me on the elevated railway overlooking the Mersey, steadying me on the wooden seats of the swaying carriage and pointing out the warehouses stuffed with grain and the rusted ships set in the black jelly of the river. Mindful of the dead we walked along the paths of St James cemetery. Jabbing with his brolly at the tombstones green with moss, he hacked aside the holly leaves to show the long flat tablets engraved with names of boys and girls all gone before their prime – the children of the Bluecoat School. He said sometimes they were whipped to death or starved, sometimes they just caught cold and died. Then, conscious of the inventive mind of man, he lectured me on Lime Street Station, describing the tunnelling into the rock and the competition held for the most efficient railway engine. Of how Stephenson's 'Rocket' won, slowing to a halt amidst a cloud of steam and fluttering flags, and William Huskisson, giddy with amazement, pitching forward in his silk top hat to die beneath its wheels. My father played a game with me called Departures. Taking me down to the Pier Head he would put me on the ferry boat to New Brighton. I would stand on the deck of the *Royal Daffodil* and watch him dwindling on the landing stage. Sometimes he waved his pocket handkerchief, and sometimes he raised his homburg hat in a last emigration gesture of farewell.

My father left school at nine years of age. As a small child, dressed in knickerbockers and a lace collar to his jacket, he had been in demand for his rendering of 'Lily of Laguna'. He had astounded his sisters by the neatness of his copper-plate handwriting and the loudness of his weeping when he read *Dombey and Son*. At fourteen he went as a cabin boy on a sailing ship to America. If he was to be believed, he'd imported the first safety matches to Berlin, dealt in diamonds in Holland, lived for some dark unspecified purpose in Dublin during the Troubles. He had been in shipping and in cotton and in property. By the time he was thirty he was in a 'good way of doing'. Doors opened to him without appointment. A carnation in his buttonhole, he pranced like Fred Astaire up the steps of his beautiful Cotton Exchange, and when he entered the massive portals of the offices of the White Star Line, men of power nodded in his direction.

As he was a proud man and a failure according to his own lights, I cannot be sure that what he told me was correct. Contradictory in his views, born with a flair for profit yet a committed socialist all his life, the few facts he told me concerning his father's family were sprinkled with business percentages and wages.

His grandfather had been called Richard and was born in 1793. In the ten years preceding his birth, the value of slaves imported into the West Indies in Liverpool vessels amounted annually to £214,677 15s. 1d. Richard had a son named William who married a girl from Scotland. They produced nine children of whom my father was the youngest. William was a cooper in a brewery and earned threepence an hour; he died two months before my father was born. The girl from Scotland, according to my father, proved to be a saintly woman; all of her nine children were respectable and God-fearing. In 1924, at the height of his success as a man of the city, my father was living at home with his mother and two remaining sisters, Nellie and Margo. He had been engaged for seven years to a young woman called Annie Mud. Margo always referred to her as Annimosity. The long engagement was because Father was busy climbing upwards and in any case his mother was in delicate health and disliked the idea of his leaving home. It was then, having clambered his way to the top deck of a tram in Lord Street, that my father met my mother. They were married in 1926, the year of the slump, and moved to a large house on the Wirral Peninsular, complete with a living-in maid named Matty. Two years later my father had lost his house, his money, and been declared a bankrupt.

Buildings, my father said, put men in their proper perspective. You knew where you were with a lump of stone that had been standing long before you were a twinkle in your grandfather's eye. Men died, he said, but the stones piled up by the sweat of their labour, survived. He was forgetting the Germans and the Town Planners, but it didn't do to contradict my father. He said memories escaped if there were no walls to keep them trapped.

The building he rented to encapsulate my memories was built in 1932. We moved to it in 1935, six months after I was born. Twelve miles from Liverpool, red-bricked and semi-detached, it was set on a road that led directly to the sea-shore. The house had four small rooms upstairs, three downstairs plus a scullery, and a long thin back garden separated from a field by a timber fence and a row of poplar trees. The lounge and the dining-room were never used, save on those rare occasions when my maternal grandparents or my aunts came to tea. We occupied only two bedrooms out of the four available; my brother slept with my father and I kept my mother company. It was generally understood that the mattresses in the other rooms were mildewed with the damp and unfit to lie on. The tiny room downstairs – wisely never referred to as a living-room –

was almost entirely filled with a table and six chairs. My brother sat by the door with his legs in the scullery. Above the fireplace was a mantelshelf of iron. When Father bent down to poke the coals he cautiously rested his hand on the shelf above. Mostly he misjudged the distance and straightened up too soon, striking his head in the process. He had a small scab, dark brown and never quite healed, to show for it. We turned round and round in that room, jostling for position, eating and doing our homework and snapping at each other as we fought for space. When we were old enough my brother and I went out as much to stretch our limbs as anything else. He went to the church, the youth club and the bowling green. I went to the pinewoods and the sea. My mother sat and read a library book at the bedroom window. Downstairs my father listened to the wireless or paced the garden in the dark, so that years later in a theatre, watching with tears the play *Death of a Salesman*, I recognized the set, the light in the upstairs room, and Willie Lomas – a dead ringer for my Dad – stumbling about the yard in a dream, muttering of business deals.

My earliest memories are of fear and anxiety. Once those pre-school days had passed, when pixie-hooded I had trotted round the town with Father, I never spoke to him again for fourteen years with either respect or tenderness. By the age of ten, hearing his voice raised against my mother, I was in the habit of hurling myself through the scullery door and leaping on him from behind. With my knee in his back and an arm about his throat I would bring him, commando fashion, crashing to the floor.

There was a song popular at the time, that my mother used to sing when dusting the furniture.

> When that man is dead and gone
> We'll go prancing down the street
> Kissing everyone we meet,
> When that man is dead and gone . . .

It was of course about Hitler but I thought she was referring to Father.

His moods were regular and followed a pattern. Anything

could spark off the initial fit of rage. A political opinion, a lump in a potato, a lost collar stud. Transformed in seconds from a reserved, rather courteous man into Frankenstein's monster – his back grew a hump, his mouth became a gob – he would call my mother a whore and a dirty bitch, accompanying these choice words with a kind of frantic Zulu dancing on the spot. For two or three days after such an outburst he was violent in all his movements. He kept verbally silent but he slammed doors, hurled plates. On the few occasions he did structural harm to the house, Mother told everyone it was delayed war damage. Once safely through these days of smouldering containment, he fell into a sullen depression which lasted several weeks and sent him slinking through the house like a dog that had been muzzled. We left his dinner on the landing in a bowl. Recovering, he would emerge sheepishly one night and join us at the table, and if it was summertime he might be full of fun for weeks at a stretch, listening to the wireless in the dark, taking us for runs in the car, treating us to afternoon tea in Southport. Until, almost at a point when we had forgotten what it was like before, something or someone gave offence and off he would go again, kicking the hose across the lawn so that the rose bush snapped or slinging the tea-pot, snug in its striped cosy, clear over the fence into next door's nettles. Then we would run in all directions to avoid the blast.

Despite the quantity of relations my father recalled standing guard in his own childhood, there were very few in mine. There was my Uncle John whom I met twice, his son Jack who was a butcher off the Priory Road, my maternal grandparents and Margo and Nellie.

My mother, who had a very different view of the saintly Scottish widow, long since buried, said Nellie had been sacrificed. She'd given up her prospects in order to take care of a selfish old woman. And both Nellie and my father had wrecked Margo's chances, refusing to let her marry Mr Aveyard. For a brief period during the first world war, Margo had been a bride. She set up house three streets away but her husband, George Bickerton, came back mustard-gassed from France and died in the upstairs bedroom. After the funeral Margo wanted to live on her own; Father said it was not right and persuaded her to come home to Nellie and Mother. Then later, Mr Aveyard, who was no better than he should be, wanted to marry her, only Nellie thought it would be madness for Margo to give up her pension. My father said she was a foolish girl – she was over fifty at the time. My mother, who had no fondness for either of my aunts, on the principle that they were related to my father, supported Margo over the business of Mr Aveyard. Considering her own unfortunate experience of marriage, it was possible she was prompted by malice. Auntie Nellie's house was small and dark with a yard at the back that sloped down to an alleyway. It was always referred to as Nellie's though in fact Margo was the wage earner. She was a dressmaker and for a time during the war she took a job in a munitions factory. My mother said there were certain indications of hysteria in her appearance, a kind of giddyness. She tended to wear cocktail dresses with white wedge-heeled shoes. She smoked continuously and her eyes were over-emphatic; they glittered with drama and fatigue. She bought a lot of material for the dressmaking from shops that had been bombed, and seeing her in a frock made of slightly charred cloth, a diamante clasp at the hip and a scorch mark on the shoulder, she looked like a woman ravaged by fire. There was the occasion, never to be forgotten, when the Dutch seaman billeted on Nellie in the first year of the war had given Margo a length of satin from the East and secretly, behind Nellie's back, she'd sewn it up into a sarong – appearing in it at a meeting of the Women's Guild, with a slit up the leg and all her suspenders showing beneath the baggy edge of her green silk drawers.

Mr Baines, my mother's father, was tall and portly. He was a director of Goodlass Walls, the Liverpool paint firm. He'd bettered himself with a vengeance and he collected butterfly specimens. My father hated him because my mother loved him. Before the war my grandfather went on cruises, leaving my grandmother behind. She had failed to rise with him. She was small and bent over and stored a humbug in her cheek. She made a habit of coming over queer when she went down town and accepting brandies from sympathetic passers-by. My mother treated her with contempt and was always telling her to pull herself together. When my grandparents came for Sunday tea we played cards. My brother fetched the Indian table with the brass tray from under the stairs. Father went to his room and brought down his cotton bag full of pennies. He enjoyed the thought of winning a few pence off his father-in-law. He gave them back when the game was over. He enjoyed that even more; he said Mr Baines was a rotten old skinflint and it gave him pleasure to show him up. It made me unhappy watching Mother gazing beady-eyed at Grandfather, hoping he'd refuse and being disillusioned time without number. My grandmother once told me she'd had rickets when a baby and she'd worked in a boiled sweet factory at eleven years of age. My mother said it was a dirty lie. If we went out to tea in Southport and my mother left a tip under the plate, my grandmother used to pick it up and pop it in her bag.

All my childhood was spent with people who were disappointed. They'd married the wrong person, failed in business, been manipulated by others. They took a fierce pride in knowing themselves for what they were. Not for them the rosy view of life, the helpful excuses that might explain and mitigate. They gave each other labels – fifth columnist, skinflint, hysterical baggage, Wreck of the Hesperus. Class conscious, they were either dead common or a cut above themselves. In the family album it was true there were some faded snap-shots of holidays at Blackpool, with everyone smiling and fooling on the sands, but it must have been a trick of the camera.

Liverpool people have always been articulate and my family used words as though they were talking to save their lives. Facts might be hidden, like income and insurance and sex, but emotions and judgments flowed from them like water. If you sat in a corner being seen and not heard, in the space of a few minutes you could hear a whole character being dissected, assassinated and chucked in the bin, to be plucked out and redeemed in one small sentence. Thus my mother, in a discussion with Margo concerning Aunt Nellie, would say how lacking in depth Nellie was, too dour, a touch of the martyr. And Aunt Margo, heaping on coals of fire, would mention incidents of malice and deceitfulness, my mother nodding her head all the while in agreement, until just as Nellie lay unravelled before my eyes, Aunt Margo would say, 'By heck, but you can't fault her sponge cake.'

There were always words in our house, even when Father was in his silent periods. There was the wireless. It was balanced behind the curtains; it was too big for the windowsill and jutted out into the room. The valves never burnt out but it had cracked across the front in three places and been patched with black adhesive. Because of its size, whoever took the chair under the window was forced to sit at an acute angle to the table and eat their food hunched over the cloth. Mother wanted the wireless thrown out. Once she nearly succeeded. She was upstairs shaking the bath mat out of the window. It was damp and heavy and slipped from her fingers on to the aerial stretched from the outside wall to the top of the fence post. Father was listening to the news at the time. The wireless leapt on the sill and toppled between chair and table. A man inspired, Father flung himself forward and caught it in his arms. He loved the wireless, not for music but for the voices talking about poetry and politics, which were the same thing for him.

There are people who live in the present and those who live for the future. There are others who live in the past. There would seem to be little choice. Early on, life dictates our preferences. All my father's bright days – the boy before the mast, the man of substance – had ended before I was born. He faced backwards. In doing so, he created within me so strong a nostalgia for time gone that I have never been able to appreciate the present or look to the future. And my own past, when it was over and I was grown, was so determined by his present, that I went into the future in a dream and never noticed it.

Continually I try to write it down, this sense of family life. For it seems to me that the funny noises we make with our mouths, or the squiggles that we put on paper, are only for ourselves to hear, to prove there's someone there.

November 1977

Bard on the Road

—— HUGO WILLIAMS ——

The railroad follows the Hudson river north. The glare of industry stings your eyes. Sidings and sheds and smoking chimneys. Hardware scattered haphazardly beside the river as if a bad child has left his things out to rust. A refuse skip labelled 'Monument Valley' trundles by. Here's a place called 'Auto-Wreck'. One freight wagon has come all the way from Genesis, Wyoming, with Sterling Salt for Baltimore. Another contains 'Liquid Flo-Sweet – Sugar for Industry'.

Hazy cliffs rise majestically on the far shore. I can almost make out the line of Indians, their arms folded, looking through half-closed eyes at this Guernica-scape. A partially-sunken speed boat has a luminous orange buoy attached to it. Nearby stands Roxy's Lighthouse. At Greystone there's a thick white dust in the air and motionless old men with faces like clowns where they have licked their lips clean of the powder. Perched on top of a factory an enormous plaster eagle clutches a tiny shrivelled globe. Stencilled on a tanker, the words 'Shock Control' are dragged slowly across my vision. Outside Tarrytown giant letters exhort me to 'Think About The American Flag'. Then an old train moves backwards along the 'Route of the Vista Dome'. I wonder why huge sheets of ice, four inches thick, are piled beside the river. Now we're at Albany. The little white HMV dog squats on the tallest building, his ear cocked crazily to the wind. The Pacific Fruit Express rots in a siding.

'In case you're so bored you haven't got anything better to do . . . this here is the Mohawk Valley we're entering . . .' I looked round and there was the ticket collector, a smart, moustachioed man, addressing us from the back of the carriage.

'If you care to look out of the left-hand window . . . ,' he said, 'we're just about to pass the first stone house to be built in the valley. It was built by Sir William Johnston from England for his daughter in 1794. There it is now.' And he passed on to the next carriage. 'He was in the paper not long ago,' said my neighbour. 'They did a series on the last of the patriots.'

Sponsored by the famed purveyor of tooth-brightener, Colgate is a pleasant, pastoral establishment on a hillside in upper New York. I thought I was staying with Peter Redgrove, the University's current O'Connor Professor of English Literature, but when I got to the house of Bruce Berlind, head of the English Department, there was a letter from Peter explaining why he had to leave Colgate the next day. 'We regret very much missing your reading,' he wrote with Penelope Shuttle, 'as we admire your poetry. Unfortunately we can't meet the English Department – the enclosed cutting will explain our situation.' Under 'Redgrove Quits', the *Colgate News* reported that Redgrove's expectations of his visit had not been realized. He had been displeased with his teaching requirements and lack of visits to neighbouring schools, but stated that it had been 'no fault of the students'.

I was to hear a number of lurid variations on this tale during the course of my visit. One was that Peter's teaching duties had interfered with his and Penelope's research for a book on menstruation. Another was that he was obsessed with the subject, had tried to introduce it into the syllabus and had resented the College's reservations on the matter. When I spoke to him on the phone he seemed sane enough. He said he'd been led to believe Colgate was a university, but there were in fact no post-graduate courses available and the college had only recently grown out of its reputation as a rich man's sporting club, famed more for its possession of a manuscript screenplay by Joseph Conrad than for its grasp of the three r's. 'There are no poets here,' he told me. 'Only one rather good prose writer, Fred Busch, who has not been a friend either – I cannot understand why.'

I was taken round the campus by Mrs Berlind. She showed me the marks of Indian bullets on the wall of the old library.

'When the first school was established here the master had to keep a rifle beside his desk apparently.'

'It was whites-only then?'

I looked at the campus neatly counterpaned in snow: the new sports centre, the sloping park with its oaks, more like a health spa than a frontier, and tried to imagine the starving redskins against this backdrop of academic routine. They flickered jerkily for a moment in black and white, then succumbed to their usual fate. I remembered standing at Epidaurus and feeling the presence of Greek heroes pricking my skin. Was it because their deeds were never shown on stage that they could never really die? The Indians were not so lucky. What the US Cavalry left standing of them were finished off in replica by Hollywood, its carnivorous smile polished with Colgate's.

When it was time for the reading I realized we were a small group marooned for the evening by various hotly competing events: 1) Jack Anderson of the *Washington Post* on Christianity and Gossip Columny, 2) the female head of a law school on women's rights and opportunities, 3) a show of short films by local film-makers, 4) the finals of the ice hockey championship. The reading came a good fifth though.

Ah, Sodom Road! Canadian Niagara Power Company. Niagara Protective Coatings. King Edward Motel. The Modern Air Motel. The Eyrie Jockey Club. British Cars. Soft grey sunset with pale brown scrubland bandaged here and there with snow. Ochre smoke from a distant chimney. Burning Springs Wax Museum. The man ahead of me at the Canadian Customs looked very reluctant to say out loud what he did for a living. 'Import clothes from Guatemala', I heard him whisper. The officials looked dubious about this, so the man made up something about having a ring for his girl in Toronto. No one believed this yank, but they let him go. My own cultural mission was looked on much more favourably by the upstanding frontier guard. 'Reading poetry, eh? Your own or other people's?'

A table was laid for twenty in a room off the main hall at York College, Toronto. I stood drinking with the chaplain, waiting for the special guests to arrive and identifying with the prawn cocktails waiting pinkly for the faculty jaws. Only half of them turned up, however, as Marshall McCluhan had chosen this moment to come home and was holding out his death-of-the-word tidings elsewhere on the campus. We bunched together at the top of the table, commiserating in whispers about the Canadian Cultural Wilderness. Those not of the cloth seemed either Irish or Scottish, anxious only to be reassured once more that they had done the right thing in seeking a new life for themselves in this essentially decent country. A short silence in the right place would have had them groping for their passports.

The reading was hardly the joyous affirmation of life my audience had been hoping for. I thought it was, but then I like poems on impotence and death. In fact, I was more than usually aware of the incongruity between the 'subjects' of my poems and my apparent adventurousness in travelling so far to read them to such a tiny audience till then ignorant of my existence. I was a walking contradiction and it was this I left hanging in the air after every reading. 'The age of writing has passed,' goes the Marshall McCluhan nag. 'We must invent a NEW METAPHOR.' Yes, talking about it.

After the reading I expressed some enthusiasm for seeing the city. I didn't know then that there was nothing to see. At Grossman's there was a blues group, but you have to sit down for music in Canada and there weren't any tables. One of our group said, by way of explanation, that you're a nobody in Canada if you have on a narrow tie, meaning me in my early Sixties stuff. Then we passed a tower which I think he said was the tallest edifice in the free-standing world and I was to put my head on the back shelf of the car in order better to appreciate this monstrosity. This was the last thing I wanted to do, so I said I'd take his word for it and an awkward silence fell over us as we drove on through those purged and passionless streets.

'May I have all your receipts, please,' said the secretary when I went to hunt up my cheque from Finance the next morning.

'I don't think I'm on expenses,' I explained.

'You don't understand,' she said. 'We need your receipts in order to pay you your fee. Your fare, meals etc.'

'I don't keep receipts for that kind of thing.'

'Well, I don't know what Accounts will say,' she said, realizing sadly that she'd have to give me the money anyway.

Niagara Falls is a traditional honeymoon attraction. Newlyweds find it encouraging to board the 'Maid of the Mist' and to view from close up a hundred thousand tons of foam crashing every second over an eighty foot precipice. As my Benares guide told me in the 'Nepalese Love Temple', 'It put idea of generation into mind of man.' The Canadian Tourist Board is more discreet: 'The Great Gorge Trip is an exciting and romantic experience in intimate contact with Nature's handiwork at the very edge of the awesome Whirlpool Rapids. Man and Nature come together with an unforgettable experience of sight and sound. The scenic tunnel is truly an interlude of unsurpassed excitement. Here Man has used his utmost skill and native artistry to coax from Nature new miracles of artistry and colour.' We read that the Niagara Plaza has 'the Big Look' in Observation Towers. 'The Tower Ride is the beginning of an unforgettable experience.' While for those of a more studious outlook 'Britain's Historical Past is portrayed in our London Wax Museum'. (Closed, naturally.)

Waxworks proliferate, including numerous renderings of the highly Freudian 'Houdini', who used to go over the Falls in milk churns, and Blondin, who walked across on a rope, cooked and ate his breakfast in mid-stream and once offered to convey the Prince of Wales to America on his shoulders. The Prince declined, claiming that his rank obliged him to stay on terra firma. 'See his personal lock collection,' ran the brochure for the Houdini Museum, 'his keys, handcuffs and straitjackets. Learn the secrets of some of the world's greatest illusions in magic, including "walking through a brick wall". See the original "Cremation" and "Decapitation", Houdini's Glass Box and the original milk can. Be mystified by our resident Magician. Continuous Performances.' When I got there the resident Magician was seeking his fortune elsewhere, but the redoubtable Houdini's instruments of restriction and bondage were laid out under greenish spotlights, shrivelled and ashamed-looking. Poor Houdini. He died a broken man. Not broken by Niagara or his battered milk churn, but by the march of progress. Aeroplanes and electricity, radio and moving pictures had upstaged his good faith. He was an anachronism escaping out of nowhere into nothingness.

Boston station was like a disused meat market, open on the side to driving sleet. I telephoned my host.

'Is that Mrs Hall?'

'No, this is Sue Miller,' said a firm voice. 'My husband is Ray Hall. Is that Hugo Williams? Yes, we're expecting you. Ray is at a committee meeting tonight. I thought we might go out to a meal later if I can get the child off. You've got the address? The name on the bell is James.'

I took a taxi to Berry Street.

'Number 10 seems to be a church,' said the driver. The rum-looking grey shed had 'South Boston Revivalist Chapel' written on it in red. I got his tip wrong, then couldn't open the car door.

'Anyone can see you never rode in a Cadillac before. This is the only Cadillac in the South Boston Cab Service.'

I found myself standing on a littered sidewalk, blacks slouching by me, curious or drunk, muttering. A black kid emerged. A man stood by his running motor. I went up and rang some bells. A huge black momma appeared at the top of a flight of stairs. This lady wasn't Mrs Hall surely?

'Who's you looking for, sonny?'

'Are you Mrs James?'

'No, I'se Mrs Patterson.'

'I was looking for a lady with a young child.'

'Wha's de name of de chile?'

'I don't know.'

'What street you looking for?'

'Maybe I got the wrong Berry Street.'

'This is Boston, sonny.'

'Maybe I should be in Cambridge.'

'You said it, sonny.'

I found a stinking old cab whose half crazy black driver said did I want Berry Street South Cambridge or North Cambridge. It came to me that he was asking me where it was. I asked in a garage and sure enough there was only one Berry Street in

Cambridge. I found Number 10 and rang the bell marked 'James'.

Inside all was calm. The child had not gone off so I spent the first hour talking to its black doll named Nicholas about Walt Disney's *Jungle Book*. A poster of Bertolt Brecht loomed over me.

Mr Hall was still in his committee, so later his wife and I repaired to a log-cabin type cinema-restaurant complex dedicated to Orson Welles, where we searched among the bits of food for common acquaintances and subjects fit for discourse. (Few.)

Back home, there was Ray: whiskies to drink and names of poets to knock back and forth like hot potatoes. Had I published a book myself? This was odd, I thought, as it was Ray who had invited me to read. I leant further forward to examine the situation. Had he ever heard of me, I wondered. Books of poetry were passed across to me like buckets of water at a fire. A pile developed by my chair. J. S. Cunningham, I confessed, was a poet I had never really studied. Arriving nowhere rather late, we pulled nightcaps well down over our heads and I went to bed on the dining room floor.

Early next morning I was offered more little ethnic dolls to inspect while Mrs Hall broke things for breakfast nearby. But something was amiss. Now here was Ray standing in the doorway of the dining room with a painful expression on his face. Mumps had come on in the night. The poor man was clearly terrified. Yet he was apologizing to me, and I was forgiving him. Obviously he couldn't take me to the reading, scheduled for the afternoon, or introduce me. Mrs Hall would have to do it. You know, honey, the large tower near the road. You take the elevator at the back of the refectory. As it turned out, she didn't know at all.

A garrison of the New Brutalism, stuck on a wind-raked peninsula of Massachusetts Bay. Miniature students, blown inside out by the rain-soaked wind, seemed to accentuate the desolation. Wavelets rippled across the vast puddles which had settled on the pedestrian precincts. Some students battled past in wheelchairs. No doubt the architects thought of them when they ignored the rest of humanity. The wind moaned through a beastly tunnel connecting two quads. We took the lift to the office. No one had heard of us. For whom were we looking exactly? Mrs Hall was uncertain where we were expected. We stumbled on the refectory and sat down to prune yoghurt and stuffed turkey. After further enquiries, we found our way to an obscure venue called 'The English Lounge'. This was empty, except for an agreeable-looking blonde girl who said she wasn't stopping for the reading, but could I sign here for the money, which they couldn't let me have unfortunately, as they had to send it to England later, after tax of course.

About eight people drifted in, then three more, then Mrs Hall said as there was no one to introduce me I'd better begin. I'd just got started when a fat girl came in saying we weren't to mind her, she only wanted to make a cup of coffee. She made her way to the kitchenette at the back of the room, put on the kettle and stood there staring at me until it boiled. She made herself a cup, smiled at the ceiling and wandered away with it through the door. I didn't mind when this happened a second time, but when two massive black men came in and started counting the empty chairs I had to stop and find out what was going on. 'How many chairs do you need exactly?' one of them asked me. 'Only the ones being used.' ''Cos we need them for the political meeting.' At first I thought he wanted all of them. 'How many do you want?' 'Only twenty-six.' And they proceeded to air-lift every free chair out of the door.

'Do you consider yourself to be a craftsman?' someone asked when the reading was over.

'A craftsman?'

'Do you spend a long time on each poem?'

'Yes, but it's more like gambling than carpentry. You keep thinking you're just about to hit on the winning system, the right system of mistakes. I can do the mistakes, it's the systems I have trouble with. You're betting on yourself, but the reader has to keep up with the horse – or very nearly. That's what makes the betting so difficult. Each time you say to yourself, just one more bet . . .'

'I understand,' said the questioner.

Another man, a teacher, said he was delighted someone was attempting the long poem. In the confusion over the chairs, I'd forgotten to read out the titles of my poems. Titles sound pompous-daft read out loud anyway. This man hadn't noticed. He thought I'd managed the long form magnificently. He wanted to congratulate me on the overall grandeur of my theme. He wouldn't say what this was exactly, despite my pumping him, but he did say he thought it was all rock solid. Fine.

I left the stand and looked around for Mrs Hall to guide me from the labyrinth. We approached each other across the room, our mouths open ready to reply to what the other was about to say. Neither of us spoke. I held the door open for her and she passed under my arm without a word. We picked our way among the puddles of the campus, through a cindery car park and up over a bridge to the subway. Here we contemplated an advertisement for A. E. Long's Funeral Homes. 'Service is a Long Word' it said, until the train arrived, swallowing our silence.

Mrs Hall got down in Cambridge. I said I had to return to New York, and stayed on the train into Boston. There I sat in the Station Hotel restaurant listening to the local dialogue: 'Well, I don't believe a word of it. I've heard it all before. I could see straight through him. Who did he think he was fooling? I told him, I said to him, it's your own fault you don't get on. You've got to look after yourself 'cos I'm not going to, I said. I've had it. Up to here. It's no good telling him. He won't listen. I never did like Boston.'

On the train back to New York, more and more schoolboy alarm at the three-month term stretching unpredictably ahead of me like a plot I have to get right before I can go home again. Or is it just the thought of tonight's probable bedlessness? Travel is really a test of the imagination. Homesickness its failure. So this kind of depression is just a failure to get up and see what's happening in the snack bar.

I get up. In the bar are six black boys with long-handled metal combs dug into the backs of their heads like tomahawks. They wobble their legs and bow, pour drink everywhere, slap hands and shout, spin round and stare at my woebegone countenance, suppressing their laughter. I think maybe I'll stay on this train down to Washington, then get the bus to Charlottesville from there. That'll solve the night for me. I was just thinking that when there was a grinding crash and the train came off the rails. One of the blacks fell over in mid-laugh, then burst out laughing again. Luckily the train was just entering Penn Station, New York, so we were going very slowly. But that was the end of my plan to go to Washington. I looked out the window and saw wheels embedded in cinders. Forlorn porters were staring at us incredulously. The black boys leant out the window and sang 'We're making trains worth travelling again', Amtrak's desperate rallying cry. Then some officials arrived and made us get out through another train waiting on the other side.

It was ten o'clock. The next train to Washington was at 4.15. I lay down on a bench and tried to sleep. There was an explosion in my dream as a policeman's nightstick struck the bench near my head. No sleeping. Wake up now. Where you heading? What time's your train? Somehow I remembered where I was. '4.15 to Washington.' I sat there watching a foul-mouthed old woman being thrown out of the women's toilets three times, before being finally led away. Then the cleaners arrived with hoovers like phantom dune buggies, the flexes plugged into points underfoot and vast areas of the hall roped off at a time. A camp young man sat down beside me and asked where I was going. When I told him he said he would come to Washington with me. Did I want to score some uppers or grass or go to the rest room with him? He took out his wallet and showed me a photograph of New Orleans. There was a horror comic stuck in his belt. I said, 'After Washington, it's Alaska. We could meet there.' 'O no, man, that's too cold, I'm from New Orleans and I ain't never going back there.' 'I wasn't serious.' 'No, but I am, man.' He went off and offered himself to some anoraked itinerant. I watched the Buchenwald-faced night cop toying sadistically with his nightstick like some hallucinatory drag drum majorette. With the thong round his wrist he would let the truncheon cartwheel downwards, hitting the floor with a 'clack', then richocheting smartly back into his open hand. He swung one leg forward from the hip and began to strut in the direction of the young queer. A poor paranoid black woman was kicking thin air and screeching abuse at a wall. She too had to go.

I wanted to sleep on the train, but a very old man sat down next to me and began overflowing with information in the New York way. Did I know he'd been to London when he was young? He couldn't remember which year exactly, but it was before the crash. He'd stayed in London and had met someone in the perfume business who had been a real gentleman. He himself was in the carton and container racket. Or had been before his son moved West. I wondered how and where he'd slept with his first woman, but remained silent. It was still dark, my face thinner in the window: Washington at last. I bought a post-card with these laudable sentiments:

> What is black and white and loveable to see
> Are the new pandas of Washington D.C.
> Given by the State Department to the public
> This gift was from the Chinese People's Republic
>
> Welcomed by our first Lady to their new nest
> As a symbol of peace between East and West
> These Chinese pandas came by air from Peking
> With names of Hsing Hsing and Ling Ling
>
> The popular pandas have get up and go
> And when being watched put on a good show
> Often they stand ready for a picture pose
> Holding high their two black ears and black nose
>
> The pandas are of God's creation so fine
> A great symbol of the love from the divine
> Both Hsing and Ling are at the Washington Zoo
> Living and waiting for a visit from you.
>
> Copyright 1973
> Donald F. Hurley

Rows of TV chairs in the Washington Greyhound Bus Station. On each the inscription which has branded itself on my brain: 'Chair for TV Viewing "Please"', and underneath it: 'Made in Salt Lake City'. I put in my quarter and watched the middle fifteen minutes of a comedy about a man and a woman who daren't make love because their children are holding an important business dinner downstairs. The wife runs down in her undies and the mayor leaves in a huff. Then the screen went blank and I read: 'Chair for TV Viewing "Please".'

'A brief gathering beforehand,' ran the article in the *Charlottesville News*, 'found Galway Kinnell heavy on the hors d'oeuvres, beer in hand, relaxing after a tennis match and still organizing the programme for his third reading in two days. Williams, younger, more anxious, clutched a stronger drink and conversed congenially, yet quite intensely with those who approached him.' Clutching, anxious and intense. Thanks, Barbara. But what happened to 'debonair' and 'handsome'? She moves on to the reading: 'When Galway Kinnell came into the analytical glare of the Chemistry Auditorium it was like a lumberjack replacing a songbird.'

Readings make me squirm. It's because every poem ever written falls short of 'poetry'. Yet it is Poetry a reading tries to celebrate.

'This one will gross you out,' said Kinnell, introducing his poem 'The Bear'.

When it was over Irvin Ehrenpreis, my host, came up and asked me to come to his poetry class the next morning. 'Was I that bad?' I asked.

Later I met Louise Gluck, poet in residence at Charlottesville, or rather just outside it. The delegates hadn't known about her child when they appointed her, she told me, and had swept her to the outskirts in a fit of displacement activity. She lived without a car in the ugly and inconvenient Mimosa Drive. Students came in relays of cars to her classes, but her life was unwieldy with babysitters and taxis. Virginia is very much Old South and the colour of a woman's skin turns black very quickly if conventions are disturbed. She seemed lonely, exhausted, caught in a crossfire. Half-joking I asked if she'd seen the cover of the current *National Lampoon* which had a picture of the Virgin Mary being thrown out of her home for being pregnant. She didn't respond much, but the next day I was sitting in the bus station reading the *New Yorker* when I came across a poem of hers:

> Under the thin fabric
> Of her skin, his heart

Formed. She
Listened because
He had no father.
So she knew
He wanted to stay
In her body, apart
From the world
With its cries, its
Roughhousing –
But already the men
Gather to see him
Born; they
Crowd in or stand
At worshipful
Distance, like
Figures in a painting
Whom the star lights, shining
Steadily in its dark context.

'Where you heading?' said a voice at my elbow. An old
woman was moving up the bench towards me. Bus stations are
like chessboards. If you don't keep an eye on your diagonals
you're liable to get checked. Your opponent opens with a
question which can't have the answer 'no'. 'No' is where they
live and they want to get out of there.

'Where you heading?'

'North.'

'I'm heading north. I've been travelling for a month. You
wanna see the map? My cousins live in Lake Charles. They
needed the room. They said I'd set fire to the house with my
newspapers. But I like to keep up with what's happening, don't
you? Of course, I had to leave them behind when I left Lake
Charles. But I can sleep on the buses. I've been on the road a
month and only one night in a motel . . .' She tucked some
grey hair back under a kind of bed-cap.

'If you look after God, he'll look after you,' she told me, as
she found half an apple in her plastic bag bulging with newspapers. 'I'm gonna meet a reverend gentleman in Idaho. You
want I should write you from there? You Jewish? No, I can see
you're a nice boy . . .'

'All aboard now. And thanks for going Greyhound.' It's the
fuel crisis and posters along the way show two smiling men –

one white, one black – sitting in the front seat of a car, the white man driving. Another says 'Don't be Fuelish!' with a picture of a boy switching something off – downwards of course in the States. There's a 'Drug Fair' and a sign in a bush says 'Our Lady of Angels'. This is Stamford, Virginia. Or rather 'Stiamford'. It's the South at last. In Woodbridge there's a Buffeteria with 'hot coffee brewin''. Burgher King purveys 'The Whopper'. There are bright yellow fire engines in this part of the world. It's started to look like the storybooks, with little shacks like old shoes in among the cheap brush and winter trees. Much 'Real Estate' up for grabs. Random weatherboard dolls' houses in Dumfries are painted pale pink and green, the vagrant grass between them parched, appearing summery already. No fences anywhere, American style. Just houses on the land or built on stilts with mosquito-wired stoops.

Behind me on the bus a young man is giving his girlfriend a terrible ear-bashing. He has a hectoring told-you-so Southern self-righteousness with which he lays down the laws of history. 'After every war there's a depression,' he observes. No matter what she says he repeats his last remark. 'After every war there's a depression.' He's just admitted he was born in 1951, now he's telling her England was conquered by Hitler. Where did he get that from? She tries to check him but he goes right on. 'Yeah, the English were conquered by Hitler all right.' I imagine he must be some big handsome lad to be so confident, but when I turn round he's a little squirt in specs. What's more surprising is they're both black.

'This Coach is Rest Room Equipped.' Yes, it is, but it's not restful keeping your balance in there in the chromium-plated dark. So I wait for the bus to stop again. A kid with a broken neck gets on. Are we going to Quantico? 'No, straight over.' This is Prince William County, where mobile homes grow like mushrooms. Chaplinesque prefabs litter the woods near Stafford. Things a shade run down. A pit full of old cars is probably some old character's livelihood, with a case of rattlers 'in back'. Now here's a big muddy river full of islands at shacky Fredericksburg. 'White Rock Cream Soda' sounds tempting, but you can't risk getting down when it's 'No time at Bowling Green' or somewhere.

I had a window seat and I dozed. I had just woken up and was thinking what a daft name 'Putt-putt' was for 'America's Quality Golf Courses' when I felt a hand on my knee. I snapped round and saw that someone was offering me a bottle of whisky. 'Have a drink,' he ordered. He looked dangerous, one of those re-hash jobs which are more frightening because they are in disguise, the hairline pulled down over the stitches, the raw nerve-ends covered with a kind of suit from the waxworks: the collar, tie and jacket too flat-looking. I should have known better. If you get on a Greyhound early and get your window seat, you're a sitting duck for the company-mongering speed-freaks and queers who make up the staple diet of these voracious intestines for digesting human being and their woes. The trick is to take your place in the queue late. By the time you get on, the window seats are gone. So you walk slowly down the aisle, your eyes relaxed but vigilant, weighing the odds of progressing towards the back or settling for this cowboy here who seems to be nodding off already.

This time I was cornered. 'Have a drink,' he told me again. The scotch was Dewar's. 'I was buried in de wars,' he said. 'I never came home. You see that?' He lifted an index finger like a blasted oak. I waited to hear what he had done with this gross digit, but he didn't pursue the matter. By now the whisky had engaged my own sleepy imagination and I was going in for the uniquely intimate confidences which seem to flow from one's lips when one is crushed elbow to elbow in these flying confessionals.

'Say, you're English aren't you?' he asked. That was all I needed. I gave him a ten-thousand-word biography of myself and before I had finished I realized I had made yet another life-friend, prepared to follow me to the ends of Virginia should I so desire him. He had nowhere particular to go himself, he told me. He had thought of visiting a certain ex-jailer friend of his in Newport News, but that could wait. 'We got to know one another inside,' he told me, adding alarmingly: 'but he was no oil painting.'

By now we were hitting the outskirts of Williamsburg and Johnny was gathering up his packages in readiness to accompany me to the poetry reading. 'It'd be a gas,' he told me youthfully, drawing in his belt. 'Get pissed – I've heard about Williamsburg. That's the old-time colonial town ain't it? That why you visiting there?'

'No, no, not at all. I was just invited by the college.'

'Poetry! I used to write poetry. The Ballad of the Reading Gaol. Have a drop for the road?'

'No thanks. I'm being met by some professor. I won't be able to stay with you any more. It's been great talking to you – and thanks for the drinks – that's really set me up. I'm not looking forward to this.'

'Don't do it then. Screw them professor fellas. I'll go along with you. Say I'm your manager. I could manage you. Have a few drinks. I'll read a poem myself . . .' Here he rolled up his sleeve and showed me a great scar where he'd had a tattoo removed.

'What was it before?' I asked.

'That would be telling now, wouldn't it,' he said, still making as if to accompany me. I said goodbye and scrambled for the door. He wasn't looking when I waved to him.

I went into the station and rang up the English department. Doctor K. would be down in a minute. I was combing my hair in one of the mirrors when I saw Johnny arguing with a soldier on the other side of the hall. So he'd got down here after all. Did he mean to stay? I prayed it wasn't on my behalf he'd decided to visit Williamsburg.

Just then a naval captain approached me. This was Doctor K. He took off his yachting cap and said he would take me straight to Hospitality House. This was a vast mock-Tudor motel, 'the gift of an Old Boy in oil. But it's nearly always empty.' In the lobby a real-unreal fire 'blazed' disconcertingly beside a life-size replica of a vintage Le Mans racing car. Richly carpeted corridors led to a cavernous chamber where I was to change and wash and be ready within an hour.

There was ice in the bathroom and a colour telly at the foot of the bed. I put the telly on to keep me awake and went into a trance in front of some afternoon junk-show in which three married couples competed against each other for some heavily promoted junk consumerables, such as automobile hooverettes and inflatable drinks trays for the pool. The panel-master was describing a situation for them: 'You're driving along with your wife,' he enthused, 'you're going through this elegant suburb. You notice all the trashcans are out. Suddenly you see this antique figurine sticking out of one of the trashcans. You stop the car, but which one of you jumps out to get the figurine, you or your wife?' The couples were then separated, like hogs prior to servicing, and each one asked what he/she thought would happen. If they both agreed, for instance, that the husband would jump out and the wife grab the wheel and drive off leaving him holding the figurine, they won another infra-red rotary barbecue by Swatomatic and would leap up and down shrieking and waving both hands in the air in glee. At the end, the couple who won the most rounds, the couple who knew best what junk was swimming around in one another's minds, was handed $5000.

The house phone rang and it was Doctor K. come to collect me. This time he wore a Tyrolean jacket and perky green hat with a porcupine cockade in the side of it. He'd left off the lederhosen. He told me his uncle used to make musical instruments for 'Pound 'n Yeats'.

We drove to the Cascades Restaurant for a delicious dinner and by the time I got to the reading I was too drunk to speak. I went down some winding stairs to a gents which had special handles for cripples. I hung on to these and read: 'I was once, a long time ago, a hippie in the best suburban tradition. I am now a Virginia gentleman and a historical scholar. Vive le Bourbon. Vive la Rare Book Room.' I went back upstairs and was immediately on a stage. I stood there for a whole minute after being introduced, wondering how long it would be before someone inside me opened his mouth. Once I did open my mouth I found it difficult to stop. Every poem that caught my eye seemed worth giving an airing to. I went on and on, explaining everything in clipped but uncoherent phrases.

The audience was very nice about it, laughed, was quiet etc., so I leaned on the lectern and continued. I hadn't noticed that this lectern was a kind of science instructor's console on little castors and as I leant on it it spun out from under me and crashed down into the first row of seats, which were luckily

— 331 —

empty. I brushed my hands at this and asked if anyone else felt like taking me on. This was obviously what my poetry reading was going to be 'about'. I did a little sparring while some of the students lifted my opponent back on to the podium for another round.

It was time, high time in fact, for the 'Talk on Current British Poetry' which I had rashly undertaken to give for the same fee.

'English poetry has concerned itself with the facts of feelings. American poetry with the feeling of facts,' I began tendentiously, brain reeling with the effort, exceptions leering at me from all over the place. 'English poetry has been about love and hate, death and mortality, while . . .' Here I had to stop for cigarette lighting: suddenly there seemed nothing left for American poetry to be about. I imagined Emily Dickinson looking at me quizzically. 'Do go on,' she was saying.

'American poetry is about things,' I said triumphantly, 'a love of place, of the new land . . .' My tongue kept slipping sideways off words like a tangled lariat.

I realized soon that I had embarked on a history of poetry and that I was stuck in the seventeenth century. My problem was how to bring my discourse up to date before I passed out. 'I was buried in de wars' I kept wanting to explain.

'I must say you were very generous with your reading,' said the doctor's pretty wife afterwards, as we flowed out of the hall into cars and through the night to a party in a bungalow in some woods. 'I chose it from a catalogue,' a man was telling me, 'the house. It had a number. I went to Europe and when I came back there it was on stilts.' Another man called Scott Donaldson had written a book on minor William Carlos Williams follower Winfield Thurley Scott.

This should have been where the girls were, but poetry never seems to be the right water for them. They are at the Godard film and the Karate club. A mature-looking student introduced his wife. He talked about the New York School, so I asked him if there were any drugs to hand. First we went to someone's house where there had been a party. Some grass was dug up for the tipsy visitor and we staggered off to a truck stop for 'grits'. I can't remember what 'grits' were exactly, only their glutinous and inappropriate consistency which everyone rhapsodized over until we were asked to leave. Then it was back to Hospitality House for the perusal of the mature-looking student's New York School poems which he happened to have about him.

Already dazed with travel, booze and dope, I read these disturbed syntheses like a credulous child. The man was a genius! Or was he a pretentious bore? His poems certainly looked original. But did this matter? I tried to remember some criteria. 'The History of Poetry' passed unwelcomely through my brain. Lines like 'staid phenomena uprooted the chinchilla patch all right' sent me groping for my iced water. I realized why certain modern poets like to live close to their mothers. I talked guardedly about texture, but my interlocutor was on top of the situation. He didn't agree with me at all. He gave me some more poems to read: the coup de grâce. I thought of running outside and burying them in the garden, but read on. Johnny, where were you when I needed you?

I slept a few hours and was woken by a friendly lecturer called Tom Heacox, who insisted on writing me out the addresses of everyone he knew in America on a paper place mat while I stuffed down the huge Hospitality Breakfast (grits again). The phone rang and someone told me my next reading was impossible to arrange at such short notice. My letter hadn't arrived in time and indeed I had only just posted it. Depressed, I allowed myself to be shown the 'Wren Building', the only building in the New World designed by C. Wren. I tried to cash last night's cheque, but the bank wanted a signature verification. Tom turned up again and fixed it for me. He said I could stay the night at his cabin in the woods.

Then I was happy and wandered up the famous Duke of Gloucester Street, a reconstruction of the original colonial avenue which was partly burnt down a hundred years ago. They found the original plans, demolished the newer Victorian stuff and set up this perfect-in-every-detail colonial main street, complete with milliner, wig-maker, boot-maker, even a 'music instructor'. I went into the stationer's and was amazed to see the shopkeeper in eighteenth-century clothes. I asked for one of the notebooks in the window. 'They're not for sale,' he said. 'May I see your ticket?' So this whole street was a museum!

Only the camera shop, a discreetly period frontage with the single word 'FILM' in classical lettering, actually purveyed reality.

I walked the mile-long avenue to the Pump House in the pleasant late afternoon cold. Here were detached weatherboard houses with verandahs, except where the lovely 'Flemish Bond' brickwork had survived the fire. I turned back at about five when all the shopkeepers were hobbling homewards through the painterly dusk, the women bonneted and basketed, the men in frock coats and white stockings.

Later that night Tom's log cabin on a deserted stretch of the Chicohominy river was another reconstruction from former days: Tom Sawyer's raft drifting just out of sight, smoke rising in a column from somebody's camp fire. Pine needles cushioned one's footsteps right up to the front door, while pine branches made another roof over the cabin. Indoors the stove made the logs ooze perfume. My bed had a view straight over the river and I woke at dawn to see the river and sky flooded with a brilliant sunrise which filled the room with fluorescent pink light. We breakfasted on the river bank. The great dane called Oak sprang off to investigate a strange rowboat which we found to contain illicit muskrat traps.

On the way back into town we picked up a copy of the local paper. Tom found the piece about the reading and showed it to me.

'Poet shaves part of himself,' I read out.

'Shares,' said Tom. He left me at the Greyhound station and I sat there reading about myself while I waited for the bus. 'I like things to be said as they are and to mean something. I think a poem has to go somewhere,' claimed a Mr Williams.

December 1977

Two Poems

──── SEAMUS HEANEY ────

An Afterwards

She would plunge all poets in the ninth circle
And fix them, tooth in skull, tonguing for brain;
For backbiting in life she'd make their hell
A rabid egotistical daisychain.

Unyielding, spurred, ambitious, unblunted,
Lockjawed, mantrapped, each a fastened badger
Jockeying for position, hasped and mounted
Like Ugolino on Archbishop Roger.

And when she'd make her circuit of the ice,
Aided and abetted by Virgil's wife,
I would cry out, 'My sweet, who wears the bays
In our green land above, whose is the life

Most dedicated and exemplary?'
And she: 'I have closed my widowed ears
To the sulphurous news of poets and poetry.
Why would you not have, oftener, in our years

Unclenched, and come down laughing from your room
And walked the twilight with me and your children –
Like that one evening of elder bloom
And hay, when the wild roses were fading?'

And (as some maker gaffs me in the neck)
'You weren't the worst. You aspired to a kind,

Indifferent, faults–on–both–sides tact.
You left us first, and then those books, behind.'

The Skunk

Up, black, striped and damasked like the chasuble
At a funeral mass, the skunk's tail
Paraded the skunk. Night after night
I expected her like a visitor.

The refrigerator whinnied into silence.
My desk light softened beyond the verandah.
Small oranges loomed in the orange tree.
I began to be tense as a voyeur.

After eleven years I was composing
Love–letters again, broaching the word 'wife'
Like a stored cask, as if its slender vowel
Had mutated into the night earth and air

Of California. The beautiful, useless
Tang of eucalyptus spelt your absence.
The aftermath of a mouthful of wine
Was like inhaling you off a cold pillow.

And there she was, the intent and glamorous,
Ordinary, mysterious skunk,
Mythologized, demythologized,
Snuffing the boards five feet beyond me.

It all came back to me last night, stirred
By the sootfall of your things at bedtime,
Your head–down, tail–up hunt in a bottom drawer
For the black plunge–line nightdress.

February 1978

The Loneliness of the
Short Story Writer

—— SHASHI THAROOR ——

There was only one thing wrong with Jennings Wilkes's writings. Verisimilitude.

His stories reeked with it. No one ever accused him of not being true to life, because if anything he was too true to it. He never concocted his plots: he found them in the quotidian experiences of living. He never created characters: he borrowed his friends, and occasionally his enemies, and populated his manuscripts with their likenesses. He never struggled with dialogue; blessed with almost total recall of anything that was spoken to him, he set down others' words as he remembered them. And since in his endeavours he proved unfailingly accurate, lack of realism was never his problem. His stories were overpoweringly realistic.

Needless to say, publishers loved him. Magazines overflowed with his work; scarcely a fortnight passed by without some periodical decorating the stands with yet another Jennings Wilkes short story. Editors would rush enthusiastic letters to him every time a submission came in, and their enthusiasm did not diminish with the passage of time. 'There's a fellow who tells it like it is,' the portly cigar-chewing male from the leading women's magazine would affirm to his chief competitor whenever they bought each other grudging lunches at '21'. 'So *painfully* twue, dear,' she would emotively respond. 'So painfully *twue*.'

Of course, that was precisely the problem: Jennings Wilkes's fiction was both true and painful, and worse, it wasn't really fiction. The truths he told were about other people, people he knew and associated with – until he committed them to print and they walked out of his life. After beginning his literary career with his popularity indexed in a black leather-bound cornucopia of addresses and telephone numbers, Jennings learned to measure his success by the number of homes he was no longer invited to, the number of calls he no longer had the courage to make. Each brilliant, honest, revelatory short story proved apocalyptic for some friend, ruined some relationship, shattered some illusion.

Soon his acquaintances began avoiding him, not always subtly. 'We don't want to find ourselves splashed across the feature pages of *Harper's Bazaar*,' one couple indelicately informed him when he met them at a restaurant and invited them to join his table. 'No, of course you don't,' he muttered miserably, retreating to his solitary chair. It was a recurring pattern: sometimes he did succeed in making friends with one individual, only to wreck it all by immortalizing the individual's weaknesses in *Playboy* ('fiction by Jennings Wilkes' the byline read). And the truths he portrayed were painful to him, too: he hated losing his friends.

'Then why do you keep doing it?' an admiring young interviewer from *Writer's Digest* asked him.

'Because,' Jennings replied, a spark glowing in his eyes, 'because when I meet an individual who interests me I take possession of his character. My mind perceives him as a person, but my imagination gives him a personality. A personality *I* cause to act, to talk, to think, to breathe. And because,' he added, his gaze directing the interviewer to his note-pad, 'because I have to. Because creativity is a compulsion and my artistic integrity cannot be compromised, even by my needs as a human being.'

He watched as the admiring scribe took it all down. Later that evening he penned an acerbic, witty short story (entitled 'Naivety and the Nasty Novelist') about a journalistic ingenue attempting to probe into the profound mind of a superior litterateur. *Cosmopolitan* advertised the story on its front cover, and the interviewer admired him no more.

And so, as friends go, his went. They went angrily, occasionally threatening libel, sometimes promising murder, once in a while tight-lipped in seething fury. Some were plainly incredulous. Jennings could never forget one erstwhile friend, waving a copy of *Ladies' Home Journal* at his doorway, pages flapping in righteous indignation: 'I can't believe,' he had spluttered, 'I can't believe you did this.' Didn't it matter, the friend went on, that after this their relationship couldn't possibly continue? 'Truth is stronger than friction,' Jennings responded with a sage smile, before the spine of the magazine binding struck him squarely on the nose.

'I don't understand it myself, doctor,' Jennings said on his second psychiatrist's couch, crossing his feet and steepling his hands in genuinely perturbed introspection. (The first had cancelled Jennings's regularly scheduled sessions abruptly after 'The Shanks of the Shrunken Shrink' had appeared in *The Atlantic*, a magazine usually available in the doctor's antechamber; 'It's not so much the story I mind,' Dr Weingarten had told him, 'but the fact that you chose to put it in *The Atlantic*. Do you realize how many of my patients can no longer take me seriously?') 'But I can't stop myself – I *have* to write about people I know. And I don't even *want* to stop myself. When I'm sitting at my desk, first thing in the morning, long yellow sheets of legal-size paper before me, pen and ink by my side – I always use pen and ink, typewriters are deathly for prose – I have an overpowering urge to pick up that pen and put it to those yellow sheets of paper and produce four thousand words of publishable . . . fiction.'

'Could you speak up, please?' the psychiatrist asked. 'I couldn't hear the last word.'

'Fiction,' Jennings said, loudly. 'I said fiction, Dr Clausewitz. I *need* to write fiction. Fiction, that is, about those I come into contact with. And I know what you're going to ask me – that's exactly what Dr Weingarten asked me – you're going to ask me, why does it have to be published? Why can't I fulfil my overpowering urge to write my story and then put it in a paper-shredder or something?'

'That's not what I was going to ask you,' Dr Clausewitz said, 'but tell me anyway.'

'Well, I can't,' Jennings replied, shortly. 'Publication is important to me. *Communication* is what writing's all about. If my fiction about real people doesn't communicate something to other real people, if it doesn't disseminate the message, the insight, I feel it contains then the entire purpose of my writing is negated. I need to publish as much as I need to write.'

Dr Clausewitz caressed his goatee. 'You haven't answered one question, you know,' he said mildly. 'Why must you write about other people you know?'

Jennings was stunned by the question, much as a raconteur might be at the end of a joke if asked what the ouch-line was. 'But you don't understand, there's no answer to that question,' he mumbled. 'That's all I can write about.'

Jennings did try to restrain himself on his own. He tried getting up in the morning and *not* sitting at his desk, with its attractions of pen and paper – but he found himself writing in bed, scrawling with a pencil on the blank areas of full-page advertisements in the *New York Times*. He tried shutting himself off from the world so that he would have nothing to write about, but discovered that though shunned by his friends, he was not lacking in attraction for interviewers, autograph-hunters, salesmen, solicitors, would-be authors and could-be groupies. On the one occasion he succeeded in packing a discreet suitcase and decamping to the wilds of Aspen, Colorado, he was nearly shot by a night club entertainer, developed an unpleasant intimacy with the impediments on the ski-slopes, and barely avoided double-pneumonia after dreaming he was being pursued by one of his not-entirely-fictional characters and jumping in the altogether out of his hotel window into seven feet of accumulated snow. His resultant 'Not Quite Altogether in Aspen', rejected by the travel editor of the *National Geographic*, appeared with minor modifications in the *Saturday Evening Post*.

'Not that effective isolation would really do all that much good,' Jennings told Dr Clausewitz as he rested his sore skiing limbs on the analyst's couch and contemplated the ceiling moodily. 'I'd probably find myself penning a soul-shattering soliloquy on "The Privacy of the Persecuted Penpusher". *And* selling it to *Saturday Review*.'

'At least that way you'd only be libelling yourself,' Dr Clausewitz pointed out.

'Don't you believe it,' Jennings replied. 'One arrives at solitude only by losing the company of, or avoiding a whole lot of people – so there will always be people responsible for my solitude. And you can bet they'll feature in my – fiction.'

Dr Clausewitz coughed, but let the word pass.

'Why don't you seek some form of diversion from writing?' he asked. 'A woman? Several women? Maybe even a man?'

There had always been women in Jennings's life, but none important enough to divert him from his writing. His writing took up most of his day; his women, when he had any, occupied only his evenings and his bed. He encountered no difficulty whenever the urge to write – usually about them – came to him. What female authors have termed 'meaningful relationships' became, as a consequence, increasingly hard to come by. His primary fidelity was clearly not to them but to his literary muse, and the few ladies who tolerated Her departed in the wake of such revelatory exegeses as 'Sex and the Single Curl' (about the fourth woman in his life, an exquisite if mildly eccentric girl who had a little curl *not* in the middle of her forehead) or 'Sinning for her Supper' (about an indigent redhead who had begun to get involved with him, though Jennings was convinced she was more interested in board than in bed).

'How can you carry on a meaningful relationship with an – *individual* who transcribes your bedtime conversation for *Penthouse*?' demanded one lissome brunette as she furiously packed her suitcase. 'How can you whisper sweet somethings into the ear of a man you half-expect to respond, "Speak up, darling – it's ten cents a word"?'

'I guess you're right,' Jennings agreed with a morose sigh. 'But, darling, can't you understand – this is beyond my control. I *have* to write about you. I can't do any – ' but the door had slammed shut behind her.

Gloomily, Jennings rose, despairing of his own redemption. A pair of the lady's panties were still on the floor near the bed, omitted in her hasty departure. He rushed to the door with them, shouting as he opened it, 'Darling you've left your – ' He never finished the call; the panties in his hand reminded him irresistibly of the posterior they belonged to, the brunette's only imperfection, a hereditarily heavy derriere whose left half was, despite dieting and exercise, appreciably larger than the right half. His exclamation disintegrated into uncontrollable giggles, and he shut his door again, laughing hysterically while leaning against it.

'Left Behind' appeared in the next issue of *Esquire*.

'Forgive me,' Dr Clausewitz said, leaning forward in his chair, legs crossed at the knee, 'but if I may ask a question that is also a suggestion – why do you not, given your obsession with penning the truth, become an investigative reporter instead of a short-story writer? Your – er – talents may then serve a social good, instead of merely contributing to your unhappy state of mind.'

'But I already am, doctor.' Jennings almost rose from the couch. 'Every writer of short stories *is* a reporter, an investigative reporter of society. Besides, it's a question of the appropriate mode of expression. Do you think my perception of feminine foibles, for instance, which is after all what my stories about women depict, would belong on page 1 of the *Washington Post*, under the headline "Alleged Inconsistencies in Female Behaviour Challenged"? And I'm not interested in whether a Third Deputy Assistant Under-Secretary has accepted Swiss currency from a Chilean vice-admiral to help a Cuban megalomaniac kick the bucket. I couldn't write a meaningful piece on that kind of stuff. But if I could have a drink with the Third Deputy Assistant Under-Secretary, and discover that he's cheating on his wife, or that the vice of the vice-admiral is the rear of a rear-admiral, or that the prospective Cuban bucket-kicker smokes imported Trichinopoly cigars, *then* I could write a fascinating story, suitably garnished, but with the essential truth preserved, and that story would *have* to appear as fiction, because that's the mode in which it will receive the kind of readership and the type of attention it deserves.'

Part of the problem with Jennings was that he really believed what he said. It is an affliction common to most authors who find themselves theorizing about their art. Writers have as large a capacity for taking their profession seriously as rat-catchers and racing-car drivers.

* * *

'As I see it,' Dr Clausewitz told Jennings at what he announced ('though this has nothing to do with that admirable story in which I fancy I see myself') would be the last session, 'your problem is really twofold. On the one hand, you feel impelled to write, but on the other, you can only write about people you know, to their embarrassment and your own discomfiture. Your attempts at resolving this problem have so far dealt primarily with the first part of this dichotomy – curbing your impulse to write. It seems to me it might be more appropriate to endeavour to deal with the second part of it – writing about those you know. By all means, write; certainly, write fiction, or what you consider to be fiction. Try to concentrate your energies, however, on writing not about people you know, but about those you do not. Invent characters. Merge the traits of five people you know into a sixth, non-existent person – a truly fictional character. Try . . .'

'You don't know what you're asking of me, Dr Clausewitz,' Jennings interrupted. 'You're telling me to betray the very principle of truth I've based my fiction on. If I merge five true characters into one I lose what is true in all five and create a lie. I can't do it, doctor. I can't.'

'Then,' said Dr Clausewitz, looking very old and very tired and very wise, 'then do it not as an author but as a human being. Allow one person to matter enough to you – to matter so much to you that you do not want to, *cannot*, desecrate him or her in print. Then – and perhaps only then – will you be able to find your absolution.'

Jennings took absolution seriously, 'absolutely seriously', as he told the leggy blonde he sat next to on the closest barstool to Dr Clausewitz's office (which proved to be, as the doctor had surprisingly indicated with an uncharacteristic twinkle in his eye, seventeen blocks and a left turn from the analyst's couch). 'Personally, however,' he articulated through a thickening tongue, 'I prefer salvation in Scotch. Can I buy you a drink, my nebulous nirvana, or are authors and ambrosia off your diet this week?'

The girl laughed, tossing a cultured coiffure. 'You're funny,' she observed, not entirely soberly.

Jennings stared at her for a moment, digesting the remark.

'Yes,' he affirmed. 'Levity *is* the soul of wit. Will you try a funny fifth of this stuff, or will abstinence make your heart grow fonder?'

'I'll have a vodka,' she giggled, toothily. She was a model, all straight lines and elegance, with the kind of high-cheekboned look Faye hadn't entirely dunaway with. ('A model of what?', Jennings joked gauchely. 'Charm,' came the stunning reply. 'The perfume, that is, silly. And a lot of other things besides.') She was young and innocent and what in an earlier age would have been called cutely feminine – the kind of girl who called a spade a thpade. It transpired she had been stood up by the city's leading photographer, and was spending an increasingly aimless wait getting sloshed. Jennings, who found her more than moderately attractive, quickly warmed to her.

'I'm not much of a photographer myself,' he found himself saying on his fifth highball (and her fourth vodka), 'but why don't we make this meeting *in camera*?'

The girl didn't quite seem to have got it, and Jennings wished he hadn't discarded his alternative jokes about dark-room developments and negative answers. He leaned forward and gripped her by the arm.

'Come,' he said authoritatively.

She came. Their love-making was brief and blurred, as alcoholic amativeness so often tends to be, but she came, shuddering in his arms, and afterwards Jennings lay still, sobered by her sensual elegance, his mind caressing the perfect lines of her mannequin's body. He turned towards her, rolling over on to his belly, and she surprised him by opening her eyes and saying, 'Jennings, I love you.' The words hit him and he shook her awake abruptly.

'How did you know my name?' he demanded.

She was instantly alert. 'Of course I know your name, silly. You're Jennings Wilkes. I've seen your picture in *Playgirl*, with one of your stories – the one about the girl who took drugs, what did you call it – oh, yes, "Methedrine in her Madness". I recognized you as soon as you sat next to me in the bar. Anyone would.' Smiling languidly, she tickled him under the chin and turned back to sleep.

Watching her lying on her side, her graceful curves under his fingertips, Jennings experienced a strange sense of disquiet. *She knew who I was,* he told himself. *She knew all along.* But then why shouldn't she? He did not suffer from any sense of false modesty. His must be a fairly familiar face. Yet the girl, coming soon after Clausewitz's disturbing last session, seemed too perfectly timed to be true. What was she? A divine gift? A psycho-analytic plant? He shook her awake again.

'What's *your* name?' he asked.

She raised a sleepy hand to touch him. 'Cheryll,' she said huskily.

'Cheryll Clausewitz?' he was almost barking.

'No, silly, where on earth did you pick that name from? Cheryll Smith.'

He felt instantly ashamed. 'Go back to sleep, Cheryll,' he said softly.

She moved in a week later, by which time they had concluded they wanted each other so much it was pointless living apart. In the meantime, in the few moments he found for writing – since Cheryll demanded more of his time than her few predecessors in residence – he put the finishing touches on a second story about Clausewitz and, inevitably, began one about Cheryll.

'I've got little more than a working title right now, but a lot of empirical data will follow,' Jennings explained to Dr Clausewitz, who had allowed himself to be coerced into restarting the treatment, realizing full well that Jennings needed him only because he had no other friend to talk to. ('If I was Roman Catholic,' Jennings had admitted, 'I could at least have gone to my father confessor.') 'I think I'll call it "Vodka and the Virgin", given my penchant for alliteration. And she was, you know, incredibly enough. A virgin. I couldn't believe the stains on my sheet the next morning. Asked her if it wasn't her time of month. She – she – started weeping then.' Jennings paused, his brow clouding. 'Poor Cheryll.'

Poor Cheryll was just what she was – she hadn't proved successful enough a model to be able to maintain herself in the kind of style that successful models could afford and not-so-successful models tried to affect. Jennings, realist that he was, told himself that the saving she would make on her rent had

— 345 —

played no small a part in her decision to live with him, and yet the fact that it was *him* she had chosen proved gratifying.

Meanwhile the story progressed. She would occasionally stand over his shoulder while he wrote, give up attempting to decipher his scrawl, and retreat to a magazine or the dressing-table; but most of the time she was at a studio, or at several, trying to obtain assignments while he wrote. 'Vodka and the Virgin' caused him more trouble than he had expected. Sometimes, the creative daemon possessing him, he would write an acidic sentence, only to look up and find Cheryll smiling down at him, mug of steaming coffee in her hand. She would leave him the beverage and rumple his hair and the spell would be broken. He would score out the sentence in self-reproach.

Somehow, the story progressed.

'She's the only virgin I've ever known, doc,' Jennings said reflectively, noting idly that a section of the plaster on the ceiling had begun to crack – it'll peel before next week's session, he thought. 'You know, really – the only virgin. Doc, I'm the first man she's ever known. I think about that sometimes when I'm writing, and I tell myself, Jesus, Jennings Wilkes, you can't do this to her. You can't betray a girl who trusts you like Cheryll Smith does, who gives you as much as she has.'

'Good,' Dr Clausewitz said. That was all he said throughout the session.

Cheryll in his arms in the living-room to a Chopin waltz – biting Cheryll's neck in the kitchen as she garnished an exquisite casserole – Cheryll naked and heaving on the double-bed – soaping Cheryll's back in the bathtub – Cheryll smiling and wet and home on the doorstep – writing about Cheryll in the study. The progression always gave him a sense of guilt. Writing was more painful each time he sat down to it, entirely because he could not write beautiful, romantic, adulatory bilge; his perception was too acute and his prose too incisive, even as his preoccupation with her steadily acquired the dimensions of an obsession.

Then, one day, he finished it.

'I've done it, doc,' he said in triumph, watching the plaster peel on the ceiling with the quiet satisfaction that comes from the knowledge of inevitability. ' "Vodka and the Virgin" complete and ready for the typewriter. Five thousand intense, painful but brilliant words. It's an affirmation of literary integrity, of an author's *karma*. Doc, I don't mind admitting to you frankly that there were moments when I thought I wouldn't be able to go through with it. I think I'm beginning to fall in love with her, leggy languor, tumbling tresses et al. There's something so terribly vulnerable in her naïvety – perhaps because her essential simplicity contrasts so strongly with her outward self-possession – that I'm becoming entranced. But you've not been entirely right, doc. She *is* beginning to matter to Jennings Wilkes the human being – but Jennings Wilkes the author still exults at his completion of her literary exposé. I love the virgin but I've violated her virginity. Don't you see how deep the dichotomy you discerned in me runs?'

'Perhaps,' Dr Clausewitz responded enigmatically. That was all he said throughout *this* session.

Jennings stopped at the bar seventeen–blocks–and–a–left–turn away once more on his way home. It was a strange feeling sitting on her barstool (the one he had occupied was taken) and then drinking, deliberately, her drink (vodka on the rocks with a dash of lime). Yet Jennings could not define the feeling. He had not come to the bar in quest of anything, not for reminders or assurances or a perverse expiation. Vaguely dissatisfied, he finished the drink and left.

She was due home, he knew, but somehow he did not want to meet her, though he felt impelled to return – to return not to her in the flesh but to her in black ink on yellow paper. He took the elevator to his floor and used the key he had not given her, one that let him directly into his study from the landing. He wanted to be alone with Cheryll there; alone as only an author can be with his creation.

The manuscript was still lying on the table, 'BY JENNINGS WILKES' proudly capitalized on the top of the first page. He looked at it and his disquiet lifted. There it was, his story, a tangible embodiment of his perception, his wit, his *power* with the pen. He began to read it, watching, as if from a curiously involved but nevertheless distant vantage-point, the words flow across the page, watched them cascade and break in crested waves. He was Neptune, Ahab, Mark Spitz. He was their genesis, their conqueror, their victim. He felt himself caught up in their movement, irresistibly enthralled, felt himself swim in their ambience, sail on their current, rise from their depths. Cheryll's voice, raised outside his study door, broke into his reverie.

'It worked, darling!' The excitement was so foreign to her customary verbal lassitude that Jennings instantly turned his attention to her. She was on the phone in the corridor between his study and the living-room, apparently pacing up and down in animation. 'He did it, just as you said he would. I came home early today, knowing he'd be away, and sneaked into his study. It's perfect. "Vodka and the Virgin" – familiar Wilkesian alliteration, establishing the story firmly in the general genre. And the contents – even better than some of his other stuff. I think it's been earmarked for *Viva*. Just wait till this comes out and half of the continental United States will be abuzz with queries about who the "vertiginous virgin" is. And I'll be up to my ears in modelling assignments!'

There was a pause while the recipient of this breathless analysis responded to it. But Jennings was no longer listening. He strove to focus on the sea of words before him, but found himself drowning in them, their sparkle dulled, his limbs heavy. Clausewitz had been wrong, but *he* had been so much wronger, his perception so pathetically amiss, the truth he had felt compelled to depict now revealed as hollow, tinsel, false. He gripped the sheaf of paper tightly, and then something snapped within him. He was a beached surfer now, watching the foam retreat from the shoreline. The manuscript was ripped apart in two; he watched his hands tear the paper, making no attempt to resist their motion. The story was bisected, and then his hands moved with increasing quickness, and the sheets were torn into furious quarters, the little jagged shreds flying with each fast, flailing violation of their wholeness, till finally no piece was large enough to tear further. He found himself laughing, at first in small sobs, then increasingly uncontrollably, the tears streaming down his face to mingle with the ink on the scraps on the table. With the tears came a greater sense of release than he had ever known, an emptying of the dam-waters through floodgates he had not known could be opened.

'I'm free!' he shouted, scooping handfuls of the shredded story and flinging them into the air, still laughing. 'By the Blessed Virgin, I'm free!'

He was still laughing when the girl outside finished her telephone conversation.

'Thank you, Dr Clausewitz,' she said.

March 1978

Outstanding fiction in paperback from Grafton Books

Nicholas Salaman		
The Frights	£1.95	☐
Dangerous Pursuits	£2.50	☐
Salman Rushdie		
Grimus	£2.95	☐
Denise Gess		
Good Deeds	£2.50	☐
Christopher Evans		
In Limbo	£2.50	☐
Stephen Minot		
Surviving the Flood	£2.95	☐
Lisa Zeidner		
Alexandra Freed	£2.50	☐
Ronald Frame		
Winter Journey	£2.50	☐
Torey Hayden		
The Sunflower Forest	£2.50	☐
Cathleen Schine		
Alice in Bed	£2.50	☐

To order direct from the publisher just tick the titles you want
and fill in the order form.   **GF982**

All these books are available at your local bookshop or newsagent, or can be ordered direct from the publisher.

To order direct from the publishers just tick the titles you want and fill in the form below.

Name _____

Address _____

_____

Send to:
Paladin Cash Sales
PO Box 11, Falmouth, Cornwall TR10 9EN.

Please enclose remittance to the value of the cover price plus:

UK 55p for the first book, 22p for the second book plus 14p per copy for each additional book ordered to a maximum charge of £1.75.

BFPO and Eire 55p for the first book, 22p for the second book plus 14p per copy for the next 7 books, thereafter 8p per book.

Overseas £1.25 for the first book and 31p for each additional book.

Paladin Books reserve the right to show new retail prices on covers, which may differ from those previously advertised in the text or elsewhere.